On Time

On Time

How America Has Learned to Live by the Clock

Carlene E. Stephens

Smithsonian Institution
National Museum of American History
Behring Center

A Bulfinch Press Book
Little, Brown and Company
Boston ❖ New York ❖ London

First Edition

ISBN 0-8212-2779-3
Library of Congress Control Number 2002102350

Bulfinch Press is an imprint and trademark of Little, Brown and Company (Inc.)
PRINTED IN SINGAPORE

contents

6   acknowledgments

9   introduction

15   telling time 1700–1820

63   mechanizing time 1820–1880

105   synchronizing time 1880–1920

153   saving time 1920–1960

185   expanding time 1960 to the present

221   notes

249   illustration credits

252   index

contents

6   acknowledgments

9   introduction

15   telling time 1700–1820

63   mechanizing time 1820–1880

105   synchronizing time 1880–1920

153   saving time 1920–1960

185   expanding time 1960 to the present

221   notes

249   illustration credits

252   index

acknowledgments

This history of American time relies on not only written evidence, but also evidence derived from objects and images. Most of the artifacts, paper ephemera, photographs, and other pictures shown here are from the permanent collections of the Smithsonian's National Museum of American History, Behring Center, and are on display there in a companion exhibition also called *On Time*. The exhibition was made possible by a generous grant from the Timex Corporation, and the museum is especially grateful to Fred Olsen, Michael Jacobi, Susie Watson, and Carl Rosa for their interest and support.

For *On Time*, key objects came from elsewhere in the Smithsonian, and I am grateful for loans from the Smithsonian Institution Libraries and National Museum of Natural History.

Other institutions and individuals also lent important objects from their own collections. Thanks to the Rare Book and Special Collections Division at the Library of Congress; Gill Library, College of New Rochelle; First Congregational Church, Whately, Massachusetts; National Watch and Clock Museum; Massachusetts Charitable Mechanic Association; Timex Corporation; and Ian Cooke, the family of Suren Hekimian, the family of Beatrice M. Schwartz, Sharon Forrer, Kristina Johnson, Frederick Leach, Elaine Paulick, Lucy Neville Smith, and David Sulzberger.

The arrangement of this book and the exhibition are nearly identical. For working with me on both, I am deeply indebted to my colleagues Ann Rossilli, the exhibition's designer, and Howard Morrison, exhibition developer. Memories of our planning sessions echoed in my head as I wrote this book upon the structure we three crafted together. Howard and I wrote the exhibition script together with editorial help from Joan Mentzer, and they will undoubtedly recognize some of their prose throughout the book. Howard's touch is especially evident in the section on "Happy Hour."

Generous colleagues inside and outside the Smithsonian helped to improve the exhibition script and the text of this book. At the very beginning of the project from which this book emerged, Arthur Molella, William Withuhn, and Roger G. Kennedy freely gave crucial support and suggestions. Sincerest thanks to Dwight Blocker Bowers, Barbara Carson, Robert Cheney, Joseph Corn, Jim Gardner, Rayna Green, Robert Levine, Peter Liebhold, Steven Lubar, Nancy McCoy, Alexis McCrossen, Theresa Murphy, Michael O'Malley, John D. Prestage, Roy Rosenzweig, Mark M. Smith, Susan Smulyan, and Donald B. Sullivan for their astute comments.

David Todd, the NMAH staff clockmaker, was indispensable for his patient technical explanations and expert attention to all the museum's clocks and watches throughout the exhibition and book projects. I can write without exaggeration that neither would have been possible without him.

Colleagues inside and out of the Smithsonian also assisted with research, locating and identifying objects, obtaining photos, and providing support. Thanks to Fred Bardwell, Silvio Bedini, Larry Bird, Eleanor Boyne, Paul Ceruzzi, Amanda Dillon, Richard Doty, Nanci Edwards, Robert Edwards, Karen Linn Femina, Shelly Foote, Yuko Fukunaga, Karen Goldman, Anna Pegler Gordon, Linda Gordon, Lisa Kathleen Graddy, Frank Greenwell, Charles Handley, Jennifer L. Jones, Helen Kafka, Claudia Kidwell, Peggy Kidwell, Stacey Kluck, Laura Kreiss, Peter Liebhold, Melissa Naulin, Shelley Nickles, Nancy Pope, Rodris Roth, Harry Rubenstein, Shilpa Rustogi, Roger Sherman, Richard Thorington, Jr., Sheila Todd, Steven Turner, Harold Wallace, Jr., William Worthington, and V. Kay Youngflesh. Robert Rolfe guided me through the museum's watch collections and cleaned and recataloged too many of them to count. Maggie Dennis proved invaluable in helping to shape the electronic watch stories. Ann Seeger kept track of all the objects, and Judi Keehnen and Kristin DeGrace did the same for exhibition images. Kris deserves additional thanks for her superb organization of all the tasks related to the illustrations in this volume. The photographers of the Office of Imaging, Printing and Photographic Services, whose names are listed elsewhere in this book, performed heroic service on behalf of this project, as did the staff of the NMAH branch library.

Portions of the chapters "Mechanizing Time" and "Expanding Time" appeared in different form in the journals *Technology and Culture* and *Material History Review*. Thanks to the Johns Hopkins University Press and the Canada Science and Technology Museum for granting permission to recycle the material here.

Steven Lubar allowed me time to write this book, George Greenfield and Michael Sand guided me through the writing process, and Gary Sturm helped in immeasurable ways. I thank them all very much.

introduction

Page 8: Interior of the clock tower at Mount Royal station, Baltimore, Maryland, about 1896. In the center of the tower sits the clock movement, firmly bolted in place and elevated just enough to give its pendulum room to swing. To rotate pairs of hands outside the tower, four horizontal rods lead off from the mechanism to the center of each of the clock's four immense dials.

Mount Royal station, Baltimore, about 1900.

The Baltimore & Ohio Railroad installed a clock tower at its new Mount Royal station in 1896. Set in a grassy landscape amid the homes of prosperous northwest Baltimore, the Romanesque depot was intended to be the line's showcase, a state-of-the-art gateway for passengers bound to or from Philadelphia and New York. In keeping with the rest of the station's new fittings, the tower clock was a fine piece of modern machinery from one of the most prestigious clock firms in America, E. Howard and Company of Boston.

A photograph taken when the clock was first installed offers us a rare glimpse inside the tower and a look at the clockwork technology from the inside out. Almost no one ever saw this interior space except the clockmaker who regularly tended the mechanism. A close look at the photograph, in fact, shows his oilcan, an extra bottle of oil, and a rag, all under the clock frame awaiting his return. As unfamiliar as this behind-the-scenes view was, tower clock dials were common sights all over America when the B&O built the station near the start of the twentieth century, and just about everyone took for granted the technology behind the dials.

The giant dials told the station manager whether arriving and departing trains were synchronized with the rest of the B&O system and conductors whether they were running on time. Outbound passengers consulted the dials as they hurried to catch their trains, and ordinary citizens in nearby neighborhoods glanced up and checked their watches to see whether they agreed. The time on the dials created a network of otherwise unrelated people. The dials connected them all in time.

Looking at the role of the clock in American history is like looking at the clock in the Baltimore railroad station tower. To see just the machinery, or just the dial, is to get only part of the story. The machinery inside clocks and watches *and* the unvarying kind of time they express on their dials together make a technical system that reflects our social needs and shapes our interactions. We use the system to synchronize and schedule ourselves, and to try to make much of life predictable. To understand how we have interacted with this system requires a look from the inside out, starting with the technological innovations, as well as from the outside in, contemplating the social forces influencing how we organize ourselves in time.

When we think about time today, we mostly think of the clock dial. Hours and minutes, quarter till, half past. The dial's imprint on us is so strong that we tend to take no notice of what makes the hands rotate or the digits change on our ubiquitous timekeepers. Nor are we likely to consider for very long other ways we experience time every day – the ways that connect us with nature, like the rising and setting sun, for example, or the change of seasons. Or those that remind us of our body rhythms, like hunger and sleepiness. What the clock says tends to dominate the way we know time.

When and how did clocks and watches intertwine with our sense of time and merge with the other ways we know time? When and how did they come to play central and controlling roles in our lives? When and how did they become the most fundamental instruments we use to connect ourselves, for better or worse, to one another? To explore these questions, this book, and a companion exhibition also called *On Time* at the Smithsonian's National Museum of American History, survey the changing ways Americans have measured, used, and thought about time over the past three hundred years.[1]

The diversity and complexity of American culture make this a difficult story to tell in a simple sequence of dates, places, and people. With only a few exceptions, clocks and watches became indispensable tools over the course of three centuries gradually and unevenly, without distinct moments of universal change. Very particular historical circumstances – community values, a person's place in the social structure, life experiences – shaped every individual's sense of time and use of clocks and watches. Thomas Jefferson's twelve-year-old daughter, for example, might receive a watch as a coming-of-age gift in the late eighteenth century, but another girl of similar background and living in the same era in nearby Richmond might not. A small town in rural Pennsylvania today, originally settled by German immigrants in the eighteenth century, might never have had a public clock to provide time to its inhabitants, but a town of the same size in Maryland, with the same founding date and religious roots, might have had a clock on a prominent church tower for centuries. The history of time in American life, then, is not a

Thompson's essay on transformations in England's time sense was a powerful stimulus to further inquiry, especially for research on the American version of the story. Precisely when and where America's reliance on the clock originated is still debated, as is the precise nature of the change. Evidence is mounting that the transformation began even before industrialization altered work patterns and originated in the growing needs to coordinate lives of increasing complexity in the eighteenth century. Crucial transitions outside the world of work, especially during the eighteenth and nineteenth centuries, took people's understanding of time from a local experience rooted in God, nature, and social patterns to an abstract standard based on science and the clock.

Also still to be determined is precisely what it means to have a modern time consciousness and how Americans came to value the time-related characteristics of punctuality and speed. How did a person who had internalized clock time, that is, one who knew how to tell time and framed behavior by the clock, also acquire a set of complementary time-related characteristics, namely haste, efficiency, and a sense of responsibility for knowing the time and being on time? And how did Americans come to value these characteristics?[4]

Like time itself, timepieces inspire multiple experiences. Clocks and watches have always been much more than machines for displaying the time of day. Clocks have enduring aesthetic appeal as domestic furnishings. Watches, now as much as before, are fashion items and objects for expressing our personal style. We have admired mechanical timepieces for the sheer pleasure of watching their intricate machinery move. We have received valuable timepieces as gifts on special occasions and treasured them enough to pass them down as family heirlooms. We have layered them with moral values such as punctuality and efficiency. And we have endowed them with symbolic significance. Depending on the context, clocks and watches simultaneously stand for the positive and negative features of modernity. Especially in the nineteenth century, some saw them as the highest expressions of American know-how, efficiency, and technical superiority. But others have cast clocks and watches as the villains. Historically, people with little or no control over their time have deemed the clock the powerful and immediate source of their troubles, regardless of the actual source. The clock becomes, for them, the symbolic focus of their efforts to win back control or their resignation at having lost it.

Over the past three centuries, timepieces have embodied our attitudes, beliefs, and sensitivities about structuring our lives in time, both individually and communally. This book and the exhibition it accompanies offer a look at how and why Americans have come to rely on clocks and watches to synchronize and connect themselves to each other and the rest of the world. The ultimate goal of this rich history is to reach a deeper understanding of how the material things of American life interact with the complex reactions we have to them and the meanings we give them.[5]

telling time

1700–1820

AMERICANS ARE DEEPLY MINDFUL OF TIME, BUT NOT OF THE CLOCK.

Benjamin Banneker, a free African-American farmer in Maryland, calculated the ephemeris, or astronomical tables, for this 1795 almanac.

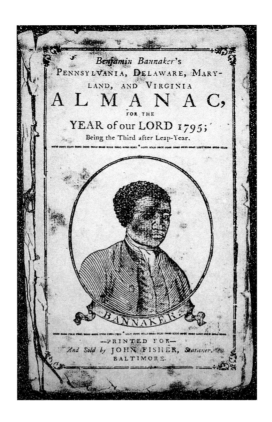

Benjamin Bannaker's
PENNSYLVANIA, DELAWARE, MARY-
LAND, AND VIRGINIA
ALMANAC,
FOR THE
YEAR of our LORD 1795;
Being the Third after Leap-Year.

BANNAKER

—PRINTED FOR—
And Sold by JOHN FISHER, Stationer,
BALTIMORE.

BANNEKER WAS A MAN AHEAD of his time. Preoccupied with coordinating clock time and astronomical events, Banneker thought about time with an accuracy that most people of his day did not. Most of his contemporaries did not have, or pay to-the-minute attention to, clocks and watches. The regularity of factory schedules, the reliability of railroad timetables, and the speed of telegraph messages were still in the future. Even though the mechanical clock had been invented nearly six hundred years before, in the eighteenth and early nineteenth centuries most Americans still mainly marked their days by the rising and setting sun, phases of the moon, cycles of hunger and sleep, and the routines of rural life. They ordered their lives by the changing seasons, calendars of religious observances, and successive births and deaths. Those who did think of time in terms of a clock might have noted the time on a church tower or town hall, neither of which was a common sight then. If they owned a timepiece at all, they still set the hour by looking to the sun or stars.

To mesh clock time with these other ways of telling time, an annual almanac like the ones Banneker calculated offered a practical guide. The basic American almanac format followed the calendar, with one month per page for a particular year. Interspersed with the days of the month, elaborate and precise timetables forecast astronomical, meteorological, and seasonal events, sometimes to the minute. The almanac's plain columns of data were seasoned with astrological predictions.

Following the pages of this calendar-based ephemeris, additional almanac pages imparted practical advice, poems and humorous stories, and other entertaining readings. The annual often concluded with schedules for local courts, college commencements, and the arrivals and departures for stagecoaches and boats. The calendar as we know it, hanging on a wall or displayed on a desk, became common only after about 1870, and until then, the almanac served the purpose. Reflections of public taste and sources of useful public information, almanacs were second only to Bibles as the most widely read books in early America.[2]

American almanacs like Banneker's, and the hundreds of others printed ever since the seventeenth century, are more than just quaint precursors to our modern calendar. They are, in fact, eloquent guides to how our ancestors measured, used, and thought about time. Even though our ancestors had few clocks and watches compared to what we have today, their almanacs show us they were nevertheless deeply mindful of time, its passing and its usefulness. The almanac pages reveal that in the eighteenth century, just as today, time in daily life operated as a kind of web, spun from ideas about nature, religion, civil authority, and mechanical timepieces. This web, a shifting network connecting people and communities, coordinated social life.

This chapter looks at a period in American history when the clock began to play a larger role in shaping the American sense of time. For organizing themselves in time, people in early America tended to look to religion and nature first, and then the clock. Those who did think of time in terms of clocks and watches set them by the sun or stars. Only a tiny minority, engaged in either scientific work or business, shared our modern preoccupations with the precise hour and minute and the time-related values of punctuality and speed. The interests of this minority would eventually come to dominate the way most of us measure, use, and behave in time.

end imposed. "Make hay while the sun shines" was to be taken literally.[4] Feeling time in nature as a kind of pressure would gradually give way to feeling the smaller increments of clock time as a kind of pressure. Making the most of time would be nothing new by the time the clock became the tool of industrial taskmasters.[5]

Sun Time

IN DESCRIBING HIS VIRGINIA JOURNEY from Monticello to Richmond in 1820, the British merchant Adam Hodgson remarked on the scarcity of clocks:

> Occasionally we heard a clock, which at first startled me, as I had not seen one since we left Georgia, and very few since we set out from Washington; everything being regulated by the sun. If you ask what time it is, it either wants so many hours of noon, or it is so much before, or so much after *sundown*. Meals are regulated by the sun, even [in] families where there is a watch or a timepiece.[6]

The sun, not clocks, ruled time in everyday life. This meant time was local. Since the sun appears to move across the sky from east to west, a community a few miles east of another would mark noon first, and would remain a few minutes and seconds ahead of its western neighbor throughout the day. So communities a few miles apart were often a few minutes apart as well. Albany, New York, for example, a little to the east of New York City, was 1 minute and 1 second ahead of the metropolis in time; Baltimore was 10 minutes and 27 seconds behind. Large cities sometimes had enough influence to impose a limited regional time on surrounding towns and farms. As late as 1880, tiny Connecticut had at least five regional standards of time, centered on Hartford, New Haven, New York, Boston, and New London.

In early America, splitting time into seconds was technically possible but still very rare. People often noted only the relative position of the sun and paid special attention to noon. To know whether the sun had reached noon for the day, that is, crossed the local meridian, or line of longitude, they might consult a south-facing noon mark. The simplest noon mark was a line running north–south, scratched onto the horizontal surface of a floor or a windowsill and read in connection with moving shadows cast by nearby trees, porch posts, or other buildings. The shadow would cross the line at local apparent noon (the moment when the sun was due south and at its

Small sundials, like this one cast in lead and marked "Jacob Leavit/1760," were made to fix to a windowsill.

This German-language almanac, *Der Hoch-Deutsch Amerikanische Calendar,* printed in Germantown, Pennsylvania, in 1750 by Christoph Saur, provided a template for those who wished to make their own sundial.

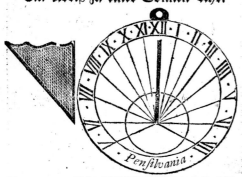

highest elevation for the day). New England farmers reportedly cut vertical meridian marks into the framing around a south-facing door. Some public buildings, such as the city hall in Albany, borrowed the European church tradition of displaying brass meridian markers.[7] The habit of noting whether the sun had passed the meridian is still part of the way we abbreviate clock time: A.M. stands for the Latin *ante meridiem,* that is, before the sun has crossed the meridian; P.M. is *post meridiem,* or after.

It was also possible in early America to mark hours, fractions of hours, and minutes using a sundial. For most of us today the sundial is a garden ornament, a charming obsolete instrument that almost always shows the wrong time. But in their heyday in Western Europe, the seventeenth and eighteenth centuries, sundials were admired products of the mathematical instrument maker's art; like the era's mechanical timepieces, they were practical and beautiful gadgets that, similar to the treasures of the Renaissance *Kunstkammer,* signaled education, wealth, and a pleasurable curiosity about nature.[8] In the United States, clocks and watches did not supersede the sundial until the second half of the nineteenth century.

Fixed sundials graced the windowsills of private houses and the walls of public buildings or sat on pedestals in gardens and plazas. But the demand for sundials wasn't so great that making, repairing, and selling them was anyone's sole occupation. Dial suppliers were, most often, instrument makers who sold and repaired miscellaneous items of their own manufacture as well as imports made by others. Stephen Greenleaf, for example, who had a shop opposite the prison in Boston, advertised in 1745 his skills in making and mending not only sundials, but also a miscellany of surveying tools and drafting instruments. Farther to the south, Goldsmith Chandlee, the son and grandson of instrument makers, ran a foundry in Winchester, Virginia, where he made, sold, and repaired not only sundials but also clocks, compasses, scales, surgical instruments, telescopes, and other metal products.[9]

Sundials marked time with approximately the same accuracy as the mechanical timepieces of the period: within about four minutes a day for the very best watch or dial; to the closest quarter hour for average ones. In fact, people who owned clocks and watches needed sundials to set their mechanical timekeepers, until the second half of the nineteenth century, when observatories and local jewelers began to disseminate accurate time by telegraph. An eighteenth-century sundial expert warned that clocks and watches were frequently "out of order, apt to stop and go wrong and therefore require frequently to be regulated by some unerring instrument as a dial;

To set their clocks and watches by the sun, people consulted an equation-of-time table like the one engraved on this sundial, made by Christopher Colles, a New York instrument maker and engineer, about 1800.

An advertisement for watchmaker Christopher Townsend, Jr., of Newport, Rhode Island, this watch paper from about 1770 bears an equation-of-time table for setting watches by the sun.

The Equation of Time. As the relationship of the Earth to the sun changes with the seasons, the sun appears to run faster or slower than the clock. The difference between clock time and sun time is the "equation of time."

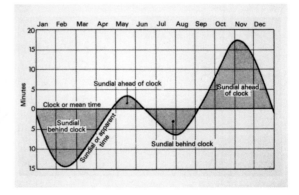

When making repairs, a watchmaker routinely inserted a watch paper between the cases of a pair-cased watch. Watch signed "L. Goddard & Son," about 1820.

Inside the case of this shelf clock, made by Eli Terry in Plymouth, Connecticut, about 1817, is a paper label printed with an equation-of-time table.

which being rightly constructed, will always (when the sun shines) tell us truth. And therefore whether we have any clocks or not we should never be without a dial."[10] The sun, not the clock, was the authoritative source of time.

Knowing the latitude of the place where the dial was to be used was essential to finding accurate time. The dial's shadow-caster, the gnomon, had to be set on the north–south axis, that is, the dial's noon line, and angled to the same degree as the degree of latitude. For a dial in Charleston, South Carolina, just south of the thirty-third parallel, an accurate gnomon required an angle of 33 degrees. For an accurate Boston dial, the gnomon slanted 42 degrees.[11]

At the end of the seventeenth century, when clocks first became accurate enough to keep time to the minute, it became clear that the sun and mechanical timekeepers do not mark the same time. Clock time is unvarying: each minute is sixty equal seconds, each hour is sixty equal minutes, and each day is twenty-four equal hours. But a solar day, from noon to noon, varies in length by a few seconds throughout the year. Days are of slightly different lengths because the Earth tilts on its axis (the plane of the equator is not the same as the plane of the Earth's orbit around the sun), and the Earth's orbit around the sun is an ellipse, not a circle. As the relationship of the Earth to the sun changes with the seasons, the sun appears to run faster or slower than the constant clock. These differences between clock time and sun time accumulate as the year progresses. In February the sun appears to be more than fourteen minutes slower than the clock, and by December sixteen minutes faster. The difference between clock time (called *mean time*) and apparent solar time, the way the sun time is indicated on the sundial, is called "the equation of time."

To account for these variations, eighteenth-century timepiece owners consulted an equation-of-time table for directions to set mechanical timepieces by a sundial. Occasionally a conversion table appeared in an almanac or directly on a sundial. More often, though, people carried the equation-of-time table with their watches. Most watches by the end of the eighteenth century had two cases, an inner one enclosing the movement and an outer protective one. Between the two cases watchmakers and repairers often inserted a round "watch paper," typically their printed advertisement which often included an equation-of-time table for setting the watch by a sundial. Even American clocks in the early nineteenth century sometimes still bore equation-of-time tables.

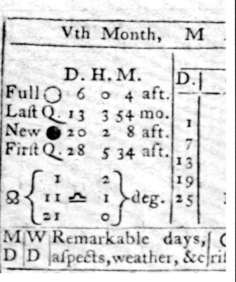

On this almanac page for May 1792, readers could find information about the moon's waxing and waning and its position in the sky relative to stars and planets.

Dial with moon phases from a tall case clock made by Peter Hill, Burlington, New Jersey, about 1800. Hill was one of the few African-American professional clockmakers working at that time. It is likely Hill made the clock movement, but the dial was imported from Wilson Clock Dial Manufactory, Birmingham, England.

Night and Day

NIGHTS WERE VERY DARK. Even with only firelight, candles, and moonlight for illumination, rural life slowed but did not stop at night. At dusk, also called "candlelighting," costly candles were brought out and used sparingly. Most houses were poorly lit, and, until bedtime, people gathered around the hearth or at a central table to finish household tasks, read, socialize, or play games. When the moon was full and bright, there was light and time for outdoor chores, amusements, or travel. Enslaved blacks in America, especially, filled the nighttime with hunting, traveling to visit friends and family, religious gatherings, and celebrations. Although time was not for slaves to pass as they wanted, they were freer to pursue their own purposes at night, once the workday ended.[12]

For those who wanted to plan for moonlight, almanacs forecast the phases of the moon, as did mechanized indicators on clock dials. The dial of a tall case clock tracked the moon's waxing and waning — the progression of the moon from first quarter, to full moon, to last quarter, to new moon. The white-painted dial, an English innovation of about 1770, was easier to see by the light of a flickering candle or the moon than a brass one.[13]

Star Time

DARK NIGHTS, without bright city lights, made it easier to see the stars. Eighteenth-century almanacs assumed a reader's ability to recognize the brightest stars in the sky, to track the planets, and to use the heavens as a way to mark time. Without any kind of instruments or advanced education, almost anyone could and did practice elementary astronomy and appreciate the lessons of the heavens. Readers of the night sky might note the time the Dog Star rose or Jupiter crossed the meridian.[14] By the middle of the nineteenth century, this kind of practical know-how was waning, if Ralph Waldo Emerson's lament in "Self-Reliance" (1841) was an accurate indicator:

> The civilized man . . . has a fine Geneva watch but he fails of the skill to tell the hour by the sun . . . the man in the street does not know a star in the sky. The solstice he does not observe; the equinox he knows as little; and the whole bright calendar of the year is without a dial in his mind.[15]

Noting the position of certain stars from one night to the next, in fact, provides a more accurate measure of time than marking the sun. But because of the difficulties inherent in making consistent night observations and the precision instruments required, using the stars to determine time to the second was the specialty of astronomers, navigators, and some surveyors.

Astronomers looked for specific predicted "clock stars" to find the time. An observer consulted published tables that correlated the recurring appearance of a star at a known meridian and then calculated the time it would appear locally. Using a special telescope called a transit and a highly accurate timekeeper called a regulator, an observer noted the instant a clock star passed the local meridian. American observers were interested in finding time not just for its own sake, but to apply it to very practical ends: determining the grid of imaginary lines for latitude and longitude in a largely uncharted country.

With so much available land, North America provided plenty of work for surveyors, especially after 1785, when Congress enacted the grid pattern that would eventually cover two-thirds of the map with orderly squares and make public lands available for settlement and sale. Initially the law required surveyors to find the true meridian (the longitude) in such surveys. Almost immediately, though, accuracy was sacrificed to speed, and Congress waived the requirement in 1786. As a result, most surveyors did not use astronomical observations in their work. Practically anyone with a little knowledge of mathematics and simple instruments — a compass to find direction, chains to measure, and a plumb bob to level — could mark town lots or township

Sandglasses with twenty-eight-second durations, early nineteenth century.

squares. Impatient settlers wanted access to the land immediately, not precise dimensions of their land expressed in terms of latitudes and longitudes.[16]

Not all surveying was local. Grand geodetic enterprises were undertaken in the eighteenth and nineteenth centuries. National surveys in France and Britain, imperial surveys in Africa and India, and other international trigonometric and chronometer expeditions established exact locations in terms of latitude and longitude, relative to each other on the globe. Determining precise locations became intimately connected with the international investigations of the size, shape, and nature of the Earth and its parts.

European academicians shaped this branch of geography into a serious science in the eighteenth century. The French, supported initially by the Académie Royale des Sciences, came to dominate the science of geodesy.[17] The British developed parallel mathematical skills and formidable instrument-making capabilities, but their emphasis for centuries had been on finding positions at sea, rather than on land. Their most famous contribution to globally linked geodetic investigations was conducted in North America. As astronomers Charles Mason and Jeremiah Dixon surveyed the border between Maryland and Pennsylvania from 1763 to 1768, the Royal Society provided them with instructions and equipment to measure the meridian arc along the western border of Delaware. Major Andrew Ellicott completed two other critical astronomical boundary surveys for the United States: the lines for the District of Columbia in 1791–92, the survey in which Benjamin Banneker participated, and the border between the United States and Spanish Florida, completed in 1800.[18]

Mariner's Time

AT SEA, TIME WAS CRUCIAL TO NAVIGATION. Since the Middle Ages, mariners had used sandglasses that measured intervals of time to calculate ship speed, distance traveled, and periods of duty.

To determine ship speed, sailors used sandglasses to time the distance run against knots in the log line. The log was a piece of wood, weighted on one side to float upright, attached to a

Durations of marine watch glasses, from
Thomas Riley Blanckley, *A Naval Expositor,*
London, 1750.

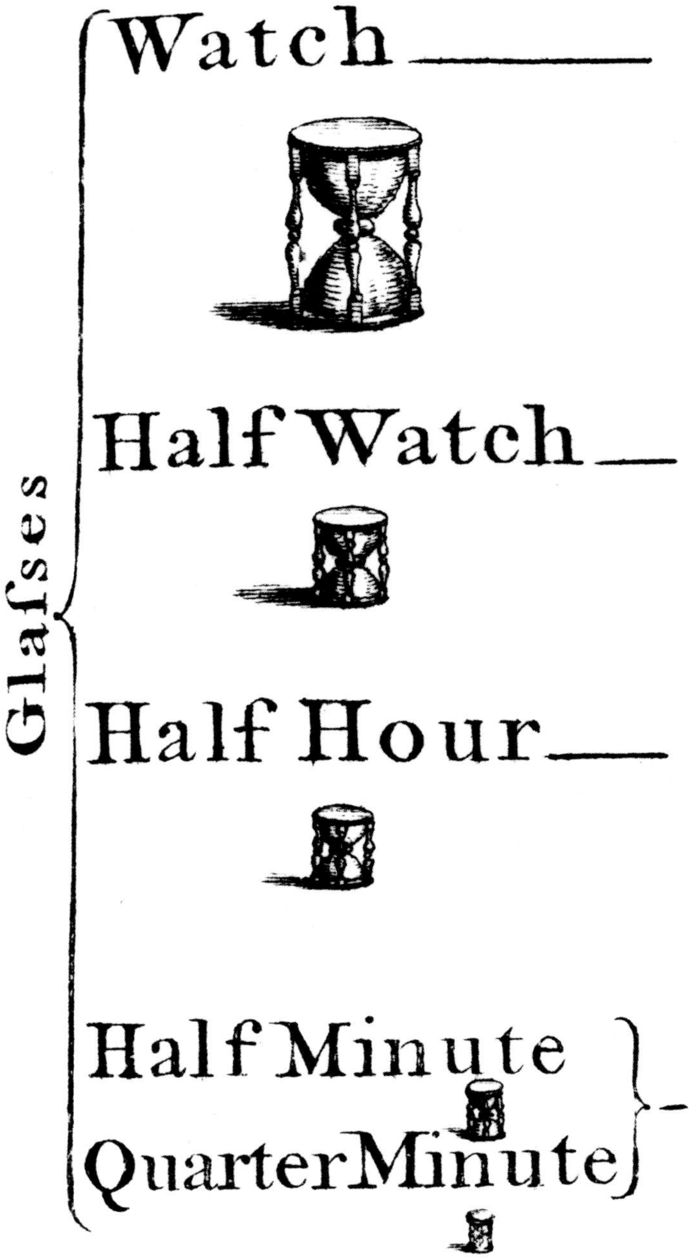

Glaſses

Watch _____

Half Watch __

Half Hour __

Half Minute }
Quarter Minute }

long rope. This log line had knots tied at regular intervals, traditionally seven fathoms, and wound off of a hand-held reel. With the log and line cast astern, a seaman counted the number of knots played out in about half a minute to get the speed in "knots." The traditional sandglass for this purpose had a duration of twenty-eight seconds. With the advent of speedier clipper ships in the 1840s, the standard shifted to fourteen seconds. Watch glasses were useful for keeping track of longer intervals – usually a half an hour, one hour, or four hours – and especially time's passage at night. The Reverend Edward Taylor noted in his diary, as he sailed across the Atlantic, "towards night we lowered sail and tarried about 2 glasses, i.e., an hour." [19]

Even more critical was using time to find a ship's precise location in the trackless seas. Even with the best compass or chart, a ship could easily lose its way at the cost of lives and cargo. In one of the worst such mishaps, the crews of four British warships – nearly two thousand men – died in October 1707 when they ran aground on the Scilly Isles. Fixing a ship's position in latitude and longitude would gradually become part of the mariners' routine, and both positional dimensions were dependent on knowing the time. To find latitude, the distance north or south of the equator, mariners used an octant or quadrant to determine the angle of the sun at noon or the star Polaris at night above the horizon. Determining longitude, a distance east or west of a reference meridian, was much more difficult.

Beginning late in the sixteenth century, Europe's prominent seafaring nations offered rewards to anyone who could find a convenient method for determining longitude. Proposals for finding longitude with a portable clock had repeatedly surfaced since Flemish astronomer Gemma Frisius first suggested it in 1530. Such plans were based on the widely recognized equivalence of time and longitude: the Earth makes one rotation in twenty-four hours through 360° of longitude, and, like the subdivisions of hours, the subdivisions of longitude degrees are expressed in "minutes" and "seconds." But actually making a timekeeper that remained reliable on a pitching ship, in ever-changing temperatures, proved a most stubborn design problem.

A stunning technical breakthrough came when John Harrison, a talented English carpenter and clockmaker, built five marine timekeepers between 1735 and 1770 that incontestably demonstrated the utility of a clock at sea. Inspired by Harrison's innovations, other makers, notably Larcum Kendall, Thomas Mudge, John Arnold, and Thomas Earnshaw in England and Pierre LeRoy and Ferdinand Berthoud in France, contributed refinements to Harrison's designs, and the standard modern marine chronometer resulted. [20]

To use a marine chronometer, outbound sailors would set their timepieces to the time of a place at a known longitude – say Greenwich, England, or Paris, France. Once at sea, mariners calculated their position east or west of that place by converting the difference between the time on the chronometer and local ship time into distance, 15 degrees of longitude for every hour.

Using an octant. To find latitude, mariners used an octant to determine the angle of the sun at noon or the star Polaris at night above the horizon.

Marine chronometer, made by Arnold & Dent, London, about 1830–40.

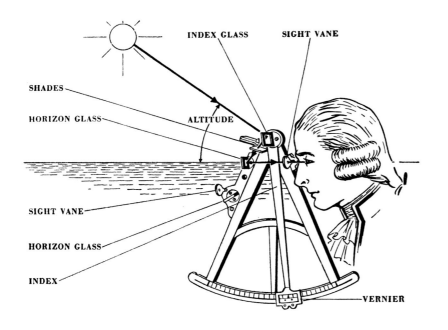

SHADES

HORIZON GLASS

INDEX GLASS

SIGHT VANE

ALTITUDE

SIGHT VANE

HORIZON GLASS

INDEX

VERNIER

1131

Marine timekeeper made by William Cranch Bond, Boston, 1812–15.

It took nearly two generations after Harrison made his models for marine chronometers to come into routine use.[21] At the start of the nineteenth century, marine chronometers were not yet standard on American vessels. Navigation was still largely conducted by "the three Ls": log (for determining speed), lead (for taking soundings), and lookout. Only as the century progressed would latitude and longitude determinations make it "the Five Ls."[22]

The first seagoing chronometer made in the United States came from the workshop of a Boston clockmaker and astronomer. Twenty-three-year-old William Cranch Bond constructed it during the War of 1812. The most striking feature of this instrument is its unconventional weight drive. By the beginning of the nineteenth century, the most common means of driving a marine timekeeper was the force of an unwinding mainspring. But Bond began working on his timekeeper during the War of 1812, when a trade embargo prevented him from procuring British spring steel, so he constructed his chronometer to run with a falling lead weight after reading about the eighteenth-century marine timekeepers that Ferdinand Berthoud made for the French navigator Jean-François de Galaup, Comte de La Pérouse.[23]

Bond's instrument went to sea only once, on a voyage to Sumatra in 1818 aboard the U.S. Navy's *Cyrus*. After numerous opportunities to test it against lunar observations, Captain Thomas B. Curtis found that the timekeeper performed "with utmost regularity," but he warned Bond to "please remember that I am not experienced in the use of the instrument, and attribute any errors you may discover to this cause." It would be another twenty years before marine chronometers were widely used on American vessels.[24]

Clockwork Universe

IDEAS ABOUT TIME, SPACE, AND CLOCKS went well beyond the practical. The clock had become a powerful metaphor for explaining how the universe worked. By the end of the seventeenth century, many Western thinkers visualized the universe functioning like a giant clockwork. Originating in fourteenth-century essays that related the clock to divine order, the metaphor evolved to describe systems – the universe, the body, and even the political state – operating under a central authority. Continental thinkers saw positive harmony in this orderly, centrally controlled cosmos and valued the clock as the symbol of authority. In Great Britain, theorists came to see the clock as a metaphor for forces that stood for the opposite of liberty: regimentation, authoritarianism, and tyranny.[25]

Sir Isaac Newton (1642–1727).

Although Isaac Newton never used the clockwork metaphor himself, he described the workings of the heavens mathematically in his celebrated masterpiece, *Philosophiae Naturalis Principia Mathematica* (1687), known more commonly as the *Principia*. There he theorized that matter moved in regular, predictable ways through space and time under the influence of gravity. For Newton, the universe was far from an ideal clock that ran flawlessly and eternally without winding. It was instead a dynamic system in need of periodic adjustments from God. In contrast to this ever-changing system, Newton theorized, time was absolute and one-way, advancing and constant everywhere in the universe.[26]

Newton's ideas about the orderly working of the cosmos shaped Enlightenment thought and science in early America. Educated Americans, typified by Thomas Jefferson and Benjamin Franklin, embraced Newtonian notions about interpreting nature through reason and mathematics. Franklin, a distinguished scientist in his own right, owed an intellectual debt to Newton and expanded Newtonian science with his experiments and theories on electricity. Franklin's mentor, James Logan, had brought the first copy of Newton's *Principia* to America, and Poor Richard, in Franklin's almanacs, often expressed himself in Newtonian verse. Thomas Jefferson understood the higher mathematics of the *Principia* and the experimental methods outlined in Newton's *Opticks*. His esteem for Newton's methods and ideas about the grand design of the cosmos was substantial: he owned not just an oil portrait of Newton, but also one of about a dozen of the great man's death masks.[27]

By the middle of the eighteenth century, Newtonian "natural philosophy" was at the core of the American college curriculum. Courses relied on textbooks written by British popularizers, who simplified Newton's *Principia* from its original Latin and dense higher mathematics. To supplement these texts, American colleges sought out master artisans to prepare three-dimensional teaching aids to link clocks, calendars, and nature. This kind of clockwork-driven model – sometimes called an orrery, in honor of the inventor's patron, Charles Boyle, Great Britain's fourth earl of Orrery – demonstrated the relative motions of the solar system, the workings of the Newtonian universe. Harvard had two such British orreries and a third by an American, Joseph Pope. Thomas Jefferson's friend David Rittenhouse, of Philadelphia, made complex three-dimensional models of the Newtonian universe for both Princeton and the University of Pennsylvania. Jefferson found Rittenhouse's work nearly perfect, except for one thing. He suggested such a heavenly model should be dubbed *planetarium Americanum,* not orrery.[28]

After midcentury, a select few of America's skilled clock- and watchmakers built domestic clocks with orrery attachments. In 1769, Pennsylvania clockmaker and millwright Joseph Ellicott completed a remarkable complicated tall case clock. It tells the time, shows the phases of the

TELLING TIME

Four-sided tall case clock made by Joseph Ellicott, Buckingham, Pennsylvania, completed 1769.

Time dial of Ellicott's clock.

moon, depicts on an orrery the motions of the sun, moon, and planets, and plays twenty-four musical selections on the hour. Some twenty years later, a Baltimore newspaper reported a curious astronomical clock made in York, Pennsylvania.[29] And in 1798, the Philadelphia watchmaker Charles Campbell advertised for sale an astronomical clock "shewing the motion of the Planets, making their revolutions round the Sun according to the Newtonian System." These eighteenth-century demonstrations of mechanical genius continued a tradition reaching back to the earliest clockmakers, in which every new generation of mechanicians sought to outdo their predecessors' work.[30]

There are those who have argued that the first clocks in the Middle Ages were invented not as automatic bell-ringing devices, but instead as grand geared models of the universe.[31] Regardless of its origins, almost from the moment the clock was invented at the end of the thirteenth century until the end of the eighteenth century, improvements in clockwork remained the cutting edge of technical achievement. Esteemed for centuries as the epitome of the machine, the clock provided the Enlightenment with a powerful symbol of rational structure and harmonious, programmed operation. Educated people wanted to own them and use them.

The orrery dial on the Ellicott clock represents the motions of the solar system known at the time of the clock's completion.

The music dial on the Ellicott clock allows the listener to choose from twelve pairs of tunes. In each pair is a short tune and a long one. On the hour, only the short tune plays, but every third hour, both play. During a tune, the automaton figures at the top of the dial appear to tap their feet in time to the music and the small dog between them jumps up and down.

Movement of the Ellicott clock. The bells that play the clock's tunes are visible through the glass, just below the arch.

Sunlight striking certain rock structures might have signaled key times in the ritual cycle for the ancient Anasazi Indians in Chaco Canyon, New Mexico.

time in religion

IN EARLY AMERICA, religion exerted a powerful influence on the way people kept track of time and ordered their lives in worship, work, and rest. The main source of time's authority, in fact, lay in religious beliefs. There the faithful found the abstract notions and practical rules, written or unwritten, that specified how people should and did use time.[32]

Every religion practiced its own calendar-based rituals cued from nature's cyclical rhythms. Every religion's calendar framed daily life, merged recurring holy days and festivals with stable astronomical cycles, and offered the most fundamental means of coordinating social time.

Early America's European population was overwhelmingly Christian, and more specifically Protestant. The source of their belief was the Bible, which described how God made time, revealed time in nature, and gave time as a gift to humans. Christianity also held that time stretched in a unidirectional line from the past through the present to a better future. Heavenly perfection was the ultimate destination, and Judgment Day the end of time. The Christian calendar, with Sunday punctuating the week, eventually came to dominate American life, but in early America the timing of religious rituals was dependent on the community practicing them. Time in religious matters, like time in daily life, was locally determined.

Calendar Rituals

This day,
My sun father,
You have come out standing
To your sacred dwelling place
Where we find our sacred spring.

– Zuni song

CALENDAR-BASED RITUALS tuned to nature's rhythms were central to every religion in the racial, ethnic, and cultural mosaic of early America. Ritual times were identified by the position of the sun, the phases of the moon, the appearance of certain stars and planets, seasonal changes. Events in nature signaled the time was right to attend to sacred matters.

Most Native Americans devised ways to reckon time to integrate themselves with nature and the supernatural elements they found there. Some were especially attentive to astronomical events. The Skidi Pawnee, the Wichita, and the Caddo of the Plains, for example, watched and heeded the stars. Others, like the Navajo, Apache, Ute, Pima, Papago, and Hopi, celebrated the sun. For Pueblo societies, determining the precise winter and summer solstice was crucial to their ceremonial and agricultural interests. They could discern their religious calendar on the landscape: the arrival of the sun at a particular feature on the horizon signaled the right time.[33]

Long before Europeans settled in America, the Christian church calendar had combined religious observances with nature's cycles and furnished a framework to structure social time in

This omer was used in the early nineteenth century during the Jewish religious year to count the fifty sunsets between Passover, commemorating the exodus from Egypt, and Shavuot, marking the giving of the Ten Commandments.

everyday life.[34] Crucial to that calendar was Easter. The most meaningful event in the church year, the annual celebration of Jesus' resurrection had occurred, according to New Testament accounts, during the observance of the Jewish Passover. To reconcile the Jewish lunar calendar with the Roman, or Julian, calendar, early Christians agreed to celebrate Easter on the first Sunday after the full moon on or after the spring equinox and to tie the other "movable feasts," holidays for which the date varies from year to year, to that date. Whitsunday, or Pentecost, for example, occurs on the seventh Sunday after Easter. Specialists responsible for calculating the church calendar issued tables to predict the appearance of the full moon year after year and to determine the possible Sundays for Easter. Theoretically, with information from the tables, which became regular features of the earliest almanacs, the faithful, no matter how scattered, could calculate the holy days and celebrate them at the same time with the rest of Christendom.

Civil governments gradually adopted the church calendar. Following Pope Gregory XIII's reform of the Julian calendar in 1582, the states of Continental Europe, one by one, made the switch. It wasn't until the mid-eighteenth century that calendar reform finally became an issue in England, the last major country still on the old-style Julian calendar. Mostly to coordinate commerce with other nations rather than for religious reasons, the British Parliament enacted a change to the new Gregorian, or new style, calendar. To realign the old and new styles throughout the British Empire, the days from 3 through 13 in September 1752 were omitted and, beginning in 1753, each new civil year began on January 1 instead of March 25.

The British North American colonies adjusted to the new calendar easily. News of the impending calendar change filled British colonial newspapers in advance, and well-prepared colonists calmly skipped the eleven days. By September 1752 the Gregorian calendar was in fact already in use in many parts of the colonies. The successful colonial merchant, for example, was fluent in both calendar systems. His transactions depended on knowing not only which countries, but also sometimes which worldwide imperial ports, used what system. And immigrants from Europe, perhaps as much as one-fifth of the American population, brought the Gregorian calendar with them from their home countries. They tended to relate important events in family life – marriages, births, and deaths – to the Gregorian calendar and to use the Julian calendar only when dealing with British officialdom. Calendar use, like other forms of time-related behavior, was contingent on community. But regardless of background, people accommodated without difficulty to the first effort to standardize time in North America.[35]

Sundays occupied a special place in the Christian calendar. Strict forms of Sabbath observance, brought to America by the Puritans, led to widely adopted "blue laws" prohibiting certain

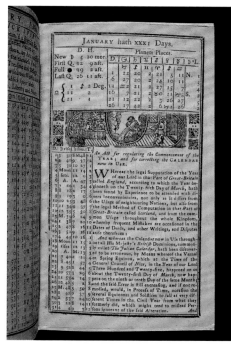

activities on Sundays. What particular activities were banned depended on local custom. Virginians could enjoy horse racing and the gambling that went with it on the Sabbath, and taverns in Massachusetts welcomed fishermen. Even for those who did not agree with setting aside Sunday for worship and rest, recurring Sundays distinguished one week from the next and provided an essential way to mark the passage of time. As the nineteenth century began, Sunday meant a day of religion-based rest from work for most Americans of every rank except slaves. As the years passed, Sunday also became a day for family gathering, cultural enrichment, and commercial forms of leisure. In our own age, as this book's final chapter discusses, economic pressures mount for a 24/7 world and threaten more than ever to turn Sunday into just another day.[36]

Scheduling the Day

CENTURIES-OLD DEVOTIONAL SCHEDULES devised by Jewish rabbis and Benedictine monks established the Western habit of partitioning the day and specifying times for worship and work.[37]

Catholic orders in the New World followed – and often imposed on others – rules that laid out highly structured schedules of work, meals, instruction, and prayer. In the American Southwest, in addition to the cyclical church calendar, with fixed and movable saints' days and religious festivals, Franciscan friars subdivided the day into hours for prayer (matins, lauds, primes, terces, sexts, nones, compline) and rang bells to alert the faithful that it was time for devotions. Like their counterparts who had cloistered themselves against the turmoil of the Middle Ages, these men and women sought order on the frontier. One cleric likened the operation of a mission in seventeenth-century New Mexico, regulated by the bells, to a clock:

> In every pueblo where a friar resides, he has schools for the teaching of praying, singing, playing musical instruments, and other interesting things. Promptly at dawn, one of the Indian singers . . . goes to ring the bell for the Prime, at the sound of which those who go to school assemble and sweep the rooms thoroughly. . . . When everything is neat and clean, they again ring the bell and each one goes to learn his particular specialty. . . . After they have been occupied in this manner for an hour and a half, the bell is rung for mass. . . . In the evening they toll the bell for vespers. . . . All the wheels of this clock must be kept in good order by the friar, without neglecting any detail, otherwise all would be totally lost.[38]

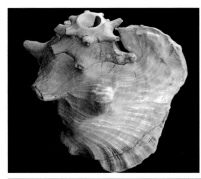

The Pueblo people who lived in or nearby the mission also understood a different kind of time, time based in seasonal changes. The summer brought different tasks from winter, and the natives went so far as to change leadership from summer to winter.[39]

Only the wealthiest colonial churches had tower clocks with bells. More often, town criers, shells, horns, and other devices served to signal time not just for a congregation but for an entire community. In some cases these signals were extensions of clock time, tolling on the hour. In others they signaled the right time to assemble, as in the words of an old hymn:

> The time we tell
> When there to come
> By beat of drum
> Or sounding shell.[40]

For centuries, European armies had instilled discipline, regulated the soldier's day, told him the time of day, and signaled what duties his superiors expected of him with drums.[41] Following the military example, some New England towns employed public drummers to "warn," or summon, citizens to upcoming important events, such as town meetings and worship. Depending on the rhythmic message, citizens within earshot knew it was time to assemble for worship, public meetings, or military obligations.[42] Drums could perform the same function for Africans in America as for New Englanders.

In responding promptly to the call of bells, drums, and horns, citizens were demonstrating an obedience to community time. Time communicated in this way meant someone was responsible for knowing the right time and sharing it with the community. The right time might have been a particular hour of the clock or some other agreed-upon cue. Each individual was responsible for obeying the summons. Still in the future was a more widespread internal time discipline, a different kind of time consciousness in which each person was responsible for knowing the correct time by the clock and being on time for the myriad social obligations of a more complex world.[43]

African slaves in Virginia used this drum in the early eighteenth century to announce celebrations and religious gatherings.

A common Puritan gravestone motif in the seventeenth century to indicate the fleeting nature of time was the winged sandglass, pictured above the skull on this casting of the headstone for Thomas Kendal, Wakefield, Massachusetts.

Improving Time

THE GERMAN SOCIOLOGIST Max Weber's classic study *The Protestant Ethic and the Spirit of Capitalism* (1920) argued that the origins of the modern drive to work hard, make the most of time, and build a progressively better life lie deep in Puritan religious ideas about time, and especially those about predestination, or election for salvation. A person's good works, according to Protestant doctrine, did not buy salvation, but they did demonstrate election.[44] Seventeenth-century New England Puritans believed that time belonged to God, who in turn gave time as a gift to his people on Earth. To show their respect for the divine gift of time, the devout diligently sought to "improve" every waking moment in an earthly life that was fleetingly short. This they did through worship and productive activity. A successful Christian, they believed, was industrious and thrifty with time. The Catholic church had similarly counted sloth among the deadly sins since the early days of medieval monasticism, but the Massachusetts colonial government took opposition to idleness to a whole new level when it joined with the Puritan clergy to enact civil laws and penalties:

> No person, householder, or other shall spend his time idly or unprofitably, under the pain of . . . punishment . . . ; and for this end it is ordered that the constables of every place shall use special diligence to take knowledge of offenders of this kind.[45]

Although the main way civil authorities regulated time was through enforcing Sunday closing laws, they also monitored on-time attendance at court sessions. Although tardiness was considered a petty breach of appropriate conduct, idleness was judged much more seriously, as a flagrant challenge to church and community. In the uncertain world of colonial New England, where people and resources were in chronically short supply, work without end seemed the only way to guarantee survival.[46]

The British historian E. P. Thompson elaborated on Weber's study when he argued that industrial capitalists, in beginning the practice of paying for workers' time and calculating labor by the clock, drew on this sense of Puritan time thrift to train and control their workforces. Critics have systematically dismantled many of the arguments Weber and Thompson made. Christians in general, not just Puritans, they point out, believed that time was precious. Not all Protestants participated in hard work, industrial capitalism, and running by the clock. But regardless of their origins, prescriptive ideas about using time to the utmost would eventually permeate nineteenth-century American life. Gradually and unevenly, the clock would join God and nature as the sources of time.[47]

Coordinating Community Life

THE GERMAN IMMIGRANTS who founded Frederick, Maryland, believed, much like the Puritans, that time was a divine gift to be spent in productive work. According to their Calvinist values, temporal order was an important component of godly and disciplined behavior. They relied on a tower clock to help them organize and coordinate their daily lives in time. The congregation of Frederick's German Reform Church (now Trinity Chapel) installed a clock in the church tower in the 1790s. The entire town contributed to buy the clock for about $800 and paid for its maintenance. This clock coordinated activities for the town's intertwined sacred and secular communities for nearly 140 years.[48]

The first tower clocks appeared in Europe in the early 1300s. They were not designed to show the hour, but to ring bells. In fact, the word *clock* has its origin in *clok*, a Middle English word for bell. Clocks and bells in church steeples, town halls, and city gates provided time cues for the daily rounds of urban life. Their influence increased after dials were added in the fifteenth century.[49]

The leading technology of its day, the medieval European tower clock symbolized a community's wealth, the value it placed on civic order, and its modernity. European settlers in America continued the practice of installing tower clocks and bells in churches and community buildings throughout the eighteenth and nineteenth centuries all over the country. The sound of the bells came to signal the passing hours as powerfully as the clock dial. And the same bells that announced the hours of prayer synchronized the housewife's and the merchant's and the artisan's and the laborer's day.[50]

Subdividing the day and sounding time's passage, the community bell delighted some and

Tower clock movement made for the German Reform Church, Frederick, Maryland, about 1790.

troubled others. Repairs to the Fort Bell in New York City in 1733, for example, prompted one artisan to predict that the renovation would restore order to life and would "produce a great Reformation . . . we shall breakfast, dine and sup, according to Rule and Compass, and know how to square our work as in the days of our Forefathers."[51] But in Newport, Rhode Island, a new service of public bells at sunrise, at one in the afternoon, and again at nine in the evening elicited an objection to a new kind of time pressure from at least one, undoubtedly fictional, citizen. Housewife "Patience Meanwell" complained to the local newspaper that her husband, "a labouring man," now arrived home after the one o'clock bell expecting a meal. "Before the bell was rung at one o'clock," she explained, "if my husband came home, and his victuals were not ready as neither he nor I really know the time of day, I could easily make an excuse." To restore "family peace," she asked that authorities either skip the one o'clock bell or add one at eleven to alert housewives to begin meal preparations.[52]

TELLING TIME

This lantern clock has only an hour hand. London clockmaker Joseph Hall made it about 1680, and its English owners moved with it from Bermuda to Massachusetts around 1700.

status symbols

Tall case clock with only an hour hand, made by Peter Stretch, Philadelphia, about 1700–1715.

Dial for tall case clock made by Peter Stretch.

FOR CENTURIES, mechanical timekeepers had been uncommon and costly symbols of a person's wealth and social standing. In 1700, the rich were still the most likely to own clocks and watches. By 1800, timepieces were becoming cheaper and more widely available to a growing American middle class that included artisans, shopkeepers, and professionals.

Domestic Clocks

ENGLISH GOODS DOMINATED the material life of the English colonies. American colonists imported clocks and watches from England as early as 1703; newspaper advertisements document a vital trade in complete clocks and horological materials throughout the eighteenth century. Relatively few clocks were made in the colonies until after the Revolution.

Clocks were among the most expensive items their seventeenth- and eighteenth-century owners possessed. Along with fully furnished "best" beds, looking glasses, sofas, silver, and case furniture, clocks were the household possessions consistently assigned the highest value in probate inventories.[53]

The earliest English type was the lantern clock, with brass gear trains held between pillars, an elaborately engraved dial, and a bell mounted above the movement with brass straps. Such clocks were usually small, roughly fifteen inches top to bottom, and usually without a case of any sort, but sometimes with brass doors enclosing the movement like a box. Lantern clocks hung directly on the wall with pendulum and falling weights exposed.

By the eighteenth century, the most common style of domestic clock came to look more like a piece of household furniture.[54] A wooden case enclosed the movement, weights, and pendulum. Through a glass window the dial was visible.

Although critical technical improvements in the 1660s permitted the best clocks to keep time to the second, clockmakers at the end of that century were still making some domestic timepieces with only one hand, the hour hand. These clocks were usually reliable to the closest quarter hour, rather than to the minute and second. Colonists in New England certainly understood and applied the concept of the minute, whether they had clocks to mark them. John Winthrop, for example, reported an earthquake in the Narragansett Bay area that sounded "like a continued thunder or the rattling of coaches in London" lasted "about four minutes."[55]

Emblematic of the changing relationship of the clock to how people used time was the timekeeper that Thomas Jefferson installed at Monticello by 1805. Specified in detail by Jefferson himself and made, under the supervision of Philadelphia clockmaker Robert Leslie, by Peter Spruck, the clockwork hung inside the house just over the entrance. There it operated a dial with three hands to indicate hours, minutes, and seconds for scheduling the household indoors. The same clockwork connected to a second dial outside the house, but the outside dial had only one hand. According to Jefferson's prescription, a gong in the cupola over the front door sounded the hours "all over my farm." The clock indicated Jefferson's own preoccupation with keeping close track of time and making the most of it. More than that, the clock with two different dials stood for a momentous transition taking place in American life. For the rhythms of agricultural work, keeping time to the closest hour seemed sufficient. For the tightly coordinated world to come, tracking minutes and seconds would scarcely be enough.[56]

The domestic craft of clockmaking grew steadily in eighteenth-century America. Clockmakers – men trained in making, finishing, or repairing clocks – emigrated to the colonies, north and south. Their numbers increased, and the trade prospered. But precisely how many clockmakers worked in America before 1820 is difficult to determine. One count of seventeenth-century clockmakers and dealers in New England listed only seven in four towns – Boston and Sudbury, Massachusetts, and Hartford and New Haven, Connecticut – but in the eighteenth century more than 300 craftsmen worked in 113 towns. Another tally shows the geographical distribution across the country. Between 1650 and 1750, 98 clockmakers worked in Northern and Middle Atlantic colonies compared to 26 in the South. Between 1751 and 1800, the numbers jump to 796 in the North and 177 in the South.[57]

Clockmakers, like today's shoemakers, often did most of their business in repairs rather than in making new clocks, and even when he undertook a new project, a clockmaker generally did not make the entire clock. In the horological trades, both in America and abroad, a long-standing practice permitted the finisher–retailer of the timepiece to put his name on it. A commentator explained:

> [S]ince clocks have become so common as to be considered an article of household furniture, the art of making them has not been confined, as at first, to one department of mechanics, but has gradually ramified into various branches, so distinct from one another, that the maker of one part is frequently unacquainted with the operations required for the manipulation of another, equally essential. . . . From custom, however, that man is called a clock-maker who finishes or puts together the different constituent parts of a clock when made, and who has his profit from the sale of the machine.[58]

Although a successful clockmaker doubtless possessed considerable metalworking skills and put them to use, he also would have enlisted others, either in England or America, to cast the

Tall case clock, signed Simon Willard,
about 1799.

pendulum, movement, dial plates, gear blanks, weights, and bell. These additional artisans had shops of their own. Small workshops of fewer than four people were the norm, although in some urban centers the staff might be larger. Country clockmakers usually began work only after a customer placed an order, but a city clockmaker might keep a small stock. Clockmakers subcontracted cases from cabinetmakers, and even then, depending on the decorations, the work of many specialists might go into the case. It was even common, and certainly economical, business practice to import a finished English movement and dial, to mark them with the American retailer's name, and sell them to waiting customers. Toward the end of the eighteenth century, customers had a range of American and imported clocks to choose from; the most popular were tall case clocks.[59]

By the end of the eighteenth century, as demand for clocks rose, two brothers from rural Massachusetts coordinated the most extensive network of independent artisans for making clocks ever attempted. Simon and Aaron Willard set up two separate workshops in Roxbury, close to the Boston market and shipping routes, and employed more than a score of people to assemble clocks. Furthermore, they attracted to the locale additional independent craftsmen with related skills – more than twenty clockmakers, cabinetmakers, dial painters, and gilders worked for the Willards in Roxbury by 1807. With this critical mass of skilled artisans and additional help from workmen in England, the Willards introduced an American style of quantity production before industrialization. To meet customer demand for things with English style and quality, they provided English-made clocks under their signatures, assembled imported English clock kits, made clocks from English components. They even made clock parts of their own.[60]

Without abandoning the traditional tall case clock, the Willards successfully experimented with two completely new American clock styles. Simon Willard and another brother, Benjamin, developed the elegant Massachusetts shelf clock, or half clock, in the 1770s. Standing only about three feet tall, the clock was in essence a tall case clock with the trunk left out. Its brass movement resembled that of the traditional tall case clock, but simplified and much reduced in size. In 1802 Simon Willard obtained a U.S. patent for a wall-hung timepiece as original as it was successful. The "patent timepiece," or banjo clock, named for its distinctive shape, established the independence of American clockmaking from European traditions. Vast numbers have been manufactured to this day without notable modifications to its design since the early nineteenth century. Several thousand banjo clocks were probably built by Simon Willard's own shop. But he also freely permitted his numerous clockmaking relatives, former apprentices, and other clockmakers to produce them according to his design. They generally sold for about $30.[61]

At the close of the eighteenth century, some American clockmakers abandoned the English tradition of making high-style clocks with movements of scarce and expensive brass. Instead, they built movements entirely from native wood, except for the brass escapement. Benjamin and

49

Timothy Cheney near Hartford made wooden movements that ran
for thirty hours rather than the eight-day norm for brass movements. Eager consumers balanced the inconvenience of daily winding with the new-found ability to afford a tall case clock, one that
only a practiced eye could tell contained a cheaper, cruder wooden
movement. A homeowner could pay $50–$60 for a fine tall case
clock from one of the Willard brothers, or as little as $18 to $25 for
a wooden clock from Connecticut's Naugatuck Valley.[62]

The wooden movements had their detractors, notably clockmakers hoping to continue selling the more expensive brass products. The wooden clocks would shrink, swell, and crack with
changes in humidity and temperature and, because of this sensitivity,
were unsuitable, some said, for shipping long distances to market.
And wood was clearly not as durable as metal. But Timothy
Dwight, who was a Congregational clergyman, author, and grandson of the Puritan theologian Jonathan Edwards, expressed his
enthusiasm for the wooden clocks being made in Waterbury, Connecticut, in 1798:

> These are considered as keeping time with nearly as much
> regularity, as those which are made of customary materials.
> They also last long: and being sold at a very moderate price, are spread over a prodi-
> gious extent of country, to the great convenience of a vast number of people who oth-
> erwise have no means of regulating correctly their various business.[63]

The flood of tall case clocks with wooden movements prompted the Connecticut legislature in 1798 to tax all timepieces in the state, $10 on a brass clock, $3.34 on a wooden one.
Nevertheless, on the brink of the nineteenth century, only one household in twelve in the state
owned a clock.[64]

Precisely who owned clocks and watches in early America, when did they acquire them, and
for what reasons? Clock owners, like the American colonists themselves, were not a homoge-
neous group. Where a person lived and what a person did for a living influenced the probability
of owning a timepiece. In 1774, for example, New Englanders and Middle Atlantic colonials
were equally likely to own a timepiece. In those regions roughly 13 or 14 adults out of 100 had

Tall case clock, made by Eli Terry, Plymouth, Connecticut, about 1795.

a clock among their possessions when they died. Among Southerners at that time, only about 6 in 100 had a clock. Not only the rich, but people of all ranks owned timepieces, and not just as status symbols, but for telling the time. More merchants and professionals owned timepieces than the very richest, and a group consisting of innkeepers, shop owners, and artisans, who had roughly one-tenth the wealth of the wealthiest, owned timepieces in the same proportion.[65] In the homes of the refined, a tall case clock might stand in a dining room, a hallway, or on a stair landing. In 1830 a Philadelphian remembered many a genteel parlor he had visited: four corners decorated in balance with a chimney in one and, in each of the others, a tea table, a cabinet for silver and china, and a clock "reaching the ceiling." But those who lived in houses with only one or two rooms might stand a clock against a wall in the room with the hearth.[66]

Connecticut's head start in manufacturing clocks from abundant native wood would enter an entirely new phase in the second decade of the nineteenth century. The state's entrepreneurs would transform clockmaking into one of the proving grounds of the American Industrial Revolution and make a wide range of clocks available and appealing to entirely new segments of the country's growing population.

Watches

FEWER THAN TWO THOUSAND WATCHES were made in America before 1849, but Americans imported tens of thousands – and the chains and trinkets to go with them.[67]

Spurred by improvements in timekeepers for navigation, watchmaking had been the leading edge of advanced technology since the mid-seventeenth century, with centers in England, France, and Switzerland. By the end of the eighteenth century, it is likely that worldwide watch production was about 350,000 to 400,000 annually. Great Britain's output alone was three-fifths of that amount, and she exported more than half her watches.[68]

As with England's clockmaking, the success of the watch industry there rested on a highly specialized division of labor, with scattered workers responsible for only one part or subassembly – the "putting out" system of manufacturing. The custom of the wholesaler as "maker" prevailed:

In this portrait of Daniel Boardman, a Connecticut dry-goods merchant, painted by Ralph Earl in 1789, the fob chains for his watch are visible at the waistline of his breeches.

An unknown artist painted Hannah Maley Cuyler of New York in 1790 with her finest possessions, including a watch worn at her waist.

The half-dollar bill designed by Benjamin Franklin for the Continental Congress, 1776, features a sundial; a reference to the fleeting nature of time in the Latin word "fugio," or "I fly"; and timely advice in the phrase "Mind Your Business."

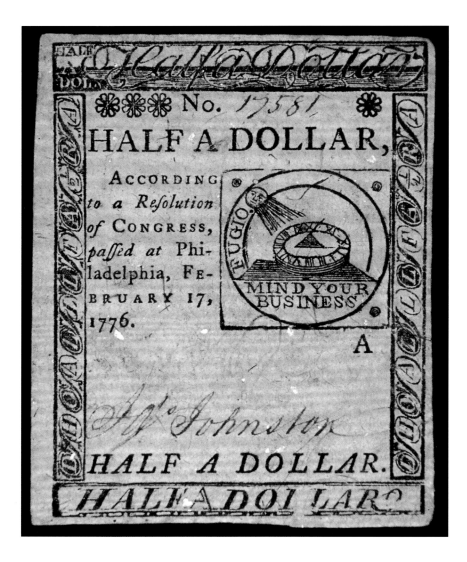

time is money

Remember that TIME is money.

— Benjamin Franklin, "Advice to a Young Tradesman, Written by an Old One," 1748

BEFORE ABOUT 1820, the time-related values of regularity, speed, and promptness were highly important to only certain segments of the American population: men engaged in business, those involved in providing transportation, and officials of the Post Office.

The economy of the American colonies depended on merchants trading in the Atlantic marketplace. Since the Middle Ages, when European men of commerce first used the public clocks on churches and palaces to count hours and coordinate transactions, time gradually came to be seen not only as God's order for the universe and government's authority over the populace, but also the basis for profitable business.[78]

But merchants in colonial America were comparatively more relaxed about schedules and appointments than today's business executives are. On a typical workday, a merchant might spend three hours attending to commercial matters, with the rest of the day devoted to government, church, or social obligations. Business hours might extend to evening meetings at a local tavern. Some merchants of New York City, for example, gathered to swap financial news and launch new ventures every weekday evening from 7:30 to 10:00 at the Baker City Tavern on Wall Street or the Tontine Coffee House near the docks.[79]

As the new republic began to convert from predominantly agricultural and commercial pursuits to an industrial economy, success depended, just as it had in the mercantile economy, on the timely exchange of goods, payments, and information. Lost time meant lost money. Key changes in shipping and the postal service would shape the growing importance of being on time and acting with a sense of urgency and reliability.

The Brilliant, Macpherſon, and Bland-
ford, Troop, are arrived in James river,
from Glaſgow; this laſt veſſel only left
Col. Burwell's office the 15th of April,
getting home in 23 days, and had a paſ-
ſage of 31 days out.

Shipping On Schedule

FOREIGN TRADE WAS CRUCIAL to the existence of the newly independent United States. But sailing ships crossed the Atlantic only when their holds were full of cargo and the weather was fair. Newspapers carried notices of their random arrivals and departures. In January and February, shipping all but shut down because of the bitter North Atlantic weather. Coastal vessels linked American port cities on equally unpredictable schedules.

Change was in the wind on a snowy morning in January 1818, when the merchantman *James Monroe* set sail for Liverpool from New York. The prompt departure of the ship marked the maiden voyage of the Black Ball Company, the first packet line to offer *scheduled* service between the United States and England.

The line was the idea of the American textile merchant Isaac Wright, his son William, and three English partners. The Wrights regularly exported cotton to England, and the partners lived in New York to handle wool imports. Many of their fellow merchants had long been impatient with the unpredictability of transatlantic navigation, but no one before their time had ever thought to regularize sailing with a schedule.

Within the first year, each of the lines' four ships completed three round trips – on schedule. The competing Red Star and the Swallowtail Lines soon followed with service also from New York. In order to meet their new timetables, speed was of the essence. Packets made crossings under full sail, day and night, in all kinds of weather. This pressure to keep to a schedule shortened crossing times. The eastbound voyage shrank from a month or more to an average of twenty-four days, and the westbound from three months to about forty days.

The word *packet* acquired a new meaning. Previously, any ship that had carried wrapped cargo might have been so identified. Now it meant a ship on a regular route and on a schedule, reliably and punctually delivering cargo, passengers, and mail. And although Boston, Philadelphia, and Baltimore would eventually run packets of their own, the New York lines gave that city a near monopoly on being first with international news and information.[80]

American Stage Coach by T. Storer after Isaac Weld, Jr., from *Travels Through the States of North America, and the Provinces of Upper and Lower Canada,* 1807.

Information on a Timetable

THE U.S. POSTAL SYSTEM became an agent of revolutionary change in the country's communications in the 1790s. A powerful influence on politics and commerce, the mails also altered the way Americans experienced time.

The Post Office Act of 1792 established a nationally coordinated system to speed delivery of the mail. Within four years, the Post Office announced a day-by-day timetable for the post road that stretched from Canada to South Carolina. A relay of post riders and stagecoaches operated on a regular schedule, with announced days and hours of departure. Until the coming of the telegraph in 1844, these mail carriers epitomized speed and punctuality.[81]

Before the 1792 legislation infused the postal system with a new dynamism, the mails were much as they had been since before the Revolution. Just under seventy coastal post offices operated in British North America, stretching from Virginia to Canada to link the port cities along the way. Regular mail ships sailed from Falmouth, England, to both New York and Charleston.[82]

The success of the national postal system after 1792 depended on sustained congressional and executive-branch support for the democratic ideals of a well-informed populace and the timely exchange of information for everyone. Moving the mails without hindrance, with all "celerity, certainty and security," as the Post Office put it, fitted with the notions of maintaining national unity. And the emphasis on a national effort meant that the developing postal network spread west and south as settlement did. Federal funds went to building nearly every road built west of the Alleghenies by 1812, because they were post roads.[83]

A national stagecoach network used the roads. To deal with contract mail carriers accustomed to setting schedules to suit themselves rather than the government, Postmaster General Samuel Osgood established by 1796 an hour-by-hour schedule for the north–south mail route. One way the public learned of this schedule was from Abraham Bradley's maps of the United States, which carried the elaborate schedule in a corner. Bradley, a Connecticut lawyer and topographer, served as assistant postmaster general beginning in 1800. Displayed in post offices everywhere and included in Jedediah Morse's widely read *Geography*, Bradley's maps received wide circulation.[84]

Once the schedules were set, the Post Office enforced them. Local postmasters kept track of contract stage and post riders' on-time performance, often using reports from coach passengers. Postmasters could impose fines for tardiness, and in the worst cases they could simply refuse to renew a contract. The American measures might have been even stricter. In Britain, post coach drivers were required to carry a clock with a tamper-proof locked dial, so there would be no mistaking what time the mail arrived.[85]

People came to expect the mails would be regular, and, mostly, the Post Office delivered. A guidebook warned visitors to Philadelphia in the 1820s about the strictness of that city's postal system:

> Great punctuality is observed in closing the respective mails at the minute, and strangers wishing to transmit letters by mail, are advised to be a little before the time, as it is impossible to send a letter by that day's mail, even should it come but a moment after it is closed. This rule has been established and acted upon for many years, and is never deviated from, except where letters containing information of sickness or death are requested to be forwarded, in which cases, the postmaster, being convinced of the contents, will forward such letter, if it be deposited any time before the mail leaves the office.[86]

The mail routes between Boston and Washington, D.C., had the quickest and most reliable service, but even there the mails could go only as fast as the transportation system allowed. Bad roads and bad weather, tired horses and stage breakdowns frequently hindered the pace. Four miles per hour for stagecoaches on the main routes was the average. Top speed was 12 miles per hour, and only a special horse express could sustain it. Even at that speed, the delivery between New York and New Orleans took seven days. Southern cities were particularly isolated from each other, and commercial information from the North often went by boat from New York to Charleston and Savannah or overland by private riders.[87]

Speeding up delivery and expanding service were among the postal system's top goals. In the 1790s, reported postal clerk Jesse Dow, it took forty days for letters to be exchanged between Portland, Maine, and Savannah and thirty-two days for the exchange between Philadelphia and Lexington, Kentucky. By 1810 the delivery time between Portland and Savannah had dropped to twenty-seven days and between Philadelphia and Lexington to sixteen. During the War of Inde-

pendence, the editor of the *Farmers' Monthly Visitor* in 1852 noted, the local post office had been open only twice a week, "but now our go-ahead-ativeness is hardly satisfied with three mails a day . . . Of a surety this is an age of progress."[88]

Who was using the postal system to send what? Before the middle of the nineteenth century, almost no one in the United States ever sent or received a letter by mail. In 1790, the postal system handled about 300,000 letters which, by one count, works out to one letter that year for every ten free people in the country. To post a letter was expensive, sometimes as much as a dollar, a day's wage for a working man. Those who were sending letters by mail were mostly merchants, brokers, and retailers.[89]

By the 1820s, between a third and a half of the mail by weight was newspapers, and the rate that news traveled was often the rate of postal delivery. Because of a news lag, the Battle of New Orleans occurred two weeks after the peace treaty ending the War of 1812. New York learned of the battle twenty-seven days after it ended, and the treaty signing forty-nine days after the fact. It was seven days between George Washington's death on December 14, 1799, in Virginia, and publication of that news in New York City.[90]

By 1828, a complete national postal network was firmly in place, with Postmaster General John McLean firmly committed to making speedy mail service not just an ideal but a reality. In professing a gospel of speed, McLean acted with a new sense of time urgency that coincided with the age's business revolution, an upheaval that transformed the American economy with expanding foreign and domestic trade, transportation improvements, increasing population, and rich merchants ready to invest in new industries.[91]

Until the invention of the telegraph, the mails provided regular communications faster than any other means. Whether the postal system was responding to increasing demands from businessmen to move the mails more quickly or, on its own, setting a pace that business found appealing, the timely delivery of information was vital to merchants and businessmen of all sorts, to politicians, and to printers and publishers of news and advertising.

Not only improved mail delivery, but also technical and organizational changes were under way, all aimed at speeding up the pace of business life and making transactions more regular. But it was still difficult to be punctual in the modern sense of the word. Originally *punctual* described a person who was a stickler for details of conduct – the word *punctilious* carries that meaning today. By the end of the seventeenth century, just as clocks improved enough to keep time to the closest minutes and seconds, *punctual* came to mean exactly on time. *Punctuality* entered the language by the end of the eighteenth century.[92]

Time is money, admonished Benjamin Franklin in the eighteenth century. Men in business throughout the new country had merged the Puritan understanding of time and its emphasis on time thrift with their own secular, materialistic behavior. Although associated with Philadelphia, Franklin was the Boston-born son of Puritans, and his aphorisms about time, money, and efficiency were straight from the New England creed. Men in commerce in the American South, largely settled in the seventeenth century by Calvinists, had much the same principles. In a process that had begun in the Middle Ages, American merchants adopted the relentless rhythms of civic and church clocks to regulate business life.[93]

The emerging business community in the new republic found itself impatient with time-consuming obstacles to trade and eager for improvements in commercial methods. Borrowing money "on time" to finance inventories or construction heightened awareness of the link between time and money and fostered a desire to accelerate every aspect of business, from manufacturing to customer payment. Improving the speed of transportation and communication would be among their most important goals.[94] They would move beyond just noting the passage of time to embrace the gospel of speed.

mechanizing time

1820–1880

INCREASINGLY, AMERICANS LET THE CLOCK TELL THE TIME AND
REGULATE THEIR LIVES.

For a great many years past there has been a wood-cut on the cover of the Farmer's Almanac, pretending to be a portrait of "Father Time." Father Time has exchanged his hourglass for a gold . . . watch, which he carries in his vest pocket.

– Nathaniel Hawthorne, "Time's Portraiture," 1838

EVEN IN THE FINAL STRETCH the bay held his fluid stride. After nearly four miles, he still galloped along with easy strength.

With just a short distance to go, Gil Patrick, Lexington's elfin jockey, had his hands full to keep the spirited horse in the center of the track, where the course was packed hard for running fast. Lexington instead preferred the soft shoulder and repeatedly tried to swerve right, against his rider's wishes. Running there would surely slow him down, Patrick knew, and seconds, even quarter seconds, were going to count.

When Lexington crossed the finish line moments later, those timing him with their own watches knew at a glance that they had witnessed an extraordinary event. The crowd of thousands roared as one when the official time was posted – 7 minutes 19¾ seconds – a world's record for a four-mile race. The time was all the more extraordinary since Lexington had run alone. His only opponent that day in New Orleans was the clock.[1]

The record Lexington set on April 2, 1855, stood for nearly twenty years. He raced the clock that day on the Metairie Course, the hub of Southern racing before the Civil War, as part of a dramatic challenge to his archrival and half-brother, Lecomte. Up to that moment, the two great horses had battled to a draw. Lexington had won the first race between them, and, in a very tight contest, Lecomte had won the second, with a record time of 7:26. Lexington's owner, Richard Ten Broeck, had then asked for a decisive rematch, and, for a controversy-filled year, Lecomte's owner had refused. As publicity reached a crescendo, Ten Broeck staged Lexington's race against the clock. In a runoff with Lecomte a week later Lexington was again victorious with another amazing time of 7:23 ¾. By the 1850s, Americans had become conscious of time as a standard of excellence at the track.

Lexington's career in the 1850s consisted of just seven races, during which he won an unprecedented $56,600 for his owner and incalculable amounts for those who bet on him. During the seventh race, his rematch with Lecomte, it was clear Lexington was going blind. Afterward he retired to stud, and his reputation as a sire eclipsed his fame as a racer. Between 1855 and 1880, 236 different offspring, a critical portion of the century's thoroughbred line, won almost 1,200 races and earned more than $1 million. Lexington was nothing short of a legend, praised only in hyperbole:

> There came a day when any little child of America could have told you the story of Lexington. And the time is not yet past when that name is synonymous with everything that is greatest in a horse. Lexington belonged not alone to the turfmen. He was the heritage of the nation. He was Lexington in the minds of the people, and after him there were merely other horses.[2]

Lexington, the Great Monarch of the Turf and Sire of Racers, lithograph by Currier and Ives, 1855.

Lexington's accomplishments in American horse racing represented a critical transition from an emphasis on endurance to a fascination with speed. For decades, American racing had followed British tradition, with horses known for their stamina and strength against the competition, not their times. But by Lexington's era, speed was ascendant at American tracks. Thanks to telegraphed reports and widespread newspaper coverage of his feats, the stallion enjoyed a national reputation in the decade before the Civil War as the epitome of American speed.[3]

Lexington's fame and the interest in split-second timing that accompanied it undoubtedly influenced product designers at the American Watch Company in Waltham, Massachusetts, to risk manufacturing the first mass-produced stopwatch. At the end of the 1850s, the firm sought a market for its four different products: three conventional pocket watches and a sports timing watch they called the chronodrometer. The chronodrometer's dial could mark quarter seconds, but was unlike any stopwatch in use then or now. A sweep hand in the center of the dial revolved once every four minutes; at the bottom of the dial a small hand revolved once every four seconds; and at the top was a conventional dial with numerals 1 through 12 and hour and minute hands for the correct time of day. But when the watch was used as a timer, the time train inconveniently stopped. Between 1859 and 1861, the American Watch Company made only about six hundred chronodrometers – not a huge number by mass-production standards. It sold for $50, compared to $150 to $350 for a high-grade import, but at that time, stopwatches of any kind were still rare.[4]

Waltham watches and the racehorse Lexington were destined to play pivotal roles in demonstrating American accomplishments on the international stage. From shaky beginnings as America's first watch business, the Waltham firm would go on to pioneer mass-production techniques and teach the rest of the world how to make watches by machine. Lexington's reputation as America's most remarkable horse continued even after his death. When he died of a skull abscess in 1875, he was buried in front of his stable door at Woodburn Farm, near Lexington, Kentucky, where he had spent the two decades after his brief racing career. Six months later, he was exhumed with the hope that his skeleton could be displayed at the Philadelphia Centennial Exposition, the international world's fair marking the hundredth birthday of the Declaration of Independence. Although Waltham watches were prominently displayed at the fair, Lexington's bones were not ready in time. His final owner, A. J. Alexander, donated the skeleton to the

Skeleton of the racehorse Lexington on the lawn of the Smithsonian Castle.

Smithsonian Institution "in the interest of science" for display in the U.S. National Museum as the epitome of speed.[5]

Speed at the track was only one part of the profound changes in the sense of time in nineteenth-century American life. Although the rising and setting sun continued to determine daily rhythms, the significance of time expressed on clocks and watches began to increase, both in material and symbolic ways.

The growing importance of time by the clock, felt already in the eighteenth century in the postal system's prototypical scheduling concerns and the accelerating course of commercial information in the mercantile community, intensified under industrial capitalism.[6] Based on mass production and mechanization, the American Industrial Revolution profoundly altered not only the organization of manufacturing but also markets and commerce. The daily rhythms of men and women in cities and rural communities were transformed in the emergence of a new industrial economy in the North around 1790. Cloth was the American Industrial Revolution's most important product. The railroads were the most important industry. The changes from an agrarian to an industrial society were rapid. In 1820, industrialization had scarcely begun in America; by 1880, the country was poised to become a global industrial power.

In New England, the clockmaking and watchmaking industry participated very early in the changes from craft to mass production. More clocks and watches were available to more people at cheaper prices, just as more people began to pay more attention to time as a means of coordinating schedules. For many, the pace of life seemed to increase, distances seemed to shrink, and noting and heeding clocks and watches became a habit. Gradually and unevenly, nineteenth-century Americans found themselves governed by machine time, the mechanized regularity and insistent pace of the clock.

A shelf clock, prominently
displayed, kept time for these
women making straw bonnets in
New England, from *Harper's New
Monthly Magazine,* October 1864.

Workers kept to strict schedules at
this New England textile factory,
about 1850.

NEW ENGLAND BONNET MAKERS.

MECHANIZING TIME

Timetable for the Holyoke Mills, Hadley Falls Company, Holyoke, Massachusetts, about 1852.

Time Table of the Holyoke Mills

TO TAKE EFFECT ON AND AFTER JAN. 3d, 1853

The standard being that of the Western Rail Road, which is the Meridian time at Cambridge

MORNING BELLS

First Bell ring at 4.40, A.M. Second Bell ring in at 5, A.M.

YARD GATES

Will be opened at ringing of Morning Bells, of Meal Bells, and of Evening Bells, and kept open ten minutes.

WORK COMMENCES

At ten minutes after last Morning Bell, and ten minutes after Bell which "rings in" from Meals.

BREAKFAST BELLS

October 1st, to March 31st, inclusive, ring out at 7 A.M., ring in at 7:30 A.M.

April 1st to Sept. 30th, inclusive, ring out at 6:30 A.M., ring in at 7 A.M.

DINNER BELLS

Ring out at 12:30 P.M., ring in at 1 P.M.

EVENING BELLS

Ring out at 6.30[†], P.M.

[†]Excepting on Saturdays when the Sun sets previous to 6:30. At such times, ring out at Sunset.
In all cases, the *first* stroke of the Bell is considered as marking the time.

like clockwork

Factory wall clock made by Benjamin and Truman Hanks, Mansfield, Connecticut, 1808–24. The clock has multiple dials for indicating both time of day and hours of running the factory machinery.

Hanks clock dial.

THE CLOCK HAD BEEN THE DEFINING MACHINE FOR THE ENLIGHTENMENT, both a real technological object and a symbol of the rational workings of the Newtonian cosmos. As machines of all sorts captured the public imagination in nineteenth-century America, the clock continued to have a significant place. With its characteristic steady regularity and utility, the clock became a crucial link between the new industrial order and how people behaved in and thought about time.[7]

Factory

THE ENTREPRENEURS OF THE AMERICAN INDUSTRIAL REVOLUTION fashioned a new kind of workplace, the mechanized factory, and in doing so reshaped both economic and social life. Although not all industries developed in the same way at the same pace, work gradually moved out of homes and small workshops to large factories powered by special-purpose machinery and staffed by scores of wage earners. Because these were expensive investments, too costly to be idle, managers devised new ways to use time to run the factories profitably.[8] Wages based on time – paid by the day or by the week worked – became the norm. Time, for owners and employees alike, became money.

To maximize work time, managers fixed strict schedules for the workday, installed factory clocks and bells to signal the hours of operation and to summon workers, and even experimented with new kinds of clocks connected to the factory machinery. They rang bells to wake workers early in the morning in their nearby homes, to summon them to the factory, to send them to and from meals and breaks, to mark the end of the workday, and sometimes to toll a curfew. Managers expected workers to obey the bells.

A machinist named John Rogers described his schedule at Horatio Allen's Novelty Works in 1830s New York:

> In the first place the bells are rung at 4 ½ in the morning that is to get up at seven minutes before five they ring a second time and then we have to go into the shop and commence work. At seven we wash and go to breakfast and come back a quarter before eight. At half past twelve to dinner and back quarter past one and to tea at seven when I have felt so tired I have been to bed soon after.[9]

Catharine Beecher, author of the very popular home advice manual *A Treatise on Domestic Economy*. Beecher was the daughter of the prominent New England theologian Lyman Beecher and the sister of Harriet Beecher Stowe, author of *Uncle Tom's Cabin*.

To accompany the increasing separation of family life from work outside the home, a new view of the role of women emerged, "the cult of domesticity." Domestic advice manuals, women's magazines, and influential clergymen urged women to assume a new and special role. The ideal woman would, according to these advisers, shape the social and moral behavior of her family. By running a steady and secure household, she would create a haven from the outside world. According to this ideology, women would practice systematic habits of using time – especially to maintain regular mealtimes – in order to ensure the well-being of their families and, by extension, the nation.[20]

Woman aspiring to live the middle-class life could consult scores of advice books. Perhaps the best known and most popular of these were volumes by Catharine Beecher. In *A Treatise on Domestic Economy*, first published in 1841, she established herself as an eloquent voice for the new ideas about women's place in the home. Relaying to an eager audience the Protestant credo of hard work and time thrift as a duty to God, she emphasized household habits of industry and regularity. She wrote:

> A woman is under obligations to so arrange the hours and pursuits of her family as to promote systematic and habitual industry; and if, by late breakfasts, irregular hours of meals, and other hindrances of this kind, she interferes with, or refrains from promoting regular industry in others, she is accountable to God for all the waste of time consequent on her negligence.[21]

Only in one later edition of her popular book does Beecher mention using a clock to aid in establishing the kind of domestic order she advocated, but the ideal household she prescribed nevertheless ran like clockwork.

Not all women participated in this cult of domesticity. The prescriptions for ideal middle-class living were hard to follow, especially for farm women, factory girls, and schoolteachers, many of whom had goals different from those of housewives: productivity, self-improvement, and financial independence. Throughout the nineteenth century, life remained primarily rural, and fluid in terms of work. Neither men nor women expected a lifetime job in a single place of employment. They alternated between stints on the farm and factory jobs.[22] Agrarian rhythms coexisted with new industrial schedules in most households, not just on a daily basis, but across lifetimes.

A wall clock hangs above the hearth on the frontispiece to *The Skillful Housewife's Complete Guide to Domestic Cookery, Taste, and Economy* by Mrs. L. G. Abell, 1853.

Wall clock from Jefferson Junior High School, 6th and D Streets S.W., Washington, D.C., about 1880.

Clock-dial lesson card, about 1830. Learning to tell the hours "of the clock" became an important part of childhood education.

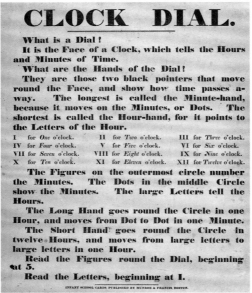

School

AS EARLY AS THE 1830S, white children were attending free public elementary schools where they were conditioned to the clock-regulated day. A ringing bell called them to class. A clock in each classroom organized their lessons, and among the first things they learned was how to read the clock dial. Strictly enforced schedules instilled time discipline, intended to preserve social order and moral values. Students were punished for tardiness and awarded certificates for punctuality. Time discipline was also central in the lessons taught at specialized schools to "civilize" non-white children and "Americanize" adult immigrants.[23] Although Puritans had long ceased to govern New England, their ideas about time thrift persisted. Lucy Larcom, one of the Lowell mill girls, remembered a childhood "penetrated through every fibre of thought with the idea that idleness is a disgrace. It was taught with the alphabet and the spelling book; it was enforced by precept and example, at home and abroad; and it is to be confessed that it did sometimes haunt the childish imagination almost mercilessly."[24]

Certificate of punctuality on parchment from the Female Seminary, Georgetown, D.C., 9 February 1844. It reads: "This certifies that Miss Elizabeth Grant Davidson during the term ending this day has been present at the calling of the Role One Hundred and Eleven times, thereby meriting approbation in a high degree and ranking in the Second Grade for Punctuality. L.I. English, Principal."

TIME TABLE.

Rising Bell	-	-	-	-	5.30 o'clock,	A. M.
Breakfast	-	-	-	-	6	" "
Work Bell	-	-	-	-	6.55	" "
Study Hour, from	-	-	7 to 8		"	"
Inspection of Men in ranks		-	-	8.15	"	"
School Bell	-	-	-	-	8.25	" "
Devotions	-	-	-	-	8.35	" "
General Exercises	-	-	-	8.45	"	"
Recitations until	-	-	-	10.20	"	"
Recess for 15 minutes	-	-	-			
Recitations until	-	-	-	12	"	M
Dinner	-	-	-	-	12.15	" P. M.
Work Bell	-	-	-	-	1	" "
School Bell	-	-	-	-	1.20	" "
Recitations until	-	-	-	3.30	"	"
Recall from Work	-	-	-	5.55	"	"
Supper	-	-	-	-	6	" "
Devotions	-	-	-	-	6.30	" "
Study Hour, from	-	-	7.15 to 9		"	"
Lights out	-	-	-	-	10	" "

During study hour the students are all assembled, the men and women in separate buildings under the direction of a teacher who is ready to render assistance when needed. There is no session on Saturdays.

Schedule for Hampton Normal and Agricultural Institute, Hampton, Virginia, a school for African-American and Indian children and young adults, 1878–79.

Native American students at Hampton Institute, 1870s.

connecticut clocks

Wherever we have been in Kentucky, Indiana, in Illinois, in Missouri, and here in every dell of Arkansas and in cabins where there was not a chair to sit on, there was sure to be a Connecticut clock.

– English traveler George Featherstonhaugh, 1844

DURING THE AMERICAN INDUSTRIAL REVOLUTION, clockmaking was one of the first crafts to change to a full-scale industry. Before the transformation, artisans working in small shops made clocks one at a time for local customers who had ordered them. The traditional methods gave way to small factories, powered by water to run machines that churned out clocks by the thousands for a nationwide market. By the 1870s, just seven companies, all born in western Connecticut, were producing millions of timepieces. The use of machines made clocks cheaper than they had ever been, and just about everybody could afford one. With appetites whetted by the growing abundance of other home furnishings, many people *wanted* to have a clock, whether or not they needed one or even knew how to tell time by it. As clock ownership increased, more people began to think about time in terms of time "of the clock," or "o'clock." On the threshold of the nineteenth century, a home with a clock would have been unusual. By the 1830s clocks seemed to be everywhere.

Making Clocks by Machine

IN THE OPENING YEARS OF THE NINETEENTH CENTURY, a handful of Connecticut entrepreneurs transformed the way clocks were made in the United States. Recognizing a vast potential market for low-cost domestic clocks, Eli Terry and his associates Seth Thomas and Silas Hoadley applied water-powered machinery to clockmaking. Although never a large industry compared to others in the American economy, clockmaking was nevertheless one of the proving grounds of the Industrial Revolution. New factories pioneered the use of machines for mass-producing uniform, interchangeable clock parts, a manufacturing style that came to be applied to other products and known as "the American System" of manufacturing.[31]

Eli Terry of East Windsor, Connecticut, began as a builder of movements for tall case clocks. About 1807 he accepted a challenging contract to produce four thousand wooden movements for tall case clocks within three years. Awarding the contract were the Reverend Edward Porter

Shelf clock by Eli Terry, Plymouth, Connecticut, about 1816.

and his brother Levi, two merchant-enterpreneurs in Waterbury with a diverse array of business enterprises. They were already in the clock business, having financed a shop for assembling parts, and they foresaw a bigger market. Terry converted a gristmill into a water-powered space full of saws and planes, organized the shop for the mechanized production of clock parts, and met his deadline. These Porter contract clocks were the first mass-produced clocks with interchangeable parts in the United States.[32]

In 1816 Terry patented a distinctly American clock small enough to set on a mantel or shelf and shorter by about a foot than the shelf clock popularized by the Willards. Determined to make the clock as economical as possible, he chose a simple wooden box with a glass door. Numerals painted in reverse on the inside of the glass served for a dial. The movement was made of wood too, instead of the more traditional, more expensive brass.

By talent and inclination, Terry was an inventor and mechanician, preferring to leave to others the marketing of his products. Closely associated with Terry's earliest productions was Seth Thomas, a joiner by trade who had started as one of Terry's employees. He went on to case and sell Terry movements and to produce Terry clocks under a license agreement. Ultimately Thomas became a major clock manufacturer and a rival of Terry.

Terry immediately proceeded to refine his box clock, and after his first patent he took out five more by 1826. The plain box case acquired a pair of slender pillars on the sides, scrollwork on top, and a set of graceful feet. A dial was added, and the lower portion of the glass door was reverse-painted, mostly by women recruited from nearby villages. In the movement, Terry experimented with modifications to the escapement, revised the gear trains, and replaced the rack-and-snail striking mechanism with the more economical count wheel. The result of these efforts, patented in 1823, was another wooden, weight-driven, hour-striking, thirty-hour clock that soon became widely known as the Connecticut pillar-and-scroll clock. As the design of the clock was perfected, Terry set about organizing its manufacture. Production was under way in 1822. By 1825, Eli Terry, in partnership with his brother Samuel and his sons Eli, Jr., and Henry, was operating three factories, each turning out two to three thousand pillar-and-scroll clocks a year. Terry sold his first shelf clocks for $12 to peddlers or other merchants, who would retail them for between $15 and $18. By the early 1820s, in the face of competition from other makers, the wholesale price of wooden clocks dropped to $10. By the middle of the decade, some peddlers were paying as little as $3.50.[33]

Terry's success spawned imitators eager to capture part of the market for machine-made clocks. By 1830, western Connecticut was home to over a hundred firms, large and small, making clocks with wooden movements.

Samuel Slick, a fictional clock peddler, from *The Clockmaker; or the Sayings and Doings of Samuel Slick, of Slicksville* by Thomas Haliburton, 1837.

Pillar-and-scroll shelf clock by Eli and Samuel Terry, Plymouth, Connecticut, about 1825.

Selling Clocks

WOODEN CLOCKS FROM CONNECTICUT were among the earliest mass-produced consumer products made in the United States. Sold largely to rural buyers by itinerant merchants, these clocks played an early and significant role in transforming the rural North from overwhelmingly agricultural to a modern market society based on industrial capital and consumerism.[34]

Before the Revolution, wealthy urban households had acquired goods from importers or city retail shops, especially after about 1740, when colonials enjoyed a dramatic increase in nonessential goods like textiles, ceramics, glassware, and utensils. But rural people had much less, mostly relying on country stores, making things themselves, or acquiring them from local craftspeople. These rural transactions were largely cashless, involving the exchange of goods for crops, other goods, or labor.[35]

Itinerant merchants also carried products to rural dwellers. They had more to carry beginning after the War of Independence, which brought an economic revolution as well as a political one. Local manufacturers increased their output of items like tinware, chairs, shoes, and clocks.

The first clocks peddled to country customers were the artisan-made wooden tall case clocks. But clock sales were insignificant until 1816, when Eli Terry's shelf clocks entered the market. Terry's timing was excellent: he invented a new product just as agricultural surpluses and rural consumer demand for decorative home furnishings both began to rise.[36]

Peddlers simultaneously responded to rural desires for consumer goods and created markets for them where none had existed before. They successfully saturated Connecticut with clocks – the number of timepieces in the state grew sixfold between 1779 and 1820. By 1820, peddlers could be found carrying clocks from western Connecticut to the Gulf Coast, the Mississippi Valley, and eastern Canada.[37]

Young men in search of riches and adventure were attracted to the peddler's footloose life. A typical route took about one year. The peddler would set out from Connecticut in the fall, making frequent stops to sell clocks and collect payment for clocks he had delivered the previous year. In late spring he would return to Connecticut. Summer was for organizing finances and goods for the following season. In fall the cycle would begin again. In 1822, for example, Rensselaer Upson, an established peddler, purchased 198 clocks at $10 each and sold them all, either for other goods, currency, or notes of $35 to $50. Between September and November, his route took him from Connecticut through New York, New Jersey, Pennsylvania, Virginia, Tennessee, and Alabama.[38]

MECHANIZING TIME

This unidentified girl, right, wears her watch on a neck chain, about 1850.

In this photo by Mathew Brady from about 1865, Mrs. Ramsey wears her watch pinned at her side.

choice. Open-face cases, a style that reduced the amount of time required to check the time, gradually became more popular than "hunting" cases (or "hunters") with covered dials that had to be opened. Stem-winding and stem-setting watches became practical, replacing those wound and set with a separate key. *Stem-winder,* in fact, entered the language as a term for something that was a first-rate example of its kind.[46]

Making Watches by Machine at Waltham

THE AMERICAN APPETITE FOR WATCHES in the first half of the nineteenth century was huge: about $46 million worth were imported between 1825 and 1858, especially from England and Switzerland. To tap in to this market, a few Americans attempted to develop a domestic product, but probably no more than two thousand were made here before the 1850s.[47]

Boy with watch, painted by Ruth Whittier Shute and Samuel Addison Shute, mid-nineteeth century.

Watch suspended from bow-knot pin, about 1870. The watch and pin are studded with diamonds.

The open-face case, like the one on this watch, grew more popular than the hunting case, one with a cover that snaps open and shut over the watch crystal and dial. On a watch without a cover, it was quicker to read the time. The movement of this watch, wound and set with a key, was made by the Rockford Watch Company, Rockford, Illinois, about 1876.

In the last quarter of the nineteenth century, stem winding and stem setting began to replace key winding and setting on American-made watches. This movement, in a hunting case, was made by E. Howard and Company, Boston, about 1876.

93

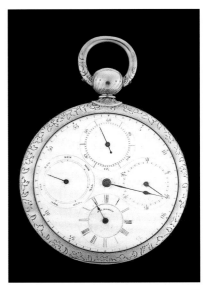

Waltham prototype watch made by Oliver B. Marsh, Roxbury, Massachusetts, between 1849 and 1851.

Waltham watch, 1852, movement marked "Howard, Davis & Dennison, Boston No. 1," designed by Oliver B. and David Marsh, and once owned by company founder Edward Howard.

In the 1850s, watchmakers at what would become the American Watch Company of Waltham, Massachusetts, developed the world's first machine-made watches to establish an American foothold in a lucrative business. They completely redesigned the watch so that its movement could be assembled from interchangeable parts made on specialized machines they had invented. They also developed a highly organized factory-based work system to speed production and cut costs. The nineteenth-century workforce was, for the most part, educated and well paid. Like the nearby Lowell textile mills, the watch factory recruited young native-born New England women from nearby farms and taught them to run production machinery and assemble parts. The firm also employed skilled male mechanicians and watchmakers, some of them Americans and others immigrants enticed away from the British watch trade.

The firm was launched in 1849 in a corner of the Howard & Davis clock factory in Roxbury, near Boston, where Edward Howard and Aaron Dennison experimented with completely new designs for watches and the machines to make them. Howard had earlier apprenticed with clock-maker Aaron Willard; Dennison had learned his trade in Brunswick, Maine, and absorbed techniques for the mass production of firearms with interchangeable parts during a visit at the Springfield Armory. Why not, he thought, try it with watches? With expert help from a cadre of experienced mechanicians and funding from Howard's father-in-law, the Boston mirror maker Samuel Curtis, the enterprise got under way.[48]

The primary measures the new firm adopted from arms making were a tight organization, a critically important machine shop, and a manufacturing system that relied on models. Waltham designers made a model watch and a master set of gauges to fit it, and every watch part made thereafter was measured against the corresponding model part. The goal was real interchangeability, that is, making watch parts that would fit any movement without the need for any hand adjustments or cutting when it came time to assemble them. Although it would be well into the twentieth century before the watch industry achieved this level of interchangeability, the Waltham designers started the innovations that would eventually lead there.[49]

In its first decade, the firm's work was largely experimental, but by late in 1852, Howard and Dennison finally had products — seventeen watches, made mostly by hand by brothers Oliver and David Marsh. The design of these first watches, eight-day movements with two mainsprings, gave way to a simpler one, a watch that ran on one mainspring for a little more than a day. Although superficially similar to English watches of the time, the new American watch featured a mainspring in a "going barrel." This meant a watch without the traditional fusee and chain to equalize the force of the unwinding spring. This was a watch with fewer parts to make. The next hundred Waltham watches, built on the new model, took until the fall of 1853. The third batch of nine hundred sold for just $40 each, cased. An imported movement of the same quality cost twice as much.[50]

Watch, 1865, movement marked "Wm Ellery, Boston, Massachusetts," made by American Watch Company, Waltham, Massachusetts; gift to Army surgeon G. D. O'Farrell from his patients at White Hall, a Civil War hospital near Philadelphia.

The inscription on Dr. O'Farrell's watch reads: "White Hall USA Gen'l Hospital, Feb. 15, 1865 Presented to Dr. G. D. O'Farrell, USA by the patients of Ward C as a token of regard & respect for his ability as a surgeon and unswerving integrity as a man."

Machine shop, American Watch Company, stereograph, about 1876.

The firm's early years were also financially unsteady. The name changed repeatedly as investors came and went. Operations moved from Roxbury to Waltham in 1854, where the company settled, optimistically poised for expansion, on a hundred-acre tract of land. But the Panic of 1857 brought bankruptcy and a new owner, Royal Robbins.

Reorganization and recovery began, and output reached fourteen thousand watches in 1858. Renamed the American Watch Company the next year, the firm was on the brink of success from an unexpected quarter. During the Civil War, Waltham's watch factory designed and mass-produced a low-cost watch, the William Ellery model. Selling for an unbelievable $13, these watches became a fad with Union soldiers. Just as itinerant peddlers had aroused the desire for inexpensive clocks, roving merchants sold thousands of cheap watches to eager customers in wartime encampments. By 1865, the year the war ended, William Ellery movements represented almost 45 percent of Waltham's unit sales.[51]

One of the most remarkable features of the Waltham factory was the special machinery designed for each part and operation. To make watches by machine, mechanicians had to invent new precision gauges and automatic equipment. The Waltham factory became a wonder of production machinery, and its owners proudly proclaimed the factory a marvel of American know-how and enterprise.

The Waterbury Supplement March 1ST 1889.

Father Time Carrying the Swiss Watchmaker and His Watches back to Switzerland

"SINCE THE ADVENT OF THE WATERBURY AMERICANS HAVE NO USE FOR CHEAP SWISS WATCHES"

In this advertisement for the Waterbury Watch Company of Waterbury, Connecticut, Father Time carries the Swiss watchmaker and his watches back to Switzerland. From the *Waterbury Supplement,* 1 March 1889.

Not surprisingly, Waltham watches proved conspicuous at the Philadelphia Centennial Exposition in 1876, celebrating the hundredth anniversary of the country. Technology captivated fairgoers by promising a bright future. Joining George Corliss's four-story steam engine, Alexander Graham Bell's new telephone, and the Sholes and Glidden typewriter was Waltham's display of American-made watches. Swiss watchmakers, who had seen their exports to the United States climb to a peak in 1872 and then crash to a disturbing low by 1876, sent a representative to the fair to investigate. He had to report that the Americans were making watches as good as their own. Waltham's international reputation was made. To remain competitive, the Swiss learned American techniques and gradually mechanized some aspects of their own operations.[52]

American Competition

WALTHAM REMAINED AN IMPORTANT INNOVATIVE FORCE in both watch and machinery design for the rest of the century. The firm's success spawned a raft of competitors who turned out movements and watches by the millions. In 1857 Edward Howard left the firm he had helped found and set up a rival company. As the Civil War ground on, a number of skilled Waltham watchmakers defected for another rival start-up in Elgin, Illinois. Although Elgin was no immediate threat to Waltham, the two firms would eventually lead the American jeweled-watch industry. Among the sixty-some companies that followed Elgin in and out of existence, a few flourished and made significant contributions to the American watch industry, especially Illinois in 1869, Hampden in 1877, Waterbury in 1879, and Hamilton in 1892.[53]

The Elgin National Watch Company published this Elgin Almanac in 1871 to advertise its products.

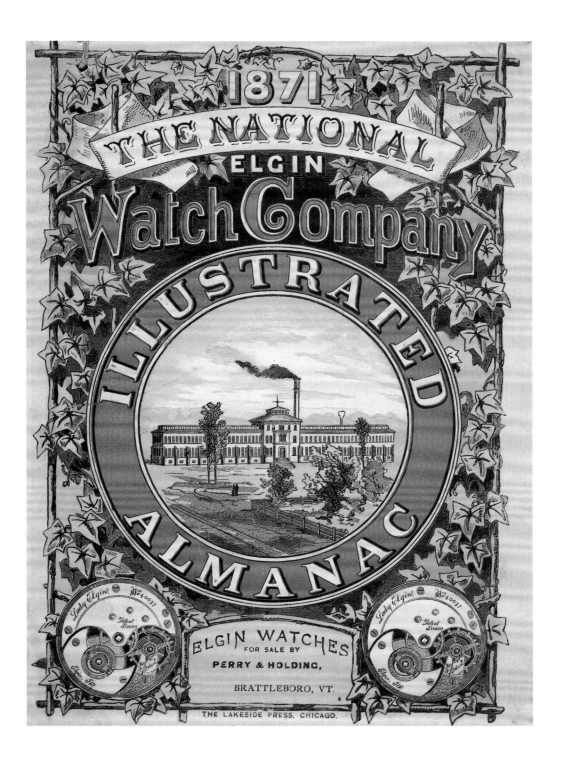

public steam railways as locomotives were. Before railroad dispatching by telegraph became common in the 1860s, timetables governed train arrivals and departures, established train priority, and ensured that trains did not collide on single-track lines.[56] Clocks in the terminals and watches held by conductors and engineers were devices to enforce the timetables.

Running on schedule was the principal railroad operating rule, and the public expected on-time performance. But the rule was not so easy to follow. On several grounds, the ideal of on-time performance was unattainable in the 1830s and 1840s.

The railroads set schedules, but for a variety of technical reasons – equipment failure, accidents, track obstructions, weather – could not keep to them. In 1831, when the Charleston & Hamburg Rail Road was still under construction in South Carolina, one of the line's commissioners predicted a need to run by established schedules: "Arrival and departure must be regulated by a system as certain and prompt as the mail arrangements."[57]

It is worth noting that the Charleston & Hamburg's officials considered the postal service the paragon of reliability. To improve on stagecoach service, which often mired in the mud in inclement weather, the Post Office began experimenting with railroad carriers in 1831, but initially found the infant transport system unfit for the job. In April 1835 the postmaster general wrote in despair: "From the experiences we have had, the adaptation of the railroad to the purposes of mail transportation is becoming every day more and more questionable." He found that the railroads could not "be relied on with that degree of certainty, which is all important in the transmission of the mail, and without which disappointments occur to the public and complaints are rung in the ears of the Department from every quarter of the country.[58] But by 1845, the railroads had improved in punctuality enough to satisfy the needs of the mail system. So railroads were allowed to compete with stages for lucrative postal contracts.[59]

To improve its own record for carrying the mails, the Charleston & Hamburg had set operating rules as early as 1834 that specified close attention to time: "With the view of attaining the greatest possible regularity in the time of running the Passenger Engines, regulations have been established fixing the hour of departure, from the 6 more important points on the line." One difficulty remained, though: "the want of a uniform standard of time at the different points." To remedy this problem and to enable engineers and station agents to "regulate their movements on the road with great accuracy," the railroad placed six clocks in the depots at the points along its 136 miles of track. The station agents were required to send a daily log of times of actual – as

The superintendent of the Boston & Providence Railroad issued these rules for running on time in the aftermath of the wreck on the Providence & Worcester in 1853.

Boston and Providence Railroad.

STANDARD TIME.

1. STANDARD TIME is two minutes later than BOND & SONS' clock, No. 17 Congress street, Boston.
2. The inside clocks, Boston and Providence stations, will be regulated by Standard Time.
3. The Ticket Clerk, Boston station, and the Ticket Clerk, Providence station, are charged with the duty of regulating Station Time. The former will daily compare it with Standard Time, and the latter will daily compare it with Conductor's time; and the agreement of any two Conductors upon a variation in Station Time shall justify him in changing it.
4. Conductors will compare their watches with Standard time in the following order.

MONDAY,..........Conductor of Steamboat Train.		
TUESDAY,..........	" Accom'n Train No.	1
WEDNESDAY,......	" "	2
THURSDAY,........	" "	3
FRIDAY,..........	" Dedham Train	1
SATURDAY,........	" "	2

5. All Conductors of Passenger and Freight trains will compare their time with Station time, Boston and Providence, every day, and report any variations to Superintendent of Transportation.
6. A record will be made by the Ticket Clerk, or in his absence, by the Baggage Master, of the comparisons required by Art. 5, to which they will certify by their signature or initials.
7. Conductors will submit their watches to Bond & Sons, 17 Congress street, Boston, for examination, and procure from them a certificate of reliability, which will be handed to the Superintendent.
8. Conductors will report to Messrs Bond any irregularity in the movements of their watches, and they will clean, repair and regulate them, at the expense of the Corporation, furnishing Conductors with reliable watches in the interim.

W. RAYMOND LEE, SUP'T.

BOSTON, AUGUST 31ST, 1853.

See vote of the Directors of all the RR Companys which leave Boston = Nov. 5/49

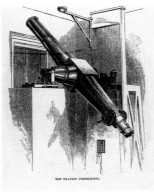

THE TRANSIT INSTRUMENT.

Samuel P. Langley, director of the Allegheny Observatory near Pittsburgh from 1867 to 1891.

To determine the correct time, Langley observed the transit of clock stars with this telescope at the Allegheny Observatory. From *Harper's New Monthly Magazine,* April 1878.

The Allegheny Observatory's clocks were wired to a chronograph (left), an instrument that produced a record that enabled the astronomer to compare clock time and star time. The chronograph's pen recorded the beats of each clock on a piece of paper wrapped around a rotating drum. Watching a star as it passed overhead, an observer marked its exact moment of transit by pressing a telegraph key, also wired to the chronograph, where the moment was also recorded. The switchboard (right) transmitted the beats of one of the clocks to time service subscribers, most notably the Pennsylvania Railroad. From *Harper's New Monthly Magazine,* April 1878.

TIME FOR SALE

By the mid-nineteenth century, astronomical observatories in the United States were not only determining time for their own purposes but were also distributing it by telegraph, in several forms. The ticking of the observatory's clock, relayed by telegraph, was the most common signal. Signals could also ring a fire bell at noon or trigger the dropping of a time ball. Several observatories across the country soon established time services and telegraphed time to jewelers, port authorities, and the railroads for a fee.

Probably the most widely publicized time service in the second half of the nineteenth century was that of the Allegheny Observatory near Pittsburgh. Its director from 1867 to 1891, Samuel P. Langley, who was one of his era's most respected scientists and eventually Secretary of the Smithsonian Institution, devised the time service as a source of income for the financially pressed observatory. While Langley's time service was not the first in the United States, it was the first to turn a considerable profit. During his administration, the service earned more than $60,000. Other observatories soon followed the Allegheny's example and began charging for distributing time.

The Pennsylvania Railroad and its many subsidiaries were the most influential customers. In 1870 the Pennsylvania system extended some 2,500 miles and had three hundred telegraph offices receiving time signals. Eventually about 8,000 miles of railway ran to the ticking of the Allegheny Observatory's clock.[67]

synchronizing time

1880–1920

THE COUNTRY ADJUSTS TO CLOCKS SET TO A NATIONAL STANDARD TIME.

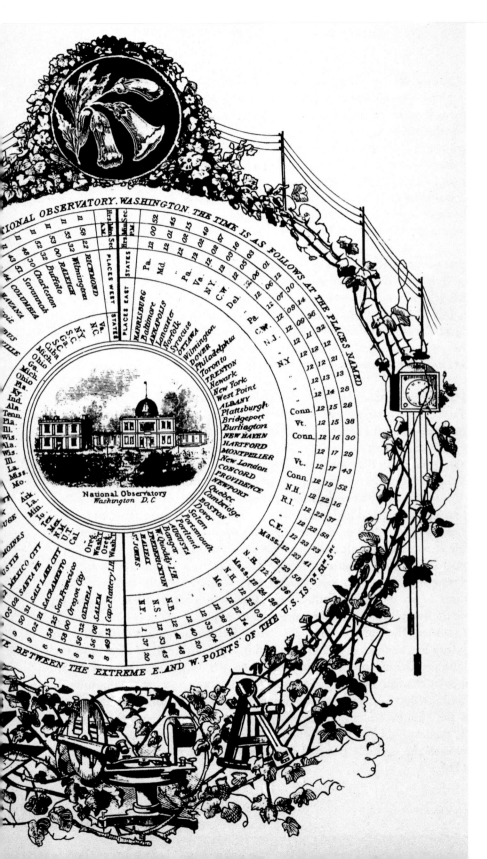

Before standard time, local times differed from one another by odd minutes and seconds. This circle of local times, an illustration from an 1869 map of New York State, is calculated from noon at Washington, D.C. Instruments for finding, keeping, and distributing time by telegraph intertwine with the decorative vines.

inventing standard time

Astronomical regulator for distributing Philadelphia time, made by E. Howard & Company for the Gold and Stock Telegraph Company, Philadelphia, 1874.

Astronomical regulator, about 1855. Most nineteenth-century American clocks were cheaply made for the mass market and domestic use. But a few firms made precision clocks for applications where accuracy was vital: determining the time of scientific observations, for example, or setting other clocks and watches. One such firm was E. Howard and Company of Boston. Howard sold this clock to James Allan and Company, Charleston, South Carolina, a jewelry firm located within walking distance of two railroad stations. Railroad employees reportedly stopped by the store to set their watches. The clock kept time there for over a century.

It is well to remember that Railways have no standard time for the Union, but usually run by the time of the principal office of the Company. In almost all hotels West, the dials of clocks indicate the railway and the time of the particular locality. To prevent disappointment, it is better to inquire at the hotel by what particular time the train one desires to travel on, runs by.

– Appleton's Railway and Steam Navigation Guide, 1857

Before Standard Time

AS NOTED EARLIER, before standard time each community determined it own time by observing the sun. A community a few miles east of another would mark noon first and would remain a few minutes ahead of its western neighbor throughout the day. This meant communities a few miles apart, east to west, were often a few minutes and seconds apart as well. Sacramento, California, was 3 hours, 9 minutes, and 51 seconds earlier than New York City, for example, but 3 minutes and 56 seconds later than San Francisco. Before standard time, there were hundreds of local time standards in use.

To complicate matters further, people had a considerable variety of public time sources to choose from. The tower clock on the local church, town hall, factory, or railroad station was the most common source. But as the nineteenth century progressed, other sources came into use: time balls atop prominent buildings, time guns at military installations, whistles and bells in factories, and precision timepieces in jewelry store windows. The railroad employees of Charleston, South Carolina, for example, often stopped in at the store of jeweler James Allan to check their watches against his fine clock. And no two public timepieces necessarily kept the same time, even in the same community. Businessmen in Philadelphia could be sure of their city's exact time if they subscribed to the time service at the local Gold and Stock Telegraph Company. A master clock in the telegraph office boldly declared it carried the true "Philadelphia Standard Time."

By the 1880s, the North American railroads ran on about fifty regional times. In practice, the boundaries between regional times lay where the railroad lines of different companies met or at the borders of a single company's divisions. The railroads were the country's biggest and most powerful business, and their regional times often prevailed over other locally determined public time.

111

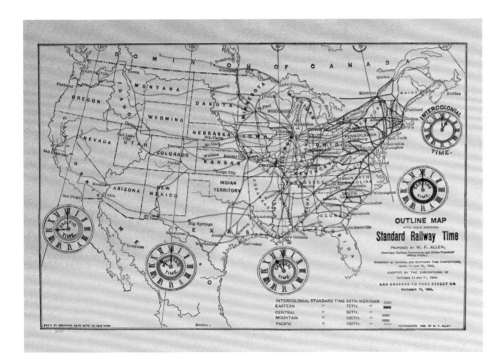

regional times then in use, with the simplified zone plan he had drawn up. His system, based on the points on railroad lines where the railroads had traditionally changed times, was one the railroads could operate comfortably. They would simply reset their clocks and watches. The Convention immediately adopted his five-zone plan for U.S. and Canadian railroads. The endorsement of the Southern Railway Time Convention followed within days.[8]

In a vigorous campaign to gain the support of the railroads and the general public, Allen enlisted an army of unpaid publicists from the railroads and scientific organizations during the summer of that year. Through private conversations, public lectures, and voluminous correspondence, Allen and his helpers persuaded businessmen, journalists, politicians, and ordinary citizens to support the new system.

Allen circulated thousands of copies of his map illustrating his five-zone plan for time reform in North America. The zones included one for the eastern provinces of Canada, known as Intercolonial (now Atlantic) Time, and four in the United States, the present Eastern, Central, Mountain, and Pacific Times. The zones were based on times determined at the 60th, 75th, 90th, 105th, and 120th meridians west of Greenwich, England.

On 18 November 1883, at noon on the 75th meridian west of Greenwich, England – roughly four minutes after the local noon of New York City – Standard Railway Time went into effect. As agreed on by nearly six hundred railroads, the fall of Western Union's time ball at its New York City headquarters marked the new system's official beginning. Cities and towns across the country had two noons that day, local time and standard time.

The cover of the *Travelers' Official Guide* for December 1883 depicted clocks set to the new zoned Standard Railway Time.

Broadside announcing standard time for the Cheshire & Monadnock Railroad, 1883.

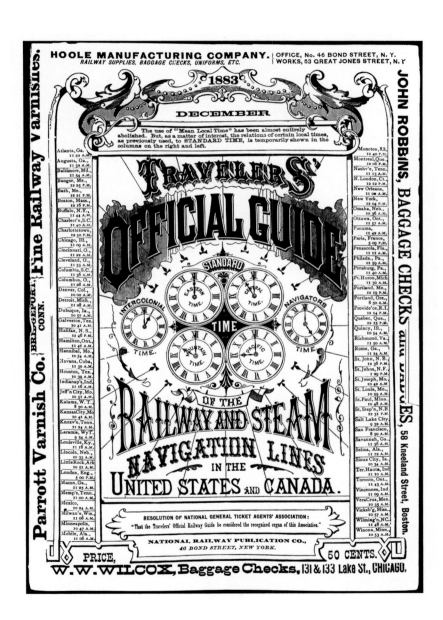

TIME BY TELEGRAPH

When Western Union's time ball in New York fell to inaugurate Standard Railway Time, it did so in response to a signal telegraphed from the U.S. Naval Observatory 240 miles away in Washington. The Naval Observatory and Western Union had already been partners in distributing public time for almost twenty years. By April of 1877, Western Union had initiated a national time service, with Washington time determined at the observatory and telegraphed for a fee to American cities of more than twenty thousand inhabitants.

After 1886, Western Union's time service delivered both time and timepieces. A national system of subscribers — businesses and public institutions of all sorts — received time signals from Western Union on clocks rented from the Self-Winding Clock Company of Brooklyn, New York, Western Union's other partner in the venture. Master clocks in Western Union offices automatically corrected the subscribers' clocks every hour on the hour.

The result of the collaboration was the nationwide distribution of a single uniform time. With the low cost and widespread reach of Western Union's service, and declining demand for local time, competing time services at private observatories one by one went out of business.[9]

Western Union time ball, 1878. From 1877 to 1914 a time ball on the roof of Western Union's headquarters marked noon in New York City. The ball, 42 inches in diameter and weighing 125 pounds, consisted of twelve copper vanes arranged radially around iron rings. Five minutes before noon each day, the ball was raised halfway up from its resting place at the bottom of a 22-foot staff. Two minutes before noon, Western Union received a signal to clear the line of regular traffic and raised the ball to the top of the staff. The noon signal telegraphed from Washington automatically tripped a magnetic latch, allowing the ball to fall.

Western Union Telegraph Company headquarters, 195 Broadway, New York City, late nineteenth century.

The U.S. Naval Observatory in Washington, D.C., transmitted time signals and rated chronometers in this room in the late nineteenth century.

SYNCHRONIZING TIME

Participants in the International Meridian Conference, Washington, D.C., 1884.

Eastern Standard Time. An election in 1884 put Cummings out of office, but a referendum returned the entire city to local time. Bangor remained out of synch until 1887, when the state legislature put all of Maine on standard time.[16]

For most people, though, the new standard time was practical and useful. It had the backing of the most powerful economic force in the country and the endorsement of the scientific community. Dissenters, no matter how vocal and reasonable, found themselves outnumbered and eventually disregarded.

Standard Time for the World

NORTH AMERICA'S ADOPTION of standard time recognized Greenwich, England, as prime meridian. But in the 1880s there was neither a binding international agreement on the use of Greenwich as prime meridian nor an international date line half a globe away.

Thinking about coordinated global time was not part of most people's experience, except for readers of Jules Verne's *Around the World in Eighty Days*. Published in 1873, the novel integrated the latest scientific thinking about world time in its storyline and used the underlying science in its surprise ending. The story pits Phileas Fogg against his cronies at a London gentleman's club, who bet him £20,000 that he cannot circle the globe in eighty days. Fogg sets off on the arduous journey, and just as it appears he has lost, he makes an astonishing discovery. By traveling eastward he had gained a day, so he wins the race in the nick of time.

Traditionally, each country used its own capital city or principal observatory for measuring time and designating lines of longitude on national land maps. After publication of the British *Nautical Almanac* began in 1767, many nations came to use Greenwich time for navigation and some scientific observations. Local mean time served for all other activities. Only long after steamships and telegraph cables linked the globe did organized international support emerge for fixing a common prime meridian. The first such meeting occurred at the International Geographical Congress in Antwerp, Belgium, in 1871. Scientists met periodically throughout the following decade to discuss the practicalities and difficulties of establishing a standard of time for the whole world.

Sir Sandford Fleming.

Sir Sandford Fleming's scheme for world
time zones, 1876. Letters correspond to
the central meridian in each zone.

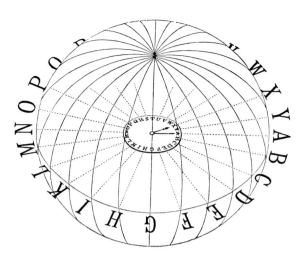

"Cosmic Time" dial of Sir Sandford
Fleming's watch, with letters corresponding
to world time zones and a twenty-four-hour
(instead of a twelve-hour) dial.

Not until October 1884 did diplomats and technical specialists gather to act on the scientists' proposals. The International Meridian Conference, held in Washington, recommended that the nations of the world establish a prime meridian at Greenwich, count longitude east and west from the prime meridian up to 180 degrees in each direction, and adopt a universal day beginning at Greenwich at midnight. Although the International Meridian Conference had no authority to enforce its suggestions, the meeting resulted in the gradual worldwide adoption of a time-zone system based on Greenwich as prime meridian.[17]

Sandford Fleming, chief engineer of the Canadian Pacific Railway, originated the idea of a system of time zones for the world. In 1876, his first notions about time reform concentrated on replacing the two twelve-hour designations of the day, A.M. and P.M., with a twenty-four-hour scheme. Almost immediately, however, he expanded his interests to propose a system he called variously "Terrestrial Time," "Cosmic Time," and "Cosmopolitan Time" – a division of the globe into twenty-four zones identified by letters of the alphabet. The military and some civilian science, aviation, and navigation efforts still use alphabet identifiers for time zones. Zone Z is governed by 0 degree longitude, or the prime meridian passing through Greenwich, England. "Zulu Time" is the time of day at that meridian.[18]

Daylight Saving Time

THE FIRST FEDERAL LEGISLATION establishing a standard time for the nation grew out of efforts to save fuel and promote efficiency during World War I. On 19 March 1918, Congress approved "an act to save daylight and provide standard time for the United States." As soon as World War I ended, a deluge of protests, mostly from farmers more in synch with the sun than with the clock, caused Congress to repeal the daylight saving provision of the act. President Woodrow Wilson vetoed the repeal twice, but Congress overrode the vetoes. National daylight saving time, in effect only for parts of 1918 and 1919, ended on the last Sunday in October in 1919. At the outbreak of World War II, the United States once again adopted daylight saving time to promote electricity conservation and evening "Victory gardening." The measure, dubbed "War Time" by Franklin D. Roosevelt, began 9 February 1942, and continued year-round until 30 September 1945.

While many states observed daylight saving time between the wars and after World War II, no national time legislation took effect until the Uniform Time Act of 1966. Arizona, Hawaii, parts of Indiana, Puerto Rico, the U.S. Virgin Islands, and American Samoa still do not observe daylight saving time.[19]

Despite the small impact on most people's lives at the moment of its adoption, standard time is in hindsight the most dramatic change in our relationship to time since the invention of the mechanical clock around A.D. 1300.[20] The mechanical clock had provided a way to represent time as numbered equal hours on a dial. The clock's dial was in fact an analog of the sundial, with its shadow moving around a ring of hours in tandem with the movement of the sun in the sky. Unlike a sundial, though, the clock is divorced from the sun. The clock's time is an abstraction of nature, and its hands are driven by the regular, invariable tempo of the clockwork behind the dial. Before standard time, when communities observed their own local sun time, clocks and the sun were already slightly out of synch. Standardized clock time, arranged in geographical zones where the sun time at a single meridian governed the time for widely distant communities, removed our idea of time even further from the sun's behavior.

Poster promoting daylight saving time, 1918.

Breakfast time, from the Healey Picture Completion Test, an intelligence test, 1918. The test, a puzzle with eleven illustrations of the events in a boy's day, challenges the test subject to place puzzle squares in the correct sequence for those events from morning to night.

time discipline

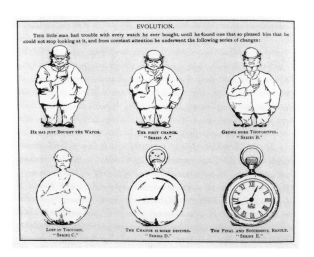

Advertisement for Waterbury Watch Company, 1888.

Do not let your child be tardy [for school]. If you do,
when he grows up he will be late at his work. Thus he will lose his job,
and always be poor and miserable.

— Amanda Matthews Chase, *Primer for Foreign Speaking Women*, 1918

IN AN INCREASINGLY URBAN AND INDUSTRIAL WORLD, people became responsible for knowing the time and being on time, all the time. They began to sleep with alarm clocks at their bedside. And owning a watch, within the reach of most working people as affordable versions were now selling in the United States by the tens of millions, and synchronizing it to the new standard time came to be seen as part of meeting that social responsibility. "The man is nothing but a botch, who tries to live without a watch," warned an advertisement for pocket watches in the 1880s. Advertising, in particular, seemed to promise that a watch once bought would convey punctuality and prosperity to the new owner. One cartoon in a trade magazine published in 1888 to promote Waterbury watches depicted a man turning into his watch, an adman's fantasy in which a person identified with his watch and lived so closely with it that they merged.[21]

Checking the time had its down side, if we are to believe physician George M. Beard's 1881 treatise on American nervousness. "The perfection of clocks and the invention of watches have something to do with modern nervousness," he wrote, "since they compel us to be on time, and excite the habit of looking to see the exact moment, so as not to be late for trains or appointments." But punctuality was still for many a distant ideal, if the following guidance from the chapter on "Business Habits" in *The Universal Self-Instructor* of 1883 is any indication: "Punctuality is a virtue that all men reverence in theory, but comparatively few carry into practice. Nothing inspires confidence in a business man sooner than this quality, nor is there any habit which

The Tornado alarm clock, made by the William Gilbert Clock Company, Winsted, Connecticut, about 1925.

Telechron electric alarm clock, made by General Electric, about 1930.

A profusion of styles soon poured from the country's clock factories. Each model had an expressive name. Some sounded like benign helpers: Big Ben or Jack-o-Lantern from Westclox, and the Tip Top Traveler or the Tidy Tot, both from the New Haven Clock Company. Others suggested a more aggressive wakeup: the Rattler, the Slumber Stopper, the Tornado. The Sears, Roebuck catalog offered the "National Call" in two styles, one with luminous hands and dial for $3.50 and another without for a dollar less. "On time!" the catalog page shouted. "Work, school, meals, appointments – punctuality is demanded by modern life and the alert and active family demands a reliable alarm clock."[28]

By the late 1920s, electric alarm clocks had entered the market. These depended on the invention of the synchronous electric motor, largely the work of engineer Henry E. Warren. Beginning about 1909, Warren experimented with, and eventually perfected, a self-starting synchronous motor to monitor generator speed at electric power plants. Such monitoring enabled the plant to generate alternating current at a constant average frequency. To connect numerous power plants into a single system, the power industry then agreed upon a standard frequency of sixty cycles per second. In addition to supplying power stations with master clocks, the Warren Clock Company of Ashland, Massachusetts, marketed with enormous success a line of small electric clocks for domestic and business use. An electric clock is little more than a synchronous motor running at the frequency of the electrical current that power stations supply to houses and other structures. Gears reduce this frequency to that required to rotate the clock hands. Warren's Telechron clocks (made later by General Electric) had synchronous motors.[29]

Mass-produced alarms appeared at a time when the changing geography of urban spaces increasingly segregated industrial workplaces from residential neighborhoods. Streetcars connected new suburbs to city hubs and new factory areas. These transformations meant that many families increasingly lived far out of earshot of work, school, and church bells.[30] Heeding their own alarm clocks, with or without assistance from public time signals, became the responsibility of men, women, and children. The domestic alarm clock, once a luxury item for the wealthy, became a widely available necessity, a technical fix for tardiness, and the mechanical assistant to punctuality.[31]

Time at a Glance: The Wristwatch

He's no parlor dude a-prancing, he's no puny pacifist,
And it's not for affectation there's a watch upon his wrist,
He's a fine two-fisted scrapper, he is pure American
And the backbone of the nation is the Wrist Watch Man.

— Edgar Guest, "The Wrist Watch Man," 1918

THE WRISTWATCH IS A RELATIVE NEWCOMER among timekeepers. No one knows precisely where or when the first appeared, but Queen Elizabeth I of England probably had one, and the few surviving examples from seventeenth-century Europe come in the form of a bracelet set with a tiny timepiece. More numerous, but still uncommon, are nineteenth-century bracelet watches made in Switzerland. The modern wristwatch dates from around 1880, when women in England and Europe began to wear small watches set in leather bands around their wrists, especially for outdoor activities like hunting, horseback riding, and, later, bicycling.[32]

Men, for the most part, did not wear wristwatches at the turn of the century. They considered them feminine jewelry. Although a pocket watch and watch chain were acceptable male accessories, men aspiring to positions of respect and status were consistently advised against ostentation. One of the period's etiquette books warned: "It is not considered in good taste for men to wear much jewelry. They may with propriety wear one gold ring, studs and cuff buttons, and a watch chain. . . . Anything more looks like a superabundance of ornament."[33] A love of display meant, to the period's arbiters of masculinity, either effeminacy or an utter lack of refinement.

Chatelaine set with a hunting theme, late nineteenth century. Worn suspended from a broad leather belt, the chatelaine accessories include a compass in the form of jockey's cap and bugle, a watch in the shape of a horse's hoof, and a perfume container in the shape of a powder flask.

Through most of the nineteenth century, an American man's pocket watch was often his most prized possession. The style of men's watches, and the way men wore them, remained relatively constant. A man wore his watch in his vest pocket and anchored it for safety with a chain draped from the center vest button across to one or both pockets. A man engaged in vigorous work or play, or a man going without a vest, might wear his watch in his trousers pocket or, less commonly, in the breast pocket of his jacket.

In contrast to the relatively constant style for men, women's styles changed often. Fashion magazines in the last two decades of the nineteenth century advocated a variety of timepieces for women who could afford luxuries. For most of the century until then, women had worn watches hung from long chains around the neck. A well-to-do woman might own a very special bracelet containing a watch, or wear a watch at her waist or on her lapel. She might also have a watch set in a ring.

Front and back of a lapel watch made in
Switzerland, 1901.

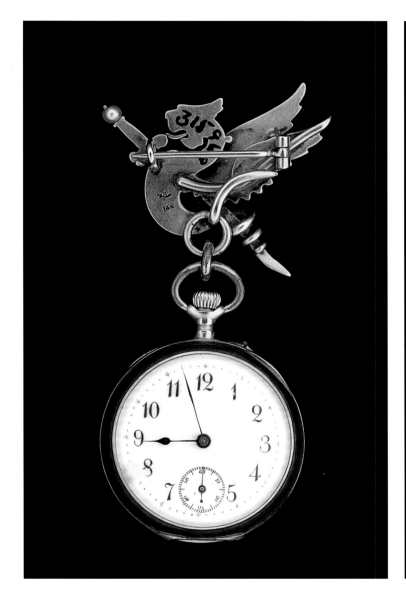

Aerial photographer wearing wristwatch, about 1918.

The practicality of having time at a glance, the feature that attracted active women to the style in the first place, changed some military men's minds about wristwatches. Reportedly, the German Admiralty ordered a few wristwatches from Swiss manufacturers in the 1880s in response to a recommendation from a naval officer who had resorted at a critical moment to attaching his pocket watch to his coat sleeve. He found he needed to be able to consult his watch *and* use both hands freely. Soldiers in the Boer War (1899–1902) wore Swiss-made Omega wristwatches, and in the first decade of the twentieth century the U.S. Signal Corps authorized the wearing of wristwatches.[37]

As soldiers entered World War I they, like the German naval officer, experimented with fastening pocket watches to their sleeves, or, in the case of airmen, to their legs. As the war progressed, the wristwatch became ubiquitous among male soldiers of all branches of the armed forces and the female nurses recruited to care for the wounded. Prebattle preparations began to include the synchronizing of watches on a scale never before undertaken in wartime. One eyewitness recalled how a runner distributed watches synchronized at field headquarters to soldiers poised for an offensive. When the synchronized watches of platoon leaders showed precisely 7:30 A.M. on 1 July 1916, they sent the men of the Third and Fourth British armies into the gruesome battle of the Somme.[38]

The fact that the wristwatch provided portable time at a glance, a much speedier read than pocket or pendant watches, was not lost on the soldiers of World War I engaged in combat with new rapid-fire weapons at a speed and ferocity unprecedented in human history. For men in the trenches, at least, the wristwatch replaced the pocket watch as the symbol of competence and efficiency. European manufacturers reportedly worked overtime to convert existing women's watches into military timepieces to meet the demand.[39]

During the war, American men began to reassess their opinion of the wristwatch, which they had previously regarded as a feminine ornament, or worse, an object of ridicule. An American correspondent for the *Horological Journal* reported in 1916 that American men had, until then, considered the wristwatch a joke, a worthy subject of comic skits in vaudeville and movies. "The objectors," he continued, "are now willing to concede the value of a bracelet watch for general outdoor life, but have not yet reached the point where, after poking fun at it, they can consistently adopt it for all occasions."[40]

Silk-mill worker wearing wristwatch, about 1925, photo by Lewis Hine.

A jeweled pocket watch, U.S. Watch Company, Waltham, Massachusetts, 1893.

Pathfinder, a "dollar" watch made by E. Ingraham and Company, Bristol, Connecticut, 1920. Such very inexpensive watches without jewels came on the market in the late 1870s.

Postwar manufacturers tried to negate the wristwatch's enduring feminine image with advertising that reassured men of its sturdy masculinity. A Benrus ad, for example, promoted "the strap watch of Sportsmen" as the perfect accessory for "a brawny, wind-tanned wrist." But even as late as 1943, wristwatches were still sometimes called "bracelet watches" or "wristlets," recalling feminine jewelry.[41]

After about 1880, most American machine-made pocket watches were remarkably alike in appearance and in the way they were made. The main feature distinguishing one type of watch movement from another was jeweling. Industrial-grade rubies, sapphires, garnets, or aquamarines were the functional jewels, distinct from decorative ones, fitted in the watch movement as bearings at points of wear. The most basic jeweled watch contained seven, but fifteen was most common, and railroad standards called for seventeen. Sophisticated manufacturing systems based on machine-made interchangeable parts allowed the cost of an average American jeweled watch to drop from $40 in 1850 to $10 in 1880. By 1900, the American Watch Company and the Elgin National Watch Company dominated the American market, but other firms, such as Hampden, Illinois, Seth Thomas, Rockford, Columbus, U.S. Watch, Lancaster, Aurora, Peoria, Howard, and Hamilton, also produced conventional jeweled watches. Inexpensive jeweled pocket watches came from such firms as New York Standard, Trenton, Manhattan, Knickerbocker, Cheshire, and Suffolk. A new kind of very inexpensive pocket watch without jewels became available in the late 1870s. Easier to make and very much in demand, these timekeepers retailed for $1 beginning in 1896. These "dollar watches," made by Waterbury, Ingersoll, and New Haven, among others, were so cheap, they were often giveaways during promotions for other products or marketed for children. In contrast, the best pocket watches from Howard, Waltham, and Elgin cost over $150.[42]

Pocket watches continued to be indicators of their owners' social status. Different grades of movement required different qualities of cases and signaled different levels of social accomplishment. The most expensive watches had gold cases and precise jeweled movements. But since a customer could buy a movement and case separately, those seeking a truly inexpensive watch opted for cases made of cheaper new materials such as silveroid (an alloy of nickel, copper, and manganese) or a gold-filled case (a layer of brass between two thin layers of gold). Horatio Alger, popularizer of American rags-to-riches stories and the status symbols of the middle class, ranked watches from most to least desirable in his novel *Struggling Upward* (1890): gold, then silver, then gold plate, and, at the bottom end, nickel or brass. Alger's characters almost always got a gold watch when they made it to the middle class.[43]

SYNCHRONIZING TIME

Railroad watch, Peoria Watch Company,
Peoria, Illinois, about 1887.

Railroad watch, E. Howard & Company,
Boston, about 1914.

Railroad Pocket Watches

ACCURATE TIMEKEEPERS WERE fundamental to safe and efficient railroad
operation. As rail traffic increased in complexity and volume after 1875, railroad managers collaborated individually with American watch manufacturers
to draw up specifications for precision watches. The definition of a railroad
watch changed over time and varied from line to line. By the 1920s, generally
accepted, closely specified standards governed almost every detail of watch
construction for railway use.

To ensure that a watch made to railroad specifications maintained accu-
racy, the railroads devised inspection systems. In some cases inspectors were railroad employees; more often, they were locally authorized, independent watchmakers who not only rated
timepieces but also cleaned and repaired them. Employees kept a record of watch inspection
dates on a card.

In 1866 the American Watch Company, under contract to the Pennsylvania Railroad, delivered the first American watches specifically ordered by a railroad for railroad use. In 1969, yield-
ing to the universal popularity of wristwatches, the Hamilton Watch Company of Lancaster,
Pennsylvania, made the last American railroad pocket watch. In the intervening century, fourteen firms had sold millions of high-grade pocket watches for the railroad market.

Presentation Watches

IN THE NINETEENTH CENTURY, pocket watches with cases of gold or silver became popular as
gifts for Christmas, birthdays, graduations, weddings, and to mark occasions of personal accomplishment or meritorious service with a lasting memento. Such gifts often bore special messages

A tiny watch made by the American Watch Company, Waltham, Massachusetts, with the monogram "A.F.S." engraved on its gold case, was the gift of Philip Cadmus to his fiancée Augusta Frances Stipp in 1906. Cadmus, a watchmaker, had his photo applied to the dial.

A Washington, D.C., policeman, Thomas Oriani, received an elaborate Waltham watch as a Christmas present in 1890 from the jewelers on his Seventh Street beat in appreciation for his keeping a protective eye on their businesses.

Blind and deaf from the age of two, Helen Keller used a special watch. The Swiss pocket watch from the late nineteenth century, called a *montre-à-tact,* has a case studded with pins that correspond to the hours on the watch dial.

On the back of the case of Helen Keller's watch, a revolving hand stops at a point between the pins that corresponds to the hour and approximate minute. Such a device permitted her to feel the time.

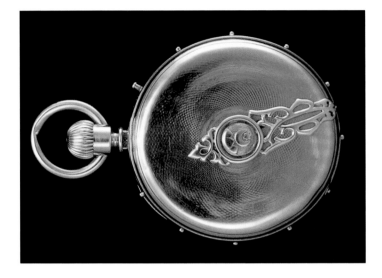

of commemoration engraved on the case, or featured dial and movement finishes customized for the recipient.[44]

An unusual watch, intended to tell time in the dark, made the perfect present for an extraordinary girl. Deaf, blind, and mute from the age of nineteen months, Helen Keller was six years old when she first met Alexander Graham Bell. (Bell's experiments with inventing a speech system for the deaf had resulted in the telephone.) In 1892, when she was twelve, Keller met John Hitz, the superintendent of Bell's Washington, D.C., establishment for the deaf, the Volta Bureau. Hitz, a retired diplomat, was the proud owner of a Swiss-made *montre-à-tact*, or "touch watch." This uncommon pocket watch has a case studded around the edge with pins that correspond to the hours on the watch dial. A revolving hand stops at a point between the pins that corresponds to the hour and approximate minute. Such a device permitted its user to feel the approximate time in the dark or, in the case of Hitz the diplomat, to consult his watch discreetly. Hitz presented the watch to Keller, who prized it and used it her entire life. Once, in 1952, she left it behind in a New York City taxi and feared it was lost forever. With ads in newspaper lost-and-found columns and the help of the head of the city's pawnbrokers, she recovered it from a hock shop.[45]

Targeted advertisements suggested which watches were appropriate gifts for particular occasions, for boys and girls, women and men. In time for Christmas shopping, an ad for the Lord Elgin pocket watch in the *Ladies' Home Journal* for December 1911 explained the watch was the "gift that a man delights to receive and show." The watch was an expensive present, to be sure, but the ad assured it was worth the price: "Men of affairs – of power and prestige – own a watch. And their reliance on its faithfulness is well founded. For a lifetime it runs true. A marvel of preciseness and beauty." In an ad for Howard watches, a mother and her son are pictured in a home decorated for the holidays. The ad advises the purchaser that her son needs a watch to assure his successful future as a grownup: "One very good way to show your affection and your high hope for the boy is to give him a HOWARD WATCH for Christmas. . . . It expresses so well your expectation for him and the work he is to do in the world." The ad promises her that the Howard "is pre-eminently the watch of successful Americans today." For a girl's graduation gift, an ad from the Elgin National Watch Company predicted another kind of future: Parents should buy a wristwatch for her because it would likely be "the last important gift to The-Girl-Who-Is-Theirs"; future gifts to their daughter, for wedding, housewarming, and anniversaries, would go to "The-Woman-Who-Belongs-To-Some-One-Else."[46]

SYNCHRONIZING TIME

time machines

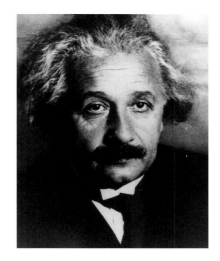

> "Upon that machine," said the Time Traveller, holding the lamp aloft, "I intend to explore time."
>
> – H. G. Wells, *The Time Machine*, 1898

AT THE VERY MOMENT the railroads put measures in place to standardize clock time everywhere in the United States, new technologies began to alter the way people experienced and thought about time. Novel inventions such as the automobile, the telephone, the phonograph, the movies, and the electric light seemed to suggest that time might be experienced in multiple ways, distinctly different from unvarying clock time. The car and the phone appeared to accelerate the pace of life. Electricity turned night into day. Sound recording and the movies seemed to manipulate past, present, and future, to bend time.

The impending dawn of the twentieth century inspired many to think about the subject of time, and especially in relation to these new inventions. Speculations about time, "the fourth dimension," as it came to be known then, preoccupied writers, artists, philosophers, and scientists. It was the scientific news of the era, in fact, that inspired the novel *The Time Machine*, H. G. Wells's literary exploration of the future. The recasting of time as personal and subjective paralleled momentous developments in physics, as when Albert Einstein suggested that time in the cosmos might, in fact, be relative to the observer, not the uniform and inalterable constant that Isaac Newton had postulated more than two centuries before.[47]

The Automobile

IN CHANGING THE WAY AMERICANS MOVED THROUGH SPACE, the car would also forever alter people's experience with time.[48] Even if they had never seen or ridden in a car, people recognized its symbolic nature almost instantly. More than just a machine for transportation, it became a mobile metaphor for speed, performance, and temporal liberation. The car provided personal transportation freed from railroad and streetcar timetables, at speeds faster than the horse and buggy had allowed. An article in *Harper's Weekly* in 1909 extolled the "feeling of independence" the car provided and listed its virtues:

the freedom from timetables, from fixed and inflexible routes . . . the ability to go where and when one wills, to linger and stop where the country is beautiful and the way pleasant, or to rush through unattractive surroundings, to select the best places to eat and sleep; and the satisfaction that comes from a knowledge that one need ask favors or accommodation from no one nor trespass on anybody's property or privacy.

A writer for *Motor World* had sounded the same theme in 1901: "In the case of a motor vehicle you have a method of moving from place to place as tireless as a train, one which for short journeys and cross journeys is as quick as the train, and yet one which is individualistic and independent, hence its charm."[49]

"The horseless vehicle is the coming wonder," Thomas Edison predicted scarcely two years after the Duryea brothers ran their gas-powered car through the streets of Springfield, Massachusetts, in September 1893 and claimed it was the first practical automobile made in the United States. No one could have foretold, though, the crucial role the automobile would play in shaping, for good or for ill, twentieth-century American life.[50]

At first only the wealthiest bought cars and used them, mostly for sports and leisure. A few doctors also purchased them to make their rounds. Poor rural road conditions also meant that America's first cars were, with only a few exceptions, the possessions of urbanites. But within a generation, Henry Ford's mass-produced Model T, introduced in 1908 – and other cars that soon appeared in imitation of it – provided nearly everyone with a new way of moving across distance through time.

Noticeably faster than the horse or the bicycle, the car created a new sense of speed. The thrill of speed tantalized many, and manufacturers appealed to them by advertising this feature. Car racing, first on roads and then on closed tracks, attracted some buyers, but antagonized a large segment of the public who thought such recklessness should not be condoned.[51] An elderly resident of Antioch, California, recalled that "when the vehicle came, horses got scared, kids screamed, and mothers pulled their children off the road." The local paper added to the hysteria with headlines like "MANY DEATHS DUE TO 'DEVIL WAGON!' Dead and Unconscious Forms Left in Wake of Speeding Automobiles Operated by Reckless Chauffeurs."[52]

As a result of incidents involving excessive and careless speed, some jurisdictions set speed limits. The earliest were unimaginably low by today's standards. The social historian Frederick Lewis Allen, for example, remembers that the first speed limit in Holderness, New Hampshire, was 6 miles an hour. A good clip on a country road was about 10 miles an hour, and the limit crept up to 20 and 25 by 1920.[53]

Speed limits were just one way to control the country's growing traffic, to move cars in time. Traffic signals were another. The new profession of traffic engineer emerged, and practitioners developed rules and signals to ensure safe and orderly flow. Engineers often preferred automatic signals to stationing a policeman at an intersection, and they experimented with systems combining lights, signs, and police. But suggestions for traffic control came from every quarter. At the behest of a local street railway, Cleveland installed a red and green signal at the corner of Euclid Avenue and 104th Street in 1914. In the same city, a collision between a car and a horse-drawn carriage inspired Garrett Morgan, an African-American businessman, to invent a new kind of sign that also signaled "caution." Detroit policeman William Potts developed an automatic green, yellow, and red light system in 1920. Nevertheless, despite the pleas to slow traffic down, Americans opted for speed. Traffic planners advocated lights to accelerate traffic, they maintained, not to slow speeders. New York City's traffic coordinators optimistically ornamented the first traffic lights on Fifth Avenue with tiny statues of Mercury, the god of speed.[54]

It's difficult for us today to think of the car as seasonal, but before about 1924, when the automobile changed into an all-weather, closed vehicle, driving was largely a recreation for fair summer days. In the small town of Oregon, Illinois, for example, people stored their cars between December and mid-March, when radiator, batteries, and tires proved no match for the harsh Midwestern winter. Snow removal in the town was nonexistent until the state began highway clearance in the winter of 1924–25. Unpaved roads could be impassable when they turned to mud in the spring. Large cities did not fare much better. They rarely cleared snow from their streets before 1915. It would be 1916 before carmakers began to offer hand-operated windshield wipers, and automatic electric wipers did not become standard equipment until the 1930s.[55]

Summer or winter, cars had a considerable effect on leisure time. Whether racing or touring, courting or simply driving to the movies, people began to spend their time differently when they had access to a car. In *Middletown: A Study in Contemporary American Culture* (1929), billed as a study of the typical American small town (Muncie, Indiana), sociologists Robert and Helen Lynd noted how the car interacted with changes in leisure time. They found autos inspired people to take vacations and offered new ways to relax after work, some of which the Lynds deplored because they appeared to undermine familial togetherness. The automobile made rural and remote areas accessible to urbanites craving fresh air and open spaces. Even more significant, it revolutionized the relationship of work and leisure for country people. And, although some writers have argued that the car sped up the pace of life because it could go faster than the horse, others have pointed out that because of its transformation of leisure, it also had the effect of slowing people down, to allow travelers to stop and enjoy the scenery.[56]

Sundays were forever changed, as the automobile made it possible to go to church and still have time for recreation. The Sunday excursion, a custom adopted from German-American immigrants, became a widespread American pastime after the Civil War; first the bicycle, in the 1880s and 1890s, and then the automobile stimulated pleasure jaunts as no other transportation modes had before. As car ownership increased, so did Sunday driving – and vocal opposition to it. One of the Lynds' informants was a minister who complained the country seemed to be infected with "automobilitis," a condition among those "who go off motoring on Sunday instead of going to church."[57] Those who considered "motoring" a violation of a sacred day continued the enduring conflict over how the Sabbath should be observed in the United States.

The Telephone

THE TELEPHONE, LIKE THE AUTOMOBILE, changed the way people perceived time and space. Both seemed to accelerate the tempo of life. The telephone allowed people to communicate instantly, over long distances. Compared with handwritten messages, which seemed slow and remote, the telephone afforded immediate responses to what people were saying and feeling.[58] And compared to the telegraph, where intermediate operators passed on terse, businesslike communications, telephone conversations seemed intimate and rich with detail.

The apparatus for which Alexander Graham Bell filed a patent in 1876 grew out of his efforts to invent a multiplex telegraph, one to carry multiple messages simultaneously over a single wire. Pressure for new telegraph technology had mounted in Bell's time, as message traffic increased and proliferating wires entangled American cities.[59] The Bell Telephone Company started providing service in 1877, and three years later Bell and his business partners had seen to the installation of more than 50,000 phones, about 1 per 1,000 people. By 1893, there were about 260,000 telephones in operation, 1 per 250 people in the United States, and by 1914, 10 million.[60] Simultaneously the Bell company actively improved the device itself, invented a switching system, and organized the business side of the service.[61]

Initially, telephone entrepreneurs pitched their new system to the same people who used the telegraph: to men of commerce for business communications and to municipalities for fire alarms. They considered social conversations, telephone "visiting," a misuse of the service. The instantaneous proximity the telephone provided tantalized businessmen, who immediately adopted it. In 1891, for example, the New York and New Jersey Telephone Company listed a total of 7,322 commercial customers, but only 1,442 residences; most of the homes with telephones belonged to doctors or businessmen.

In the first decade of the century, the business world's infatuation with "scientific management" was in full flower. Sales pitches for telephone service emphasized how the apparatus could save time and increase efficiency. Advertisements for 1910, for example, advised "Save Time by Telephone," or to make appointments: "Call Ahead for Business." Even the few marketing efforts directed to home telephone sales depicted the home as a business and the homemaker as its manager. A 1904 salesman's handbook suggested the following sales pitch:

> While residential telephone service may not directly save money for the household, yet, in an indirect way, it accomplishes the same thing by saving time, labor, and drudgery, and in making the whole household run more smoothly. It is always on duty, shops in all weather, corrects mistakes, and hastens deliveries. It saves letter writing, orders the dinner, invites the guests, reserves the tickets, and calls the carriage. It makes appointments, changes the time, cancels them altogether and renews them.[62]

By the time the United States entered World War I, in 1914, about half of middle-income Americans had telephones, but the telephone would not become an instrument for making social calls until after the war.[63]

Besides its practical uses as a time-saver and speedy destroyer of distances, the telephone had a great impact on how people experienced the present. Phone conversations permitted people to undergo multiple simultaneous events, to be, in effect, in two places at one time. Party lines increased the number of places connected simultaneously, as did public telephone "broadcasts": Sermons and music were sent to wide audiences over telephone wires in the instrument's early days, and in 1896 thousands reportedly received presidential election returns through their telephone receivers.[64]

The Phonograph

Let us glance at the promise of the phonograph in the future. . . . It will be the great collector of spoken phrases of the world. It will confer immortality on the human voice; it will be its champion against time.

— Dr. J. Mount Bleyer, "Living Autograms," *The Phonogram,* 1893

THE COMPETITION FOR AN IMPROVED TELEPHONE yielded a whole new invention: the phonograph, a machine to record and play back sound. The telephone transmitted sound, but the phonograph captured it and preserved it for later replay. In this way, the phonograph altered the experience of time, allowing people of the present to resurrect the past, preserve the present, and speak to the future. What to record and pass on became matters of debate.[65]

Although recorded sound is most often associated today with music and audio books, it was initially unclear precisely to what use people would put the phonograph. Thomas Edison's pursuit of a machine to record telephone messages led him to a patent for a "sound writer" in 1877. Enthusiastic receptions for the phonograph at numerous demonstrations made Edison think his new device might be more than just a telephone recorder. Maybe it could be a dictating machine for business, too, or a talking book, a voice for all kinds of toys, even a talking clock. But the novelty wore off, both for Edison and his audiences. Nothing came of the phonograph until the late 1880s, when Alexander Graham Bell and his associates – a cousin, Chichester Bell, and a young electrical tinkerer, Charles Sumner Tainter – produced their own version of a talking machine called the graphophone. The competition spurred Edison to make improvements in his original device.[66]

Edison and the Bell associates successfully marketed their recording machines as tools to save time and increase efficiency in business offices. The new devices were replacements for professional stenographers, called "phonographers" in that era. Due to continuing technical difficulties and managers who preferred not to use recording equipment, dictating machines did not become as widespread and crucial to business operations as typewriters and telephones. Eventually other applications for recording developed – radio broadcasting, telephone answering, and automatic responses – all of which could preserve sound in time for the present and the future.[67]

Sales of records and machines for home entertainment really took off with the introduction of products from the workshop of Emile Berliner, a German immigrant working in Washington, D.C. He invented the gramophone, a machine that played a flat, mass-producible disk. The record player evolved into an essential component of the ideal middle-class home.[68]

Edgar and Jennie Kreuger with their cat Tramp and an Edison phonograph, 1905.

First night rodeo in the Los Angeles Coliseum, 1927.

Electric Lighting

People stood overwhelmed with awe, as if in the presence of the supernatural.
The strange weird light, exceeded in power only by the sun, rendered the square as light as
midday. . . . Men fell on their knees, groans were uttered at the sight,
and many were dumb with amazement.

— *Wabash* [Indiana] *Plain Dealer* on illuminating the courthouse, 1880

HEARTH FIRES, CANDLES, AND GAS LIGHTING had blurred the line between day and night for some time. There had always been a few people who ventured out after dark for work and play. Some might be up all night, such as fishermen following night-running herring; others, like innkeepers, bakers, garbage collectors, or actors, might work the early-morning or late-evening hours on the edges of darkness. But only with the brilliance of electric light did significant numbers of people begin to experience a major shift of activities into nighttime hours. Electric lighting enabled people to expand the boundaries of daytime both indoors and out. Bending time this way was a significant challenge to long-held Newtonian notions that time was unchangeable.[69]

Thomas Edison's invention of the incandescent bulb in 1879 and the electrical power supply system for the Pearl Street district of New York three years later marked the beginning. With a reliable generator, centrally located to distribute power, electric lamps might be located anywhere wires would stretch.[70]

Edison's system initially competed for customers against brilliant electrical arc lighting, which came into wide use in the 1870s, and gas illumination systems. But Edison's light was different. His bulb depended on a glowing filament, not an open flame, as all previous lighting devices had. The new lamps had the radiance of the supernatural, and people were awestruck when they first encountered them. Crowds, mostly from the middle and upper classes, flocked to brightly lit world's fairs, beginning with Chicago's Columbian Exposition of 1893–94, to gaze in wonder at demonstrations of the newest technologies, including electric light and power. In imitation, businesses erected extravagant outdoor advertising using electric bulbs. Except for a few mansions, the first places where most people saw electric lighting were these outdoor displays or indoors at hotels, theaters, or department stores. The earliest uses for electric lighting, then, between about 1885 and 1915 were mostly in public urban settings. Lights were spectacular displays, symbolic of wealth and power, rather than utilitarian elements of the infrastructure.[71]

Practical uses came later. Utility companies formed to supply street lighting and electric transportation systems and only later sought customers more widely. Entertainment expanded into the night. And because electric lamps were cleaner and safer than gas illumination, they transformed industrial workplaces after about 1900, making possible round-the-clock shifts, keeping valuable equipment from idling, but disrupting workers' personal lives. Beginning around 1910, when only about one in ten American homes had electric lights, electric lighting for urban dwellers began to spread. Rural electrification would become a national goal in the 1930s.[72]

In the arrival of reliable electrical service lie the technical roots of our present-day nonstop Internet, overnight delivery, round-the-clock banking at automated teller machines, amusements that never close. Lighting up the night, traditionally the time for sleep, was a way of expanding in time, much the same way humans were expanding their range in geographical space.[73]

The Movies

[A movie] does for us what no other thing can do save a drug . . . it takes normal intervals of time and expands them one, two or a thousand fold, or compresses them . . .

– C. H. Claudy, "Motion Picture Magic: Playing Tricks on Time,"
Scientific American, 15 May 1915

THE MOVIE INDUSTRY PROFOUNDLY ALTERED the way Americans thought about and used time. Starting in 1895, American filmmakers learned to edit film to construct new ways of telling stories. They recorded motion in discrete parts, cut the film up, and rearranged the segments at will. In doing so they discovered that traditional notions about how time works, its supposed irreversibility and steady forward flow, no longer held – at least on film. In compressing or expanding the sequence of original filmed events, they took control of time to produce cinematic stories and illusions, enthralling mass audiences and inducing them to spend their leisure time at the pictures.[74]

Precisely who invented the first motion picture machinery was a matter of vigorous dispute through most of the twentieth century. Inspired in the late 1880s to do for moving pictures what the phonograph did for sound, Thomas Edison claimed both the movie camera and the movie projector, but many of his patents for them were challenged as other inventors, and their defenders, came forward to champion their own efforts. What is certain is the commercial success of Edison's Kinetoscope launched the movie industry in the United States.[75]

Edison's Kinetoscope was a box with a view slit, suitable for one person at a time to peer through. Inside was a celluloid film loop advancing over rollers, shown against a constant light source and intermittently darkened by a revolving shutter. The "motion picture" lasted at most about forty seconds. These early motion pictures, viewed in coin-operated Kinetoscopes set up in urban arcades, were shorts with no plots. Audiences composed mostly of working-class immigrants saw silent pictures of the local news, ordinary events like a train passing, or erotic scenes like a stolen kiss or women in their underwear exploited for comedy. Once Edison began producing his own loops, he included excerpts from vaudeville acts, and once a practical projector became available about 1896, movies were incorporated into vaudeville, itself shown between acts or at the end of an evening's performance. As the century turned, movies ran in thousands of nickelodeons, where working-class audiences saw continuous shows of brief films for as little as five cents.[76]

Movies became an enormously popular form of entertainment not just because they were inexpensive, but also because they had a magical appeal. For comic or dramatic effect in these films with no plots, filmmakers and projectionists often relied on the ability of film to speed up and slow down, to reverse and stop time. In *Star Theater* (1901), F. S. Armitage reverses and speeds up a time-lapse filming of a building under construction. In less than a minute, the building appears to dismantle itself, and the film ends with an empty lot. These film effects altered the normal experience of time and made the impossible seem real.[77]

As the twentieth century got under way, moviemakers began to tell stories, provoked in part by reformers calling for motion pictures to conform to middle-class ideas about respectability. The storytelling techniques today's films rely on had to be invented. In *Life of an American Fireman* (1903), Edwin S. Porter experimented with ways to depict simultaneous action. Viewers saw the same rescue of a mother and child twice, first from the inside of a burning building, and then, all over again, from the outside. Such repetitions appear in a large number of American films from the period.[78]

D. W. Griffith refined the film narrative technique of parallel editing, the alternation of scenes occurring in different places to show simultaneous action. In one of his melodramas, *The Lonely Villa* (1909), intruders force their way into a home, while a mother and her daughters try to keep them at bay. Alerted by a telephone call, the absent husband and the police race to their rescue in the nick of time. With extensive intercutting to build suspense, scenes alternate between the home and the route of the returning husband. The technique, used extensively thereafter by Griffith and widely adopted by other filmmakers, became a useful device not only for showing simultaneous action but also introducing the film's point of view, the omniscient narrator shaping the story in space and time. Gradually, with such techniques for manipulating stories in time, the feature film was born.[79]

Paradoxically, as time on the movie screen took on more malleable characteristics than time in real life, the timing of showings became more inflexible. When movies were short with no plots, continuous showings were the norm, with hours of operation announced, rather than spe-

Comet Theater, 100 Third Avenue, New York, 1910.

cific starting times for each film. A theater placard might say "Films shown continuously, noon to 11." Viewers wandered in and out at will and socialized in the aisles between films. But when moviemakers started producing feature films, with a beginning and end, cinemas treated them as theatrical productions, with specific show times, encouraging in the audience the same standards of punctuality in leisure time that workplaces required. Thus movies simultaneously freed the imagination from clock time and required audiences to show up on time.[80]

Such differences between clock time and other ways of experiencing time acquired sharper definition between roughly 1880 and 1920. Unquestionably, clock time acquired greater significance. As the United States spread across the continent and gained population, local and regional means for connecting citizens in time seemed no longer sufficient. Despite sporadic and lasting protests, the entire population eventually came to operate on a national zoned standard of clock time. This time was applicable everywhere, uniform, and objective regardless of geography, traditions, or personal differences. Technical systems – the railroads, the telegraph, and countless watches and clocks – assisted the transformation. The result was more people focused on the face of the clock to coordinate themselves with others.

Simultaneously, though, as multiple ways of setting and keeping clock time declined in favor of a single national system, a temporal counterpoint arose. New ways of thinking about time itself, stimulated in part by a whole different set of new technical inventions, reinforced the notion that our sense of time is made up of complex multiple strands, not just time by the clock. In contrast to the uniformity of clock time, these other experiences defined a time that was malleable, personal, and subjective.

saving time

1920–1960

AMERICANS BECOME OBSESSED WITH USING TIME EFFICIENTLY.

To save time is to lengthen life.

— slogan of the Remington Typewriter Company

WHEN IT WAS HER TURN, she'd taken her role very seriously at first. The camera filmed her as she picked up the eggs and moved them, one by one, from one container to the other. In the first test, she used only one hand. Then she transferred the eggs all over again, but with two hands. All the while, the timer counted out fiftieths of a second. By the time she'd repeated the test four times, in four different ways, she was giggling. The film was rolling, she knew she should be projecting seriousness and objectivity, but the whole experience suddenly struck her as very silly.

When she saw the finished product, the proof, nevertheless, was there on the screen. It really was twice as fast – nine seconds instead of nearly eighteen – to transfer two eggs at a time instead of one. Any housewife interested in speeding through her daily tasks, she thought, would be foolish to ignore the measurable results.[1]

In the 1950s, Jane Callaghan and Betty Jane Johnson, two teachers of home economics at the University of Connecticut at Storrs, made repeated use of the school's Motion and Time Study Laboratory to analyze and streamline the mundane tasks of housework, including making beds and putting newly bought eggs into a refrigerator container. Their consultant on a variety of projects was the noted engineering efficiency expert Lillian Gilbreth. And their research on making housework easier had taken on a new urgency, as more and more women disabled by the recent polio epidemic still had to keep house and raise children.

The laboratory, with its film unit, was one of hundreds of places across the country, in schools and industry, that studied people performing the motions of work. The professional study of work tasks and detailed designs for the most efficient ways to perform them, a movement that came to be called "scientific management," began with the work of Frederick W. Taylor in the machine shops of the American steel industry in the 1880s. As the first decade of the twentieth century ended, the engineer–managers behind the movement began to control the processes of production for both the physical plant and personnel in all aspects of American manufacturing. They also extended rational procedures to corporate administration, planning, cost accounting, office work, and marketing. Their methods emphasized order, system, and control.[2] By midcentury, the principles of efficiency and time saving were firmly entrenched in nearly every aspect of American life, including housework.

As a result, people felt pressured by the clock more than ever before. Like it or not, they found themselves preoccupied with efficiency. Even leisure – time off – became defined by the clock. It was divided up, measured out, not to be wasted.

time control

BY THE END OF THE NINETEENTH CENTURY, Americans had built a modern industrial nation, with new economic and political structures and complex systems of production and administration to sustain it. The giant, smooth-running factory was the symbol of the new industrial order. By the turn of the century, U.S. manufacturing, electrical, and chemical companies were rapidly outgrowing their physical plants. Workplaces were evolving from small-scale operations, often in family hands, to immense and complex corporate enterprises, with heavy investments in equipment and huge workforces. By 1916, for example, 15,000 workers were making agricultural machinery for McCormick. Ford Motor Company, at its Highland Park works where the Model T was first made, employed 33,000. At the end of that decade, three-quarters of all northern industrial workers east of the Mississippi staffed factories of more than 100 employees. Nearly a third worked in factories with more than 1,000 employees.[3]

Management practices suited to small workshops with a few employees proved ineffective once factories scaled up. Engineers were hired specifically to organize work processes, machinery, and employees. They designed new kinds of spaces to integrate equipment and workers; they also introduced new theories of conducting business and organizing tasks that focused on tighter and more systematic practices to control workers' behavior. New ways of controlling time on the job were part of the new practices, including how long the workday extended and how fast employees should work on the job.

Industrialization turned most employees into wage earners and structured the workplace to the time of the clock. Despite worker resistance, managers studied and standardized specific tasks in factories, often putting speed and efficiency above workers' know-how traditions, and safety. In imposing this new industrial order, managers specified who was to do what work, in what manner, and when. Workers disliked many of the new measures that altered their control over the pace of work, and they repeatedly protested their imposition. Managers, with new regulations and new technologies at their disposal, had taken away much of the power workers once had over how they organized their work and how they spent their time at work.[4]

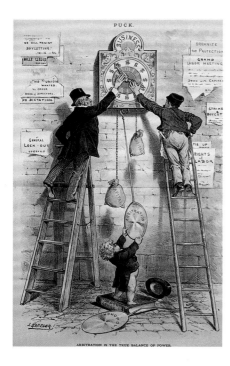

Managers and workers argue over time in this cartoon, "Arbitration Is the True Balance of Power," from *Puck,* 17 March 1886.

How Much of Life Should Be Work?

AS PEOPLE INCREASINGLY CONSIDERED the time spent at work a deduction from the time available for themselves, the length of the workday became a central issue between workers and employers. They shaped and defined work time together, in a constant exchange that sometimes erupted in fierce clashes.

Workers took repeated action to secure shorter hours through most of the nineteenth and early twentieth centuries. Their motives were both economic and social. Organized labor emphasized shorter hours as a way to make the labor supply scarcer and to raise wages, employment levels, and working conditions. Nonunion workers also wanted fewer hours at work so they could enjoy more leisure time — for their families, for participating in church and community, and for pursuing culture, rest, or recreation.[5]

The violent confrontations over the length of the workday included Chicago's Haymarket Riot, sparked by the McCormick Harvester strike in 1886, and a steel strike in 1919. But in the long run, workers were able to bargain successfully for shorter hours with employers, who gradually recognized that shorter hours could be to their advantage by increasing worker morale and reducing accidents and fatigue-induced drops in productivity. The beginning of the twentieth century saw a dramatic reduction, from ten-hour days to eight-hour days, although the six-day workweek, with only Sunday as a day of rest, remained common.

Watch fob promoting the eight-hour day, issued by the International Association of Machinists, early twentieth century.

Button promoting the eight-hour day, issued by the American Federation of Labor, 1900–10.

By the 1930s, the U.S. Congress enacted sweeping legislation governing work hours and other aspects of labor–management relations in response to the economic crisis of the Depression. As the country faced colossal job shortages and unemployment, Franklin Roosevelt's New Deal promoted each worker's right to a full-time job, rather than shorter hours. Federal projects created such full-time employment. After World War II, the eight-hour day and the five-day workweek became the rough standard, and work hours have remained essentially stable since then. The principal historian of work hours in the United States has interpreted this stabilization of the workweek's length as a shift from a vision of progress rooted in leisure to one based on work. The crusade for shorter work hours, which prevailed until the Depression, gave way to programs for full employment to ensure economic growth for the nation and wages to spend on consumer goods for individual workers.[6]

Synchronizing the Workplace

AS THE TWENTIETH CENTURY BEGAN, management specialists promised that synchronizing work to a uniform time standard would increase productivity and efficiency in industries across the country. Not just the workforce's punctuality was at issue. Cost accounting and analysis — recording and scrutinizing expenses for labor, materials, and overhead — were getting more attention than ever before. Time was money.

Showing up for work punctually, at an official time, became expected behavior toward the end of the nineteenth century, as more and more people worked for others rather than for themselves. In the 1890s, timekeepers, that is, clerks who kept track of employees' hours in handwritten logs, found that machines were beginning to replace them. Time clocks, first produced in modern form in the late 1880s, began to appear more frequently in workplaces, especially those with large numbers of employees. "Each swing of the pendulum adds to the profits of the methodical businessman," advised one clock manufacturer. "He wastes no time; neither does he countenance the waste of time by employes [sic]."[7] Thanks to the influence of the advocates of scientific management, after about 1910 nearly every industrial workplace had a time clock. So did many offices.

Workers in line to have their time recorded at Bush Terminal, New York City, 1917. Workers reported to clerks who operated time clocks.

Clerks operating time clocks at Bush Terminal, New York City, 1917.

Factory superintendents had long ago devised a variety of ways to enforce punctuality and regularity on the job. In the nineteenth century they mostly depended on the factory bell to announce the time, and factory gates to enforce schedules. At starting time, when the gates slammed shut, the punctual were inside, but latecomers, to get credit for a day's work, had to pass by office clerks who docked them for their tardiness.[8] By the second half of the nineteenth century, industrial workplaces commonly used a "check" system. Each worker was assigned a number and received a token engraved with that number; as employees arrived and departed, clerks recorded the time and attendance. The attendance records were the basis of the payroll.

The earliest mechanical attendance recorder in the United States was Willard Bundy's time recorder. Bundy, a jeweler from Auburn, New York, devised a clockwork instrument inspired by the "check" system, used it to time his own employees, and received a patent for it in 1888. Instead of relying on a token with an identification number, Bundy's invention substituted a numbered key. When entering or leaving, each worker picked a key off a board at the entrance to the workplace, pushed it through a keyhole in the clock, gave it a quarter turn, and removed it. Inside the clock, the key, the end of which bore the individual's identification number, came in contact with an inked ribbon and pressed the number onto a paper tape. Simultaneously, the mechanism printed the time of day next to the number. By 1892, manufacturing of the time

Workers in line at Baltimore Gas & Electric to clock themselves out, 1925.

Time stamp for marking task records, early twentieth century.

recorders was in full swing in Binghamton, New York, and a year later over 2,500 Bundy clocks kept time in industries across the country.[9]

The Bundy time recorder wasn't the perfect answer to recording time and attendance. Since the paper tape was continuous and recorded the times of employee after employee, to compile the records of an individual worker for payroll required laborious transcription from the tapes. In search of an easier method of record keeping, D. M. Cooper of Rochester, New York, invented the card time recorder, patented it in 1894, and arranged for its manufacture by the firm Willard & Frick. This "Rochester" system, ancestor to the time clocks familiar today, printed work hours for a week on a time card, one card per employee.[10]

In addition to tracking attendance times, industrial managers began to pay close attention to time spent on each operation or task. Automatic time stamps, or job stamps, operated by a worker or roving "time-takers," marked preprinted job cards, providing a way to document and analyze start and finish times for the most detailed operations on the factory floor. The Standard Time Stamp Company of Binghamton, New York, invented these devices and became a subsidiary of the Bundy operation.[11]

Steam whistle used at a Pennsylvania coal mine, about 1900.

Pamphlet illustrating a system for controlling time throughout the workplace, International Time Recording Company (now IBM), Endicott, New York, early twentieth century.

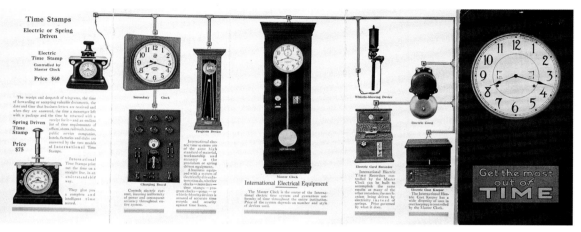

In 1900, these pioneering firms merged into the International Time Recording Company. Before the decade ended, the new firm had absorbed nearly all its competitors, and about 1920, ITRC claimed they made over 260 different styles of time and cost recorders, both electrical and spring-driven, with prices ranging from $70 to $450. They also sold paper supplies for the machinery. Reportedly one hundred million time cards were sold each year in the 1930s. The firm heavily promoted their line of electrical devices, and, in response, many factories installed integrated electrical systems. For a single building or an industrial complex, a master clock could control secondary dials, bells, and whistles, and even time stamps for marking paperwork. Advertising for the systems clearly targeted supervisors and others in authority, not workers. "Time records from which your payroll and cost data are compiled are accurately produced by the various recorders," promised one brochure, "each standing as a silent promoter of discipline, punctuality and harmony." [12]

In 1911, ITRC had joined with two other companies – the Tabulating Machine Company, makers of Hollerith punch card machines, and the Computing Scale Company – to form the corporation that after 1933 would be known as International Business Machines (IBM). [13]

Master clock made by International Time Recording Company (now IBM), Endicott, New York, about 1915. A "master" clock in a central location could send electrical signals to remote "slave" dials to synchronize time throughout a workplace, school, or other public building.

Time clock made by International Time Recording Company (now IBM), Endicott, New York, about 1916; used at Anheuser-Busch brewery, St. Louis. Each number on the iron ring around the dial represented an employee. To punch in, an employee spun the central rotating arm and pressed his or her number. An internal paper drum recorded the time.

Time clock made by International Time Recording Company (now IBM), Endicott, New York, to stamp arrival and departure times on each employee's time card, about 1915.

165

Measuring the amount of time a particular task took preoccupied turn-of-the-century managers, became one of the cornerstones of the new profession of industrial engineering, and dominated the analysis of manufacturing work until the 1960s. Among the most frequently used and most controversial tools for measuring work was the stopwatch.

The stopwatch is an indicator of interval, a tool for observing and measuring the divisibility of time. Even more than ordinary clocks and watches that indicate time of day, the ticking stopwatch fragments time, disassociating it from its perceived flow. The stopwatch, in fact, provides a way to see time stand still. It is also a device that extends perception beyond human limits, enabling the human eye to see tiny fractions of time otherwise too fleeting to be visible.

By the 1880s, stopwatches had changed considerably from the chronodrometer of the 1850s, the American Watch Company's horse-timing watch. For one thing, the time-of-day portion of the chronodrometer stopped completely when the timer function was in use, so the watch needed constantly resetting. For another, the smallest interval of time the watch could measure was a quarter of a second. Both of these limits fell to technical innovations in the 1870s, when a number of patented refinements made in Switzerland, and two new models of Waltham stopwatches, made the stopwatch more widely available to Americans, easier to use with a "fly-back" seconds hand, and, most important, more versatile in its ability to measure time in even smaller portions. These newer watches, sometimes called chronographs, could measure fifths of a second. This finer measurement was possible because of the so-called quick train watch movement, one with a balance wheel that makes 5 half swings a second (18,000 an hour). In contrast, the American Watch Company's chronodrometer balance made 4 half swings a second (14,400 times an hour). A fifth of a second was at the time believed to be the smallest fraction to which a human timer could react.[14]

These improvements in the technical operation of the stopwatch coincided with the earliest work of Frederick Winslow Taylor, a mechanical engineer, who devised stopwatch time studies of machinists at work at Philadelphia's Midvale Steel in the 1880s. He observed that a particular job could be divided into distinct parts, each of which could be timed, studied, and rearranged if necessary to speed up the task. His goal was to establish the optimum rate of work for a given machining operation.

Taylor's stopwatch studies were a small, and contested, part of a larger system of industrial management ideas he developed, a system that became known as "Taylorism." Taylor's system was renamed "scientific management" in 1910 during a highly publicized hearing before the Interstate Commerce Commission over the railroad industry's request to raise freight rates. Headlines that quoted from the testimony of one of Taylor's followers to declare that the railroads could save a million dollars a day if they would only use "scientific management" changed the concept almost overnight from esoteric engineering to a movement that would introduce modern management to American industry.[15]

A zealous reformer, Taylor set about designing systems of production that aimed to merge humans and their equipment into an efficiently running, well-oiled machine. According to historian of technology Thomas Hughes, Taylor sought efficiency, control, and order. He "asked managers to do for the production system as a whole what inventors and engineers had done in the nineteenth century for machines and processes." According to Taylor, "the system must be first."[16]

In 1911, Taylor wrote in *Shop Management* that a worker's natural inclination was to go slower, not faster, and to go slower still in the company of other workers. He described this behavior as "the natural instinct and tendency of men to take it easy," and termed it "natural soldiering." Today we'd probably use the term "goofing off." Taylor and his followers spent considerable effort to counteract these tendencies with time studies of various tasks in various trades.

Garment worker undergoing time study at Joseph Feiss Company, Cleveland, Ohio, about 1920.

Concealed stopwatch, from Frederick Winslow Taylor's *Shop Management,* 1911.

FIGURE 3. — WATCH BOOK FOR TIME STUDY

Taylor's assistants, armed with stopwatches, timed worker's motions, but went beyond merely recording the time as the men at the track timed horses for recreation. The stopwatch permitted managers to time and then rearrange the workers' motions, to assign each worker a very specific task in a preordained sequence of productive operations. Taylor advocated the stopwatch as the scientific, objective arbiter, invariable and independent of context.

To the "time study men," the stopwatch symbolized efficiency and the power of scientific authority. But workers frequently objected to being timed, and various craft unions mounted bitter campaigns against the use of stopwatches. Taylorism suffered a mighty setback at the Watertown Arsenal in Massachusetts, for example, where a follower of Taylor, Carl Barth, tried to introduce Taylor's system. His stopwatch studies triggered a walkout in August 1911, with workers claiming they suffered exhaustion from the pressure of work speedups caused by the use of the device. They also felt humiliated by it. The opposition spread to another U.S. government arsenal in Rock Island, Illinois. A special government commission was established to investigate. At one of the hearings, Watertown machinist Orin Cheney gave telling testimony: "I don't object to their finding out how long [a job] takes, but I do object to their standing over me with a stopwatch as if I was a race horse or an automobile." To many workers, the time studies were anything but impartial. And although time studies showed that some workers could work faster and more efficiently than was their custom, it didn't mean they wanted to. Time studies diminished workers' power base, devalued their special knowledge of their own work, and permitted

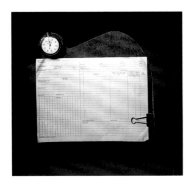

managers to speed up their work and control their time. And because the stopwatch meant different things to different people, conflict resulted over the meaning of time and the value of speed.[17] The stopwatch was a bone of contention precisely because it was visible, the single most tangible, accessible manifestation of the new management systems. Hiding the stopwatch in a book was one solution that Sanford Thompson devised to defuse rancorous objections. In just the span of Taylor's lifetime, the stopwatch acquired meanings entirely different from those it had trackside. It is not just a coincidence that the root of the word *management* is the Latin word *manus*, for hand, which originally meant "to train a horse in his paces." [18]

There is no record of precisely what kind of stopwatches Taylor used until after 1896, when his colleague Sanford Thompson surveyed all available stopwatches and then devised one of his own for reading 100ths of a minute.[19] What is clear is that after Taylor began advocating stopwatch studies, the demands of the new management style stimulated the stopwatch market and the two grew together, along with a market for accessories. Despite the prohibitions against stopwatch studies in U.S. government establishments in the aftermath of the Watertown Arsenal strike, stopwatch styles for industrial use proliferated in the early twentieth century, and the use of stopwatches to study work processes endures to this day.

Pamphlet produced to defuse employee antagonism to stopwatch studies of their work. Written by L. H. Woodman, illustrated by Don Wagnitz, and published by the Dow Chemical Company, 1946.

Poster for war work, about 1918. Posters like this urged workers to be more productive.

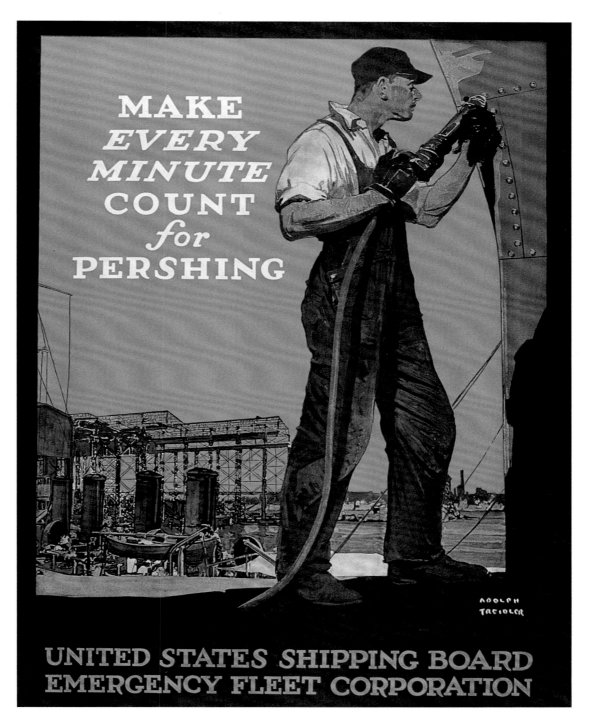

"Everybody Hustle," urged a sign in the office of Holy Name parish, Washington, D.C., about 1925. Speedy efficiency became the manager's ideal in workplaces of all kinds — from factory floors to business offices.

Office workers during World War II, about
1942. Wartime urgency added to the sense
that time was a kind of pressure.

SAVING TIME

Motion study of woman typing, conducted by the Gilbreths for the Remington Typewriter Company, about 1916.

The Gilbreth Method

THE GILBRETHS PIONEERED the use of photography in analyzing motion in time. Study subjects wore lights attached to their fingers that left tracings in multiple-exposure still photographs called chronocyclegraphs. The light paths were rendered in three-dimensional models and were studied to eliminate wasted motion. The Gilbreths also recorded subjects using a motion picture camera. They filmed tasks with a minutely calibrated timer in view of the camera to clock the worker's motions. As a backdrop for their filming, they cross-sectioned the work area (including tabletops, walls, ceilings, and floors) into a grid pattern of four-inch squares. Observers of the study subject then transferred the work process onto paper, on a form the Gilbreths called a Simultaneous Motion Chart (simochart). On the chart, each movement was broken down into a set of elements, each of which was illustrated with a symbol from the hieroglyphic-like "therbligs" (*Gilbreth* spelled backward, with the *t* and *h* switched). The Gilbreths analyzed simocharts for all filmed workers, selected motions representing "the one best way" to do the work, and established the new standard method for the task. These "micromotion" studies enabled the Gilbreths to prescribe the "one best way" to do any task with the least amount of effort and time.[20]

Frank Gilbreth, third from left, oversees filming of a work study at New England Butt, a manufacturer of hinges, 1914.

Therbligs. From Lillian Gilbreth's *The Home-Maker and Her Job,* 1927. According to Frank and Lillian Gilbreth, every motion could be broken down into a set of elements, each of which they illustrated with a hieroglyphic-like symbol they dubbed a "therblig" (roughly, Gilbreth spelled backward).

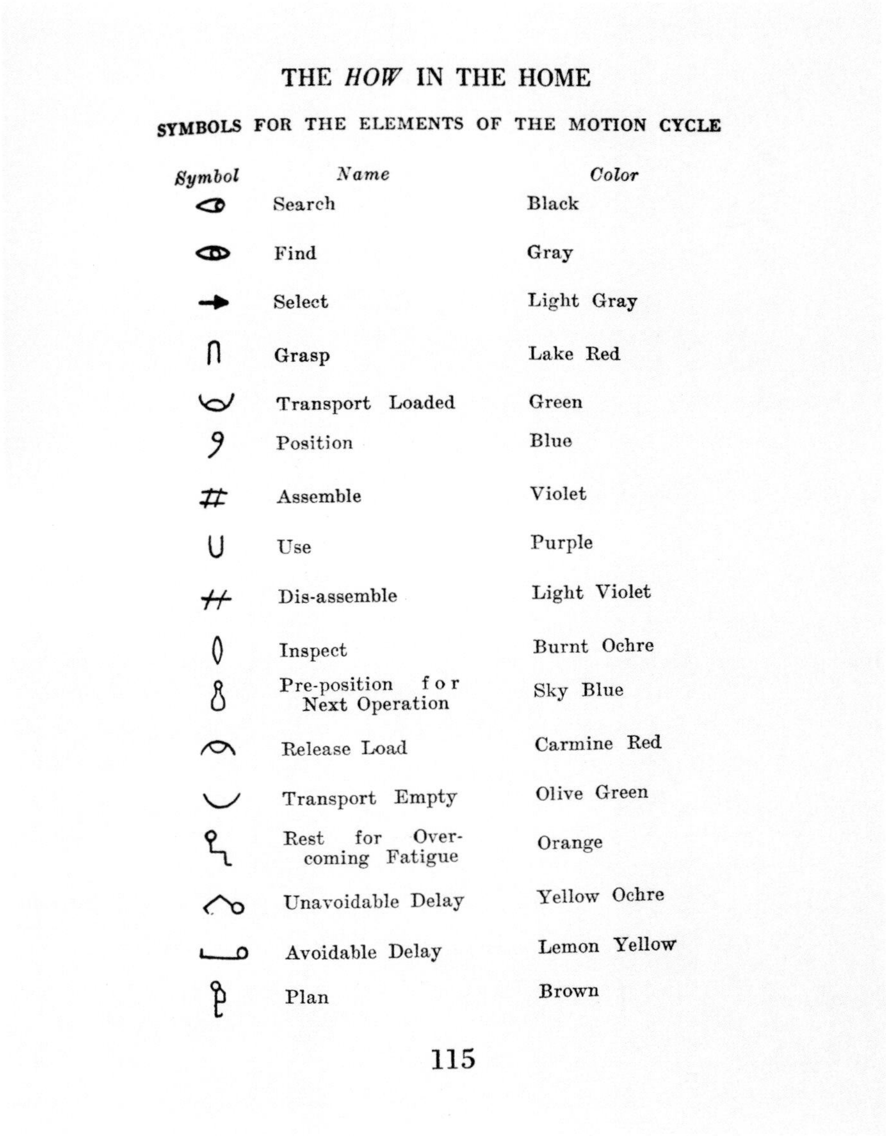

THE *HOW* IN THE HOME

SYMBOLS FOR THE ELEMENTS OF THE MOTION CYCLE

Symbol	Name	Color
☚	Search	Black
�</>	Find	Gray
→	Select	Light Gray
∩	Grasp	Lake Red
ᗐ	Transport Loaded	Green
9	Position	Blue
#	Assemble	Violet
U	Use	Purple
#	Dis-assemble	Light Violet
◊	Inspect	Burnt Ochre
8	Pre-position for Next Operation	Sky Blue
⌒	Release Load	Carmine Red
ᴗ	Transport Empty	Olive Green
ᒷ	Rest for Over-coming Fatigue	Orange
⌒o	Unavoidable Delay	Yellow Ochre
⌐o	Avoidable Delay	Lemon Yellow
ᕳ	Plan	Brown

115

Lillian Gilbreth seated at a management desk she designed in collaboration with IBM. The IBM slogan "THINK" and an IBM electric clock are part of the desk. From *The Model Kitchen Is Remodeled,* New York Herald-Tribune Institute, 1935.

Lillian and Frank Gilbreth with nine of their twelve children in the family's Pierce Arrow automobile, "Foolish Carriage," in front of the family's summer home on Nantucket, about 1920.

Manager and Matriarch

WHEN FRANK GILBRETH DIED OF A HEART ATTACK IN 1924, Lillian carried on their business for a short while, but in the face of sex discrimination, her industrial contracts dwindled.

With twelve children to support and a career crisis facing her, Gilbreth reinvented herself and turned to the study of housework, home management, and women as consumers. Her alliance with business continued, but entirely new businesses catering to women as consumers — department stores, appliance manufacturers, and the like — were opened to her. She dedicated herself to increasing the efficiencies and satisfactions of the household. To her own work she brought not only a prodigious energy, but also a background in psychology, the analytical methods she and her husband had developed together for studying motion in time, and the lessons learned while raising her large family (made famous in the 1950 film *Cheaper by the Dozen,* based on the book by two of her children). In a career that continued forty-five years after her husband's death, she wrote prolifically, lectured widely, and held a position in the engineering school at Purdue University. One of the most famous and respected women of the 1950s, she earned international celebrity for balancing career and family.[21]

Three Kitchen Floor Plans (Bad, Good, Better). From *The Model Kitchen Is Remodeled,* New York Herald-Tribune Institute, 1935.

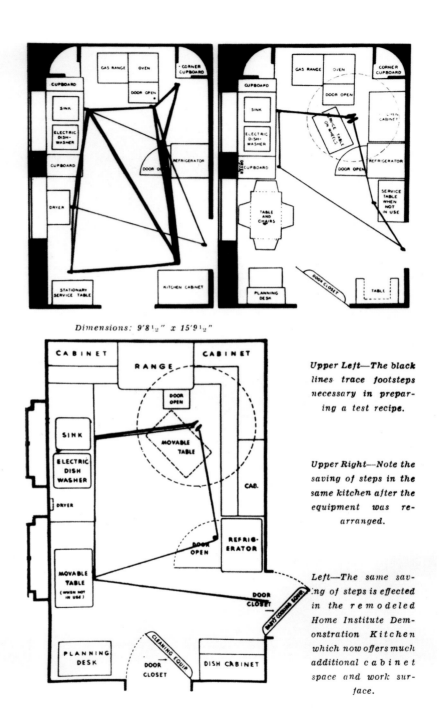

Dimensions: 9'8½" x 15'9½"

Upper Left—The black lines trace footsteps necessary in preparing a test recipe.

Upper Right—Note the saving of steps in the same kitchen after the equipment was rearranged.

Left—The same saving of steps is effected in the remodeled Home Institute Demonstration Kitchen which now offers much additional cabinet space and work surface.

Gilbreth's renown was more enduring than that of Christine Frederick, who preceded her in promoting scientific management for saving time at home. In articles for the *Ladies' Home Journal* in 1912 and two books, *The New Housekeeping* (1913) and *Household Engineering* (1920), Frederick, a middle-class housewife from Long Island, emphasized the importance of scheduling and planning. She advocated schedules for days, weeks, even years; she offered suggestions for planned meals with planned leftovers; and wrote standards for cleaning, dishwashing, and other chores. And she anticipated Gilbreth on the reason for saving time at home, where no profit motive inspired it. "The real object in saving time and effort," she wrote in *Household Engineering*, "is to enable the homemaker to have leisure time to devote to interests which are more important than the mere mechanics of living."[22]

Neither Christine Frederick nor Lillian Gilbreth was among the mainstream home economists at the beginning of the twentieth century. Seeking a professional route for women and a means of educating women to be informed consumers, pioneers in the new field of home economics did not go as far as Frederick and Gilbreth in advocating the industrialization of housework.[23]

Model Kitchens

LIKE FREDERICK AND THE HOME ECONOMISTS, though, Lillian Gilbreth paid special attention to the kitchen. She analyzed the motions involved in routine food preparation tasks, reorganizing workspaces to eliminate repetitive or unproductive steps, and promoted the use of an array of new, supposedly time- and labor-saving appliances and devices. She disseminated her ideas to thousands of homemakers in numerous books and articles and in a series of influential model kitchens.

Gilbreth had a major influence on the field of kitchen design. In the late 1920s and 1930s, she designed model kitchens for public display that incorporated the principles of scientific management. Publicity about these models, mostly in newspapers, aimed to convince homemakers to reorganize their kitchens to save time and motion.

Major utility companies and appliance manufacturers across the country sought to increase consumer demand with demonstration kitchens and customer services. They also began to employ professional women like Gilbreth and university-trained home economists to teach women consumers about how to use their products and services. Gilbreth's first model kitchen in 1929, called "the Kitchen Practical," was for the Brooklyn Borough Gas Company. A year

Circular workspace, about 1929, one of Lillian Gilbreth's kitchen ideals.

Gilbreth management desk, designed in collaboration with IBM, as pictured in the sales brochure "Planned Motion in the Home Saves: Time — Energy — Money," about 1933.

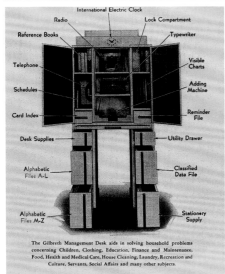

International Electric Clock
Radio — Lock Compartment
Reference Books — Typewriter
Telephone — Visible Charts
Schedules — Adding Machine
Card Index — Reminder File
Desk Supplies — Utility Drawer
Alphabetic Files A-L — Classified Data File
Alphabetic Files M-Z — Stationery Supply

The Gilbreth Management Desk aids in solving household problems concerning Children, Clothing, Education, Finance and Maintenance, Food, Health and Medical Care, House Cleaning, Laundry, Recreation and Culture, Servants, Social Affairs and many other subjects.

later she designed four kitchens for the New York Herald-Tribune Institute, a research department of the newspaper that focused on topics of interest to women, and in 1934–35 she updated her designs for the Institute.[24]

All three projects featured her notions about the ideal circular workspace, the forerunner of today's standard triangular arrangement of sink, stove, and refrigerator. To reduce fatigue and the number of steps involved in cooking, she not only positioned the appliances but also provided for a wheeled table that could serve as counter space. Her evidence of time saved was a comparison of two methods for making strawberry shortcake. One way required 97 movements and 280 steps. Her way in the newly rearranged kitchen reduced those numbers to 64 and 45. And she included a convenient planning desk, a compact little business office, right in the kitchen.[25]

If running a household was like running a business, then, according to Gilbreth, the kitchen needed a businesslike desk for the homemaker–manager. At the Chicago World's Fair in 1933, IBM unveiled the Gilbreth Management Desk, available in the latest Art Deco styles. Promoted as the "General Business Headquarters of the Household Manager," it featured built-in clock and radio and compartments for typewriter, adding machine, and telephone. There was also room for household files, reference books, schedules, and a series of pull-out charts with tips on organizing and planning household tasks. "Everything within easy reach," promised the sales brochure. As part of IBM's efforts to diversify markets and remain solvent during the Depression, Waldemar Ayres of IBM's research laboratory undertook a market study on the desk, and the company got Gilbreth's endorsement for the finished product. Although the firm never sold the desks to individual customers, they became staples in model kitchens Gilbreth designed.[26]

Maximum reach test for planning kitchen storage, 1962. Influenced by the work of Lillian Gilbreth, home economists at the University of Connecticut, Storrs, sought ways to make housekeeping easier for disabled homemakers.

Accessible kitchen workspace, 1962.

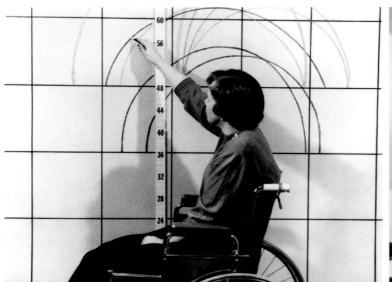

The Accessible Kitchen: Homemaking for the Disabled

LILLIAN GILBRETH CONSIDERED HER MOST VALUABLE CONTRIBUTION to have been her work for disabled homemakers. After World War II, with public awareness of disabled veterans and polio victims at a high point, she assisted with the design of special-needs kitchens for a number of universities and the American Heart Association. Clothing manufacturers employed her to design children's clothing for mothers with polio disabilities, and in collaboration with the School of Home Economics at the University of Connecticut, she designed wheelchair-accessible workspaces and simplified ways to perform housework and child care.[27]

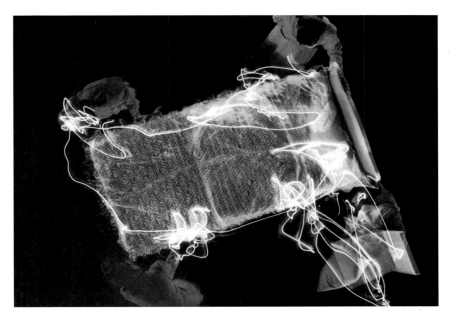

How to make a bed, 1946. In this multiple-exposure photograph, a woman wearing tiny lights on her fingers makes a bed efficiently. The streaks of light show her motions. Purdue University scholars analyzed housework in the 1940s with Gilbreth methods and recommended techniques for easier housekeeping in *Life* magazine.

Easier Housekeeping

AT PURDUE UNIVERSITY IN THE 1940S, industrial engineering professor Marvin Mundel and home economists were influenced by Lillian Gilbreth's work in time-saving methods for the home. They used Gilbreth techniques to analyze housework and devise new ways to increase efficiencies, eliminate drudgery, and save time. Their tips for easier housekeeping, featured in *Life* magazine in 1946, ranged from step-saving bedmaking to speedy cleaning. They recommended, for example, that the housewife interested in working quickly through her chores should dust using both hands at the same time![28]

Gilbreth and others like her helped raise the standard of what was considered acceptable housekeeping, so instead of helping women at home save time, the proliferation of efficiency techniques paradoxically created more for them to do.[29] Fundamentally, many of Gilbreth's recommendations, no matter how well intended, were beyond the practical reach of most homemakers. Lillian Gilbreth herself was highly successful as an advocate for organized time-saving and labor-saving methods, but she believed in the rationalization of activities that couldn't, in the final analysis, be rationalized. Although some tasks in running a household, such as meal planning and certain cleaning chores, lend themselves to scheduling and order, other aspects, especially child care and care of the sick, involve myriad interruptions that defy ruthless rational planning. The Gilbreths' methods for achieving "happiness minutes" were complex and extreme by anyone else's standards, but their goal was identical to that of those already beginning to feel time as a kind of pressure, with more to do than the day had hours. The Gilbreths hoped to carve out time for leisure rather than work.

Cocktail set with silver shaker and goblets, by Bernard Rice's Sons, used by Mr. and Mrs. Foster M. Reader, West Hatton, Maryland, from the 1920s through the 1940s.

The cocktail hour, 1920s.

HAPPY HOUR

The increasing regimentation of the workplace and the spread of the fixed-hour workday heightened the distinction between labor and leisure. "It's time for a drink!" signaled the end of the workday in many urban and suburban neighborhoods. The cocktail hour — defined, ironically, in terms of the clock, as roughly between the hours of five and seven in the evening — became the ritual transition to leisure time.

The cocktail hour was very much a twentieth-century invention — in many workplaces of the early nineteenth century, drinking alcohol and socializing were a normal part of the workday. As managers began to prohibit drinking on the job, saloons began to flourish. Many were crowded, mostly with men who were often violently drunk. In the 1920s, Prohibition shut down the saloons and generated a new, if illegal, leisure-time cocktail culture. That culture was often home-centered, organized by women and highly ritualized with specialty drinks and refined accoutrements. Following the repeal of Prohibition in 1933, the cocktail hour grew in popularity as a limited interlude between work and dinner. The evening drink served a symbolic purpose, marking the transition to personal time.[30]

Cocktail culture continued to flourish in American homes in the 1950s and 1960s. Home bars, often home-built in the basement or in the rec room, were well stocked with alcohol and the accessories required to make mixed drinks. In the 1970s, commercial bars introduced "happy hour," with reduced prices for drinks and food.

expanding time

1960 to the present

TIME SEEMS SCARCE, AND WE TRY TO GET MORE TIME OUT OF EVERY DAY.

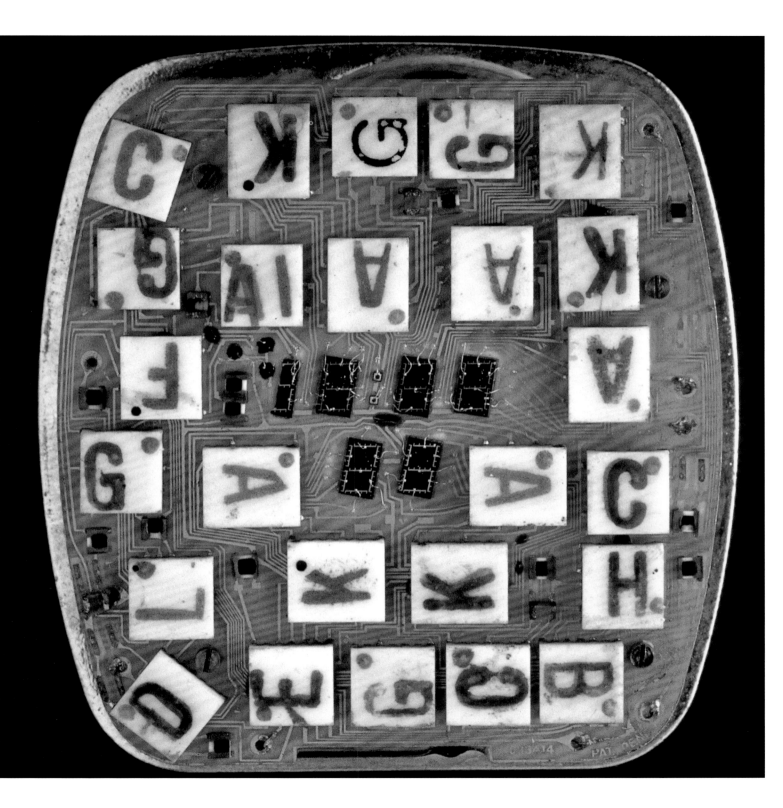

I've been on a calendar, but never on time.

– Marilyn Monroe

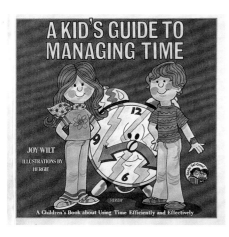

Cover for *A Kid's Guide to Managing Time: A Children's Book about Using Time Efficiently and Effectively,* by Joy Wilt, 1979.

Ask yourself these questions.

What did I spend the most time doing?
What did I spend the least time doing?
Is there something I would like to have spent more time doing?
Is there something I would like to have spent less time doing?
Is there something I would like to have done, but didn't do?
Did I have enough free time when I could do whatever I wanted to do?
Did I get to spend enough time doing things I decided to do?
Do I feel good about the way I spent my time?

— Joy Wilt, *A Kid's Guide to Managing Time,* 1979

THE DAY HAS JUST TWENTY-FOUR HOURS. Lots of people feel they simply don't have enough time to do everything they think they have to do. Feeling time as a sort of pressure and viewing it as a scarce resource aren't new in the American experience, but some of our techniques for dealing with complex lives, long to-do lists, and pressing deadlines are. How do we give ourselves the illusion that we have squeezed out more time from our day?

Some think one way to get more accomplished is to keep a tight schedule with the help of a paper or electronic calendar. Time-management texts, self-help books and courses — for men, women, and even children — spell out the steps for success to beat the clock. Who hasn't said, "I'd have more time if I could just get organized!"

Another way is to split the second into tinier usable parcels and fill them up. With inexpensive modern wristwatches, just about everyone has access to split-second accuracy once available only to scientists and technicians. It's not humanly possible to experience nanoseconds, but cell phones, power transmission systems, radio and television broadcasting, computers, and spacecraft bound for distant planets load minuscule fractions of seconds with essential data.

And still another way to find more time is to use parts of the day that haven't traditionally been used — to expand purposeful activity into the night, weekends, and holidays. Many who find themselves going nonstop, around the clock, value the vitality and opportunity that kind of life promises and simultaneously vilify its demands, as they do more and sleep less.

the twenty-four-hour society

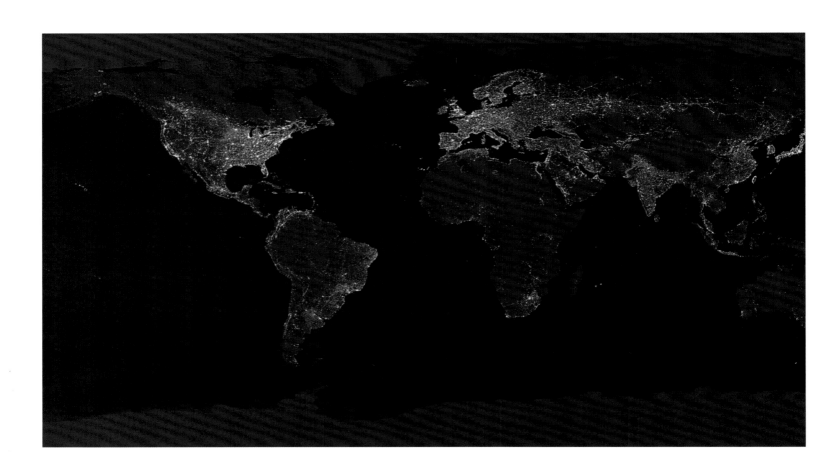

Signs announcing twenty-four-hour operations have been cropping up on the landscape with increasing frequency in recent years. Sometimes they brighten the night with neon. But more often, in the fine print of door placards listing opening and closing times, the nation's supermarkets, convenience stores, retailers, and entertainments signal their readiness for a society too busy to sleep. The popular expression "24/7" – short for twenty-four hours a day, seven days a week – officially entered the American language only recently. It's adverbial slang for "continuously" or "unceasingly" and suggests that every minute is available and usable.

More than a decade ago, sociologist Murray Melbin noted how American life had become "incessant," especially by spilling over into the nighttime hours. In his pioneering book *Night as Frontier: Colonizing the World After Dark* (1987), Melbin described a society that "has broken from the boundaries of daytime. . . . To colonize time is to annex a band of hours and fill it with active people." In this way, he argued, colonizing time is a lot like colonizing space. He found these new settlers everywhere: "food stores, metal smelting plants, freight carriers, indoor tennis courts, mayors' complaint offices, hospital emergency wards, and data-processing departments."[1]

Melbin also listed characteristics of night people that distinguish them from "daytimers," finding that people were drawn to the night by the potential for escape and widened opportunities, a broader range of tolerated behavior, fewer status distinctions, novel hardships, decentralized authority, more danger and lawlessness, and simultaneously an enhanced helpfulness and sociability.[2]

The rooster and the night owl, here depicted on store display cutouts from the 1960s, signaled to 7-Eleven customers that the store opened early and closed late. Competition from convenience stores prompted groceries and other businesses to stay open longer hours too.

Brittney Moss, age four, and friends at Toyota's child care center in Georgetown, Kentucky, just returned from an evening picnic while their parents work the late shift.

We can buy, sell, work, play, and travel around the clock. But it's really work that keeps people up at odd hours on a regular basis. Kevin Coyne, a journalist who crossed the country interviewing Americans after midnight for a 1992 book, noted: "Night workers are the taxpaying, bedrock citizens of the dark hours; the moonlighting day people who visit for an occasional dose of entertainment are just tourists."[3]

The number of people now keeping what the U.S. Bureau of Labor Statistics calls "nontraditional" work hours is on the upswing. Fewer than a third of employed Americans work what we think of as the standard workweek: thirty-five to forty daytime hours, Monday through Friday. According to 1991 statistics, one out of five employed Americans, or about 20 million people, work mostly evening, night, or rotating schedules. One in three work Saturdays and Sundays or varying days in the week. One in four two-earner couples include at least one spouse who works evenings, nights, or rotating hours. That increases to one in three when there are children under age five. These nontraditional schedules are about equally divided between men and women, and part-timers are more often working evenings than full-timers are. As always, those with less education and less wealth have less choice not only about what kind of work they do, but also when they do it.[4]

Conventional wisdom says we're a species meant to sleep when it's dark. Recent biological research shows that humans are programmed to synchronize to light stimuli and to be active by day. For most of us, whether we tend to be night owls or early birds, a complex system of body signals operates on a light–dark cycle that roughly matches the twenty-four-hour rotation of the Earth. The system of circadian rhythms, or internal clocks on a daily cycle, operates at the molecular level through chemical messengers to control sleep and wakefulness, body temperature, and metabolic rate.

In 1972, scientists discovered a circadian pacemaker in the human brain's hypothalamus, a small area in the base of the brain, located roughly behind the eyes. They thought this might be a kind of master clock, sending signals to other lesser clocks throughout the body. Since the early 1970s, researchers have also found independent gene sites and proteins called cryptochromes, located throughout the body, that detect changes in light and control the body's rhythms. These proteins, according to the current working model of this fast-changing science, perform in con-

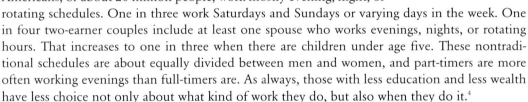

Clockwork automaton of a monk, about 1570.

cert with the gene sites of our innate rhythms. In a feedback loop with a roughly twenty-four-hour cycle, specialized "clock" genes are switched on and off by the proteins they encode. So there isn't just one master body pacemaker. Franz Halberg, the chronobiologist who coined the term "circadian rhythms," notes: "We have not just a single note in the time structure of the body now, but a symphony."[5]

Although researchers like Halberg frequently describe the body's rhythms in terms of harmonious music, more common are their references to the clock. Explaining the workings of the human body in time in terms of the clock has a history almost as old as the clock itself. Since their invention in early modern Europe, clocks and clockwork automatons – moving figures of animals, people, and mythical beasts animated by machinery – served not just as timekeepers, but also as demonstrations of how things worked. Familiarity with clockwork might have even taught Europeans how to think mechanically, that is, to identify linear linkages of cause and effect.[6] That scientists still make use of the clock metaphor to explain nature's durations, cycles, cadences, and patterns is evidence of the metaphor's enduring power and the deep roots of our equation of the clock and time.

There is growing interest in studying not just the biological mechanisms of sleep, but the social ones too, an oddly neglected field of research, considering most humans spend a third of every day of their lives sleeping. Evidence seems to suggest that the way we sleep is as socially constructed as the way we schedule our days. Investigations into the social history of American sleep show that regular bedtimes and rising times are the nighttime component of the industrial world's orderly scheduled day. In a recent cross-cultural survey, anthropologists have pointed out the modern Western way of sleeping – inside a building, on a cushioned bed, in a single eight-hour block at night, with routine bedtimes and wake times often punctuated by an alarm clock – is certainly not the only way. Other cultures, wide awake after dark for an assortment of rituals and other activities, have used the night in ways Westerners haven't even begun to contemplate.[7]

As we expand our activities into the night, the consequences have yet to be determined. There are some pluses. As a rule, people get higher pay for night work. Night workers often enjoy less supervision and more freedom, because managers mostly work during the day. Evidence is mounting, though, that there are also serious risks involved in trying to change humans habituated to the daytime into nocturnal creatures. Late-night shifts, for example, increase the risk of separation and divorce, especially in families with children.[8] As for health consequences, researchers are beginning to document the physiology of swing-shift work, prolonged sleep deprivation, and jet lag. When an external schedule alters body rhythms, the result is fatigue at the very least; if the disruption is prolonged, also possible are sleep and digestive disorders and disturbances related to lack of sleep: loss of memory, slowed reaction time, reduced manual dexterity, and impaired alertness. Critics point to the near-meltdown of Three-Mile Island at 4:00 A.M., to Chernobyl's catastrophe at 1:23 A.M., and Bhopal's at 12:40 A.M. They point to the frequent trucking and airline accidents caused by sleep-deprived drivers and pilots, mistakes in hospitals caused by physicians on stretched rotations, and a long list of other mishaps based on human limitations when it comes to round-the-clock operations. Some see a technical fix for such limitations that others deem a sci-fi nightmare: the next medical frontier just might be manipulating the human body so that we won't need to sleep at all.[9]

The technical origins of our nonstop society may lie in our changing relationship to light. The invention of gas and electric incandescent lighting in the nineteenth century certainly accelerated our journey into the night, but electrification in general, not just the electric light, greatly expanded new nighttime opportunities. Beginning about 1880, Americans enthusiastically embraced electricity and understood it as both a powerful metaphor and an exciting new technology. On a metaphoric level, according to historian David Nye, electricity stood for

> novelty, excitement, modernity, and heightened awareness. Anything electric was saturated with energy, and the nation came to admire "live wires," "human dynamos" and "electrifying performances." At the most abstract level, the intensifying use of energy represented the increasing national greatness of the United States.

Thanks to electricity, new features appeared on the American landscape: streetcar suburbs, department stores, amusement parks, assembly-line factories, electrified homes, modernized farms, and the utopian extension of all of these, the world's fair.[10]

In the factory, electricity improved working conditions by making work areas brighter, reducing the risk of fire, and eliminating air pollution from stinking oil and gas lamps. Electricity also made things worse by disrupting family and community life with round-the-clock shifts. Standardized clocks and good lighting, Nye writes, "made every minute potential work time." This expanding daytime "might have offered labor choices about when and how long to work, but simultaneous changes in factory organization moved in the opposite direction, toward more rigid control."[11]

In the past three decades, the role of technology in creating and serving twenty-four-hour needs has been enormous. By way of example, automated teller machines (ATMs) have done away with "banker's hours." Stand-alone banking machines that could both accept deposits and dispense cash were first introduced in Rockville Centre, New York, in 1969, and networks of

From the ruins of a suspected weapons plant, Peter Arnett reports for CNN in Baghdad, August 1991. CNN pioneered in round-the-clock news broadcasting.

Shee Wong Chan of San Francisco and his grandchildren read the Sunday funnies together, 1944. Sundays, once set aside for worship and leisure, are becoming indistinct from any other day of the week.

such machines appeared beginning in the mid-1970s.[12] Broadcasting and telecommunications also contribute to our move to a round-the clock society. CNN, an upstart satellite news network in the early 1980s, earned distinction for international immediacy with its continuous twenty-four-hour crisis coverage of the Persian Gulf War and the Chinese protests in Tiananmen Square. Overnight air delivery and computer networks have made on-line shopping feasible and available around the clock. And the Internet provides virtually instant access to people, shopping, and information at any hour.

There is a danger in attributing to technology too much influence over our expansion into the night, though. Changing values, attitudes, and behaviors also shape these transformations. Especially salient to the 24/7 society is the evolution of the American Sunday. Although the evolution is scarcely complete, Sunday is certainly headed toward becoming a day indistinct from any other day of the week. Beginning in the 1960s and 1970s, under heavy lobbying from commercial chains, state legislatures and courts in most jurisdictions did away with Sunday closing, or "blue," laws. With their extinction came the expectation that we can shop – or do anything else, for that matter – on any day of the week and, by extension, at any time of the day or night.

The debate over Sunday closings was a debate over the very meaning of Sunday itself. From its beginnings as a Christian day of worship and rest, the American Sunday changed, through centuries of negotiation, into a day of leisure. What American Puritans, facing work without end to build a thriving colony, had seen as God's gift of time for spiritual reflection and rest evolved into a modern consumer culture's opportunity to spend increasing amounts of free time and rising incomes on an overwhelming array of new goods and services.[13] Since the beginning of the twentieth century, opponents of laws prohibiting Sunday activities have succeeded in winning exemptions from them.

Efforts to make Sunday a day of commerce accelerated after World War II. Mushrooming suburbs attracted new business and enticed established stores away from older downtowns, with the advantage of expansive parking to accommodate ever-increasing numbers of cars. Eager customers, many of whom were too busy to shop during the week, flocked to the stores on the weekends. Churches still filled on the Sabbath, noted *Newsweek* in the spring of 1958, but so did supermarkets, discount stores, used-car lots, and real estate offices.[14]

Nevertheless, as the 1960s began, every state but Alaska had a law against some kind of Sunday activity. More than half the states banned work on Sunday, except for work of "necessity or charity." A patchwork of state laws prohibited, variously, Sunday sales of alcoholic beverages, stock-car racing, telephone solicitation, or selling anything other than vaguely defined "necessities." Clauses in the laws exempted other activities, such as selling medicines, operating public utilities, or running a movie theater. Enforcement was as haphazard as the list of prohibitions. Often, when crackdowns occurred, those charged with violations of the law were hapless employees, rather than business owners, or members of religious minorities, such as Jews and Seventh-Day Adventists, who observed their Sabbath on Saturday and were free to work on Sunday.[15]

And many of the laws were recent, rather than quaintly anachronistic leftovers from earlier centuries. On a battleground that had seen numerous skirmishes since the early nineteenth century, new retail pressures in the 1950s provoked fresh confrontations over Sunday laws. Chain stores began to threaten smaller enterprises, especially family-run businesses. Opponents of closing laws, the chains among them, mounted constitutional challenges to them, notably in the heavily populated and commercial Northeast, on the basis of minority rights and religious freedoms, especially for Jewish and Seventh-Day Adventist merchants. Defenders of the laws pointed to not only religious reasons for keeping them in place, but also the safeguards they afforded to the health and welfare of workers, their families, and their communities. Hours not spent at work, presumably, would be spent at leisure with family and friends, upholding a traditional American morality. Local and state political alliances varied in their composition, but often siding with the closing-law defenders were merchants of downtown department stores, who saw the suburban chain-store retailers as competitive threats, and labor unions seeking to preserve hard-won benefits and shorter workweeks.[16]

In 1961, the U.S. Supreme Court considered four cases challenging Sunday-closing laws. Sorting through a messy combination of volatile religious and economic issues, the court upheld their legality. In *McGowan v. Maryland* and *Two Guys v. McGinley,* discount retailers had hoped to overturn the blue laws in Maryland and Pennsylvania to stay open seven days a week. The other two cases, *Braunfeld v. Braun* and *Gallagher v. Crown Kosher Super Market,* highlighted the predicament of Orthodox Jews prohibited from operating Saturdays by their religion and Sundays by

Shopping for shoes on a Sunday in the 1960s.

state law. Chief Justice Earl Warren wrote the majority opinion, and Felix Frankfurter provided a separate appendix that traced the history of English and American Sunday laws. Frankfurter's evidence sketched an evolution from ancient origins in religious piety to the contemporary common day off – one he depicted as a secular weekly holiday for rest, relaxation, and family activities.[17]

Crucial to the future interpretation of Sunday-closing laws was the court's majority opinion that such laws were no longer religiously based. Supporters of closing laws attempted to stem the tide of commercialism on Sunday, but to no avail. People changed their minds about Sunday prohibitions. Retailers continued to lobby for the repeal of state laws. As women swelled the workforce in greater numbers and divorced dads took the children only on weekends, being able to work, shop, and make use of local services on Sunday grew more necessary and appealing. By 1986, general Sunday-closing laws persisted in just eighteen states, most of them in the Southeast.[18] Nevertheless, only a small percentage of Americans go to work on Sundays, and the day retains its special status in the week.

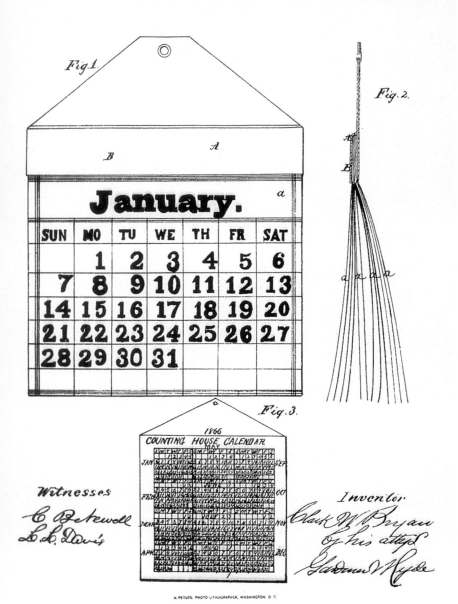

Patent specification for a wall calendar invented by C. W. Bryan, Springfield, Massachusetts, 26 February 1867.

organizing time

Next week there can't be any crisis.
My schedule is already full.

— Henry Kissinger, quoted in the *New York Times*, 28 October 1973

PEOPLE HAVE MORE TO DO THAN EVER — not just at work, but at home too. Lots of people feel compelled to do it all. And many believe they can create more time by getting organized. They divide their days into multiple usable segments. They keep elaborate personal calendars and schedules, striving to make the most of every moment and to do everything on time.

Calendars and Planners

UNTIL WELL INTO THE NINETEENTH CENTURY, many people used an almanac to mark time. Paper calendars as we know them today first appeared after the Civil War, when printers and stationers began to devise ways to show not only the passing months and days of the year, but also the daily schedule.[19]

Until recently, people were most likely to use a calendar as a diary, making notes about what happened on a particular day. Such an annotated record could be simple or elaborate — comments jotted in the margins of an almanac page, for example, or in elaborate leather-bound diaries meticulously kept day by day, year by year, over a lifetime. Today, we are more apt to use a calendar as a way to plan what is *going* to happen. In fact, the word *calendar* is no longer adequate to describe the devices many of us use for this purpose. With lots more jobs to do than track time — like keeping to-do lists, sounding alarms for meeting reminders, or storing names and telephone numbers — what we use now are called "day planners" or "personal organizers." The electronics industry dubbed the small computerized versions of the early 1990s "personal digital assistants." These days even that name is outdated, and they are now "hand-helds."

The time clock was the principle tool for noting and controlling the hours of work for the industrial labor force. Blue-collar workers punched in, but salaried managers and professionals, for the most part, were trusted to keep track of their own time by whatever system they liked.

As "scientific management" spread from factory floors to offices, businesspeople and professionals sought to increase their efficiency by mastering their use of work time. From this

Advertisement for a desk calendar by Liebenroth, Von Auw & Company, New York, 1878.

heightened sensitivity to efficiency came the paradigm for the modern personal organizer: a loose-leaf binder with calendar and add-in sheets containing useful information. Lefax, Inc. (derived from "Facts on Leaves"), was the brainchild of Philadelphia engineer John Clinton Parker, who began publishing a monthly pocket-size magazine, a self-described "digest of Business, Social and Political Progress for Business Men," as well as "Technical Supplements for Engineers and Others," around 1910. Each page of the magazine was punched to fit in a six-ring pocket binder and printed with a subject line in the upper right corner for indexing in the binder. Parker's new firm also sold supplies: a binder cover in both pocket- and letter-size versions, both available in black leather or gray canvas; filler pages to customize the binders for personal use; and "daily memo" calendar pages, seven days to a page, for a calendar year. The firm was proud to note that as of 31 May 1916, the magazine had 3,341 subscribers. Among them was efficiency expert Frank Gilbreth. A British version of the Philadelphia binder system went on the market in 1921 under the trade name Filofax.[20]

The personal organizer that came to dominate the American market after World War II happened almost inadvertently. In the late 1940s Morris Perkin, an attorney in Allentown, Pennsylvania, meticulously drew by hand a daily calendar for his own use. He devoted one page of 8½ x 11 paper to each day and provided for tracking appointments between 8:00 A.M. and

This homemade calendar hung in the kitchen of the Lindsay family of Freeland, Washington. The family used the board, made in the 1980s by Mrs. Lindsay's mother, to schedule activities, scrawl messages, and keep track of phone numbers.

Lawyer's Day prototype, 1951. Attorney Morris Perkin's hand-drawn calendar was the prototype for what eventually became the Day-Timer planner.

Brochure for *Lawyer's Day*, early 1950s.

EXPANDING TIME

Advertisement for the Synchronome Company's free-pendulum clock, promoted as "The Perfect Clock," from the *Horological Journal,* March 1928.

splitting seconds

THREE HUNDRED YEARS AGO, a second appeared to be such a tiny wisp of time that clocks had great difficulty measuring one. Now the second no longer seems fast enough. Pieces of the second, unimaginably short and beyond human perception, make a difference in the technologies we depend on, like computers, cell phone networks, radio and television broadcasting, deep-space vehicles, and electric power transmissions. Billionths, trillionths, and even smaller parts of a second are put to work. But how do we know how long a second is?

In Search of the Perfect Clock

UNTIL THE LATE 1960s, scientists defined measurable time in terms of the Earth's rotation relative to the sun and other stars. Early in the nineteenth century, astronomers had agreed to define the second as 1/86,400 of a mean solar day: one part of 24 hours times 60 minutes times 60 seconds. As recently as the mid-1950s, they further refined this definition to a fraction of the length of the sidereal year in 1900.[26]

Those of us who don't need such accuracy use ordinary clocks to mark out seconds. A precisely made pendulum clock with anchor escapement can keep time to within a few seconds a day. The pendulum is what gives the mechanical clock its regular beat, and one swing of a seconds pendulum (roughly thirty-nine inches long), left to right or right to left, is a second. But even the best pendulum clock is still not a perfect timekeeper. The biggest source of inaccuracy in a good clock is friction, an almost imperceptible resistance between the pendulum, the rest of the clock movement, and the very air the pendulum swings in.

Aiming to build a clock with almost no frictional impediments to accuracy, William Shortt, a British railroad engineer, and F. Hope-Jones, a clock manufacturer, developed a new kind of two-piece electromechanical timekeeper in the 1920s. The clock's free pendulum, hung in a vacuum and kept swinging by electrical impulses instead of an interfering gear train and power source, transmitted beats electrically to a partner clock that displayed the time.

A GPS receiver translates signals from atomic clocks circling the Earth to enable U.S. troops in Hajvazi, Bosnia, to determine their position, 1997.

more orbiting satellites to calculate the user's time, velocity, latitude, longitude, and altitude. The system, originally developed for the U.S. military, has gradually been finding more civilian applications in everything from way-finders for hikers and boaters to electronic car maps to robot grain harvesters.[34]

Even more numerous are users at the bottom of the pyramid. With the aid of commercially produced atomic clocks, hundreds of radio and television stations maintain their broadcast frequencies, electric light and power systems provide alternating current at sixty cycles a second to households, and computers in the vast Internet communicate with each other using tiny fractions of seconds.

The Leap Second

WITH THE MEASUREMENT of the atomic second now so precise, the Earth is noticeably out of synch with atomic time. Since 1972, every two or three years, we have added a single second to the calendar more than twenty times to keep atomic time, civil clock time, and the globe in synch. In the very long run, that means the time our clocks tell us and the behavior of the sun and stars overhead will basically agree.[35]

No one clock sets the time for the world. Ultimately, the Bureau International des Poids et Mesures (BIPM) in Sèvres, France, pools information from about 260 atomic clocks, most of them cesium standards, at about thirty locations worldwide to determine the official average international time, UTC (Coordinated Universal Time).[36] Likewise, no one clock provides a U.S. national time. American contributions to the pool come from atomic clocks at the National Institute for Standards and Technology in Boulder, Colorado, and the U.S. Naval Observatory in Washington, D.C.

To help audiences at her lectures in the 1980s understand the tiny fractions of seconds that computers fill with multiple calculations, computer programming pioneer Admiral Grace Hopper distributed lengths of wire like these, approximately a foot long, to represent the maximum distance electricity can travel in a nanosecond.

Grace Hopper with lengths of wire representing a nanosecond, about 1985.

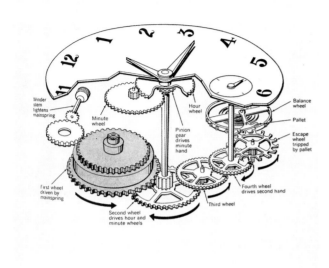

Quartz Accuracy for Everyone

LIKE WARREN MARRISON'S FIRST QUARTZ CLOCK, quartz wristwatches rely on the vibrations of a quartz crystal to keep the beat of time. Battery-powered quartz wristwatches give just about everyone access to the split-second accuracy of the quartz time standard that once was available only to scientists and technicians. When the first battery-powered quartz watches hit the American marketplace in the early 1970s, almost no one really believed they would catch on with consumers. Since then, styles have diversified, prices have fallen, and quartz watches outsell mechanical ones by a huge margin.[37]

All watches work essentially the same way with three basic components. They have a part that vibrates regularly, a means of counting and displaying those vibrations, and a power source. In a mechanical watch, an unwinding spring drives a train of wheels and causes a balance wheel to swing back and forth, usually at a rate of five half swings a second. Another set of gears, called the motion work, reduces the swings to rotate a pair of hands, the minute hand once in sixty minutes and the hour hand once in twelve hours. In an electronic watch, a battery provides the power to sustain the oscillations of a quartz crystal, which vibrates thousands of times a second. These days, the quartz resonators in watches have a frequency of 32,768 cycles per second, which divides down to rotate hands around a dial with numerals 1 through 12 or to light a digital display.

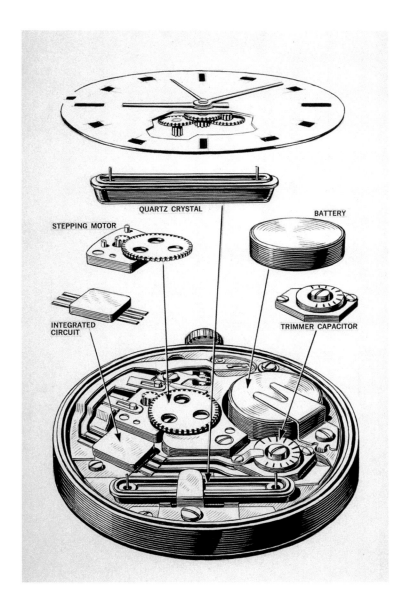

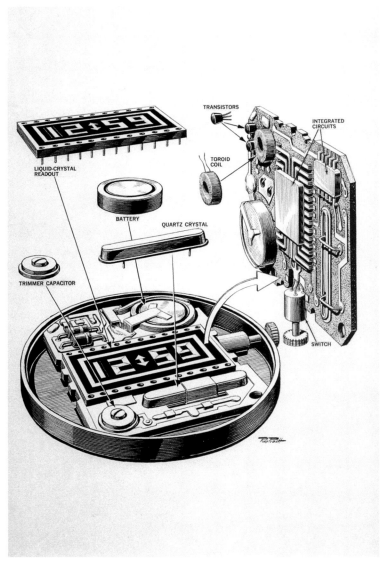

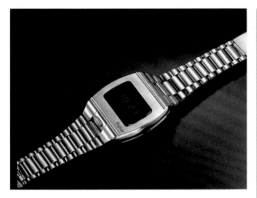

Hamilton Pulsar wristwatch with LED digital display, 1972.

Pulsar module, 1972. Inside the Hamilton Pulsar wristwatch was this electronic module with the first LED (light emitting diode) digital display.

The Hamilton Watch Company's Pulsar was the very first *digital* quartz watch. Instead of a dial and hands, it provided time on demand with lighted red numerals. The module inside the watch was unique too, with all electronic components, no moving parts. Huge and ostentatious, at $2,100 the Pulsar cost about the same as a Chevy Vega in 1972.

The ruby-colored "time screen" afforded the user a "space-capsule view" of the "read-out." The display was composed of light-emitting diodes, or LEDs, that consumed so much power, the time could not be displayed continuously. To read the watch, the wearer pushed the "command button" to illuminate the numerals. Pressing the button briefly displayed the hour and minute. Holding the button down showed the seconds. For this huge inconvenience, the Pulsar's proud owner got the most accurate time then available in a wristwatch. The new quartz technology inside made the watch accurate to within a minute a year, compared to fifteen seconds a day for the best mechanical watch.

The Pulsar was not the very first quartz wristwatch. The first ones, the vanguard of what historian David Landes has called "the quartz revolution," came from Japan in 1969 and Switzerland in 1970.[38] But those pioneering watches, as cutting-edge as they were inside, featured conventional dials and hands.

Having fallen behind its competitors, Hamilton hoped the Pulsar's unique appearance would grab consumer attention and give the ailing watch company the lead in the worldwide quartz watch market. In fact, the Pulsar was a sensation, quickly earning the reputation of a space-age gadget with sex appeal.

Module for Seiko's Astron SQ quartz wristwatch, made in Japan, 1969. The Astron was the first quartz wristwatch ever sold anywhere in the world.

Two views of the Swiss-made Beta 21 quartz wristwatch module, the dial side with calendar ring (top) and the reverse showing the battery. Watches containing this electronic module went on sale under the brand names of sixteen different Swiss watch companies in 1970.

The impulse to develop a solid-state digital watch had come not from Hamilton management, but from two electrical engineers from the company's military products division, John Bergey and Richard Walton. Their inspiration came from both science and science fiction. Bergey remembers the idea came to him when Stanley Kubrick hired the military products division to design a futuristic clock as a prop for the movie *2001: A Space Odyssey.* At about the same time, Richard Walton attended a conference, the Timers for Ordnance Symposium, where he heard a presentation by RCA engineers about their research on C-MOS integrated circuits. Walton realized that these low-power circuits developed for military purposes could be used to make an electronic watch, and he returned to headquarters to write up a proposal.

In the midst of development work, a small Texas Instruments spin-off company, Electro-Data, approached Hamilton with their idea for a digital watch. George Thiess and Willy Crabtree had been developing a solid-state watch with an LED display, and were looking for an established watch company to market their product. Bergey, by then director of the watch division, arranged a contract for the Texas company to produce six prototypes.

On 6 May 1970, a press conference in New York announced the Pulsar to the world. The watches unveiled on that occasion were still cranky prototypes that failed to work most of the time. Developing a viable watch began right after the press conference. Since the prototypes were composed of many circuits wire-bonded by hand, the design was far from ready for economical manufacturing. A single-chip module took two more years to get to market.

Hamilton needed to create a market and an identity for the Pulsar. They targeted men and placed the Pulsar squarely in the category of space-age technology. The Pulsar, claimed the advertising, was no ordinary wristwatch. It was a "wrist computer," the most up-to-the-minute know-how developed by scientists for NASA. Its very name came from outer space, from the stars that emit radio waves at regular intervals.

Hamilton also understood that watches are fashion items. The high costs of production ensured that Pulsar would be marketed as a luxury item. Designers created expensive gold and stainless steel cases for the first Pulsars, which were sold only through high-end jewelers. The price tag, unique look, and limited availability created a cachet. A Tiffany spokesman might well have been right when he said, "Every man in the world wants one."[39]

Hamilton's strategy fit in perfectly with what was happening in men's fashion at the time. Shaking off the conservative style that had persisted since the beginning of the nineteenth cen-

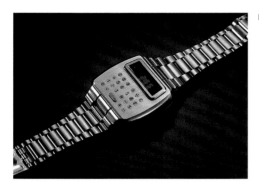

Hamilton Pulsar calculator watch, 1975.

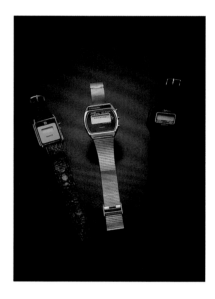

Digital watches flooded the market in the mid-1970s.

tury, men's clothing and jewelry was undergoing a period of either inspired innovation or temporary insanity, depending on your point of view, in what has come to be called "the peacock revolution." Clothes came in bright colors, bold patterns, and unexpected textures. Where once only a gold pocket watch and chain had been considered appropriate jewelry for men, now necklaces, often large and flamboyant, shone from manly chests bared by unbuttoned shirts. Bracelets, gigantic belt buckles, flashy cuff links and rings were everyday attire. In this context, a large gold LED watch reinforced the wearer's "mod" masculine image.

Sales really took off when James Bond (the Roger Moore version) wore little more than a Pulsar in a love scene in the 1973 film *Live and Let Die* and inspired a whole new category of gadget lust. Celebrities and politicians sported Pulsars too. Richard Nixon, Sammy Davis Jr., the Shah of Iran, King Hussein, and Sonny Bono all wore them. Gerald Ford received one as a gift, which he wore during House judiciary subcommittee meetings while explaining why he had pardoned former president Nixon. When an article about Ford's Pulsar appeared in the *Washington Post*, Hamilton dealers displayed the article, with photo, in their stores. With all this attention, Ford quit wearing the watch, but the Pulsar had clearly earned the reputation as the fashion item of choice for rich and powerful men. In 1975 Ford caused another stir when the public heard he told his wife Betty he wanted the Pulsar calculator watch for Christmas. With a price tag approaching $4,000, she told him no.

Hamilton's success tempted both traditional watch firms and upstart electronics companies to jump into the market with their own products. By the mid-1970s about forty American companies were mass-producing electronic watches. Prices plunged. Just four years after the debut of the costly Pulsar, consumers could purchase a digital watch from Texas Instruments for only $20. Other manufacturers quickly followed, and cheap digital watches poured by the millions out of U.S. and Asian factories. The power-hungry red lights of the LED gave way to a whole new display technology – liquid crystal displays – by the late 1970s.

This tidal wave of electronic watches, with their new kind of digital time display, provoked a lively public debate over the comparative benefits of digital versus analog. The proponents of digital displays were, predictably, watch manufacturers, advertisers, quartz watch inventors, and the enthusiastic consumers attracted to the new technology. The watch companies believed consumers had to be told how to use the new watches. Advertising campaigns explicitly aimed "to make digital watches an acceptable method of displaying time." [40]

Although he was an intelligent and successful bank - owner, Emil still had trouble figuring out how to get the clock to stop flashing 12:00.

Setting digital displays has never been as easy as setting mechanical watches.

Digital watches were a novelty, and some "early adopters" were real fans of the ultramodern look. To them, time displayed in digits signaled a much more accurate, objective, and abstract "scientific" time.

But as digital watches flooded the marketplace in the mid-1970s, and smaller models for women and children became available, criticisms about the newfangled watches began to mount. Some consumer complaints, which at first glance seemed to be about the drawbacks of reading time displayed in digits, actually had to do with poor quality and design. LEDs couldn't be read in sunlight, LCDs were invisible at night. Batteries were annoyingly short-lived. Setting the new watches was always complicated, often required extra tools, and sometimes seemed next to impossible. This design flaw persists in digital displays on many of today's watches and appliances. Cheap watches could be unreliable. Buyers returned malfunctioning watches to their manufacturers in record numbers. And many found the digital display and the plastic watches downright ugly. Manufacturers responded with product changes, and consumers had, as a result, a huge role in shaping the form and function of quartz watches.

But consumer concerns went beyond dreadful quality and design. Some began to question the very nature of digital time itself. For some adults, the transition to digital proved genuinely difficult. Their concept of time was rooted in the analog dial and disrupted by abstract numbers without the familiar context of hands rotating in a circle. A frequent complaint was that digitals showed only a given moment in time, a kind of incomplete information. Others criticized the digital display because it was *too* precise. The language of time-telling, long ago established through reading analog dials, is inexact. When faced with the question "What time is it?" the analog-dial user may say "About quarter till eight." Ask someone who wears a digital watch, though, and the answer is "7:43." As *Good Housekeeping* magazine noted in its 1976 consumer guide, "Whether or not we ordinary mortals need such accuracy is a debatable point."[41] Some parents and teachers worried that children would forever fail to learn to tell time using a traditional clock dial. In a 1975 *New York Times* article, one mother warned "The same kids who can't read now because of the television and who can't add because of calculators won't be able to tell time soon either."[42] But by the late 1970s, resistance to digital watches in the classroom subsided. It became clear that analog displays weren't going to disappear. In fact, since the mid-1980s people have bought more watches with analog dials than with digital displays.

The Swatch marketers appear undaunted by anyone else's difficulties with switching time standards. Before long, they predict, we will all be moving to their "beat." Nicholas Negroponte, one of the fathers of the Internet and director of MIT's prestigious Media Lab, agrees, and portrays the new system as the ultimate 24/7 tool. "Cyberspace has no seasons and no night and day," he noted as he helped Swatch launch Internet time in the fall of 1998. "In the future, for many people, real time will be Internet time."[43] If we look beyond the hyperbole and jargon, we can see at work a recognition that boundaries between people are changing and perhaps even dissolving. And as people's perceptions of space change, usually their ideas about time do too.

Most of us don't think about how and why we keep time as we do, either when we strap on a watch or glance at a nearby clock. Our timekeepers, after all, are more than just keepers of time. Watches can be disposable fashion items or complex wearable technologies, status symbols or heirlooms. In their vast variety they offer us ways to express and change our personal styles. Clocks share many of the same decorative and symbolic characteristics. Both are everywhere in the public and private spaces of our lives.

Whether we heed them is another matter entirely.

notes

Introduction

1. This book focuses on the interaction of clocks, watches, and time and does not attempt to offer a comprehensive guide to how timepieces work. No one volume provides an overview of the business, technical, and social history of American clocks and watches. For a survey of prominent individual makers and manufacturers see Chris H. Bailey, *Two Hundred Years of American Clocks and Watches* (Englewood Cliffs, N.J.: Prentice-Hall, 1975). For the underlying science, see James Jespersen and Jane Fitz-Randolph, *From Sundials to Atomic Clocks: Understanding Time and Frequency,* 2nd rev. ed. (Mineola, N.Y.: Dover Publications, 1999). Among the countless printed explanations of how mechanical clocks and watches work, see the simple and clear illustrations in David Macaulay, *The Way Things Work* (Boston: Houghton Mifflin, 1988), 46.

2. Lewis Mumford, *Technics and Civilization* (New York: Harcourt, Brace & Co., 1934), 14.

3. E. P. Thompson, "Time, Work Discipline and Industrial Capitalism," *Past and Present* 38 (December 1967): 57.

4. The recent literature on shifts in American senses of clock time includes Mark M. Smith, *Mastered by the Clock: Time, Slavery and Freedom in the American South* (Chapel Hill: University of North Carolina Press, 1997); Paul B. Hensley, "Time, Work, and Social Context in New England," *New England Quarterly* 65 (December 1992): 532–59; Martin Bruegel, " 'Time That Can Be Relied Upon': The Evolution of Time Consciousness in the Mid-Hudson Valley, 1760–1860," *Journal of Social History* 28 (Spring 1995): 547–64; and Michael O'Malley, *Keeping Watch: A History of American Time* (New York: Viking, 1990). For the European context, see Gerhard Dohrn-van Rossum, *History of the Hour: Clocks and Modern Temporal Orders,* trans. Thomas Dunlap (Chicago: University of Chicago Press, 1996); David Landes, *Revolution in Time: Clocks and the Making of the Modern World* (Cambridge, Mass.: Belknap Press, 1983); and Nigel Thrift, "Owner's Time and Own Time: The Making of a Capitalist Time Consciousness 1300–1800," in *Space and Time in Geography: Essays Dedicated to Torsten Hagerstrand,* ed. A. R. Pred (Lund, Sweden: Gleerup Studies in Geography, 1981), 56–84.

5. David Nye discusses the power of objects in these terms in *American Technological Sublime* (Cambridge, Mass.: MIT Press), xv.

Telling Time 1700–1820

1. Banneker lived the modest life of a tobacco farmer and died shortly before his seventy-fifth birthday in 1806. Just as friends and neighbors watched his burial, Banneker's house burst into flames and burned to the ground. For the definitive biography of Banneker, see Silvio Bedini, *The Life of Benjamin Banneker,* 2nd ed. (Baltimore: Maryland Historical Society, 1999); for mathematical and astronomical techniques used in the compilation of almanacs, see John T. Kelly, *Practical Astronomy During the Seventeenth Century: Almanac-Makers in America and England* (New York: Garland, 1991), 127, 130, 245.

2. Daniel Boorstin, *The Americans: The Colonial Experience* (New York: Vintage Books, 1958), 325–26; Bedini, *Benjamin Banneker,* 86, 336.

3. Jack Larkin, *The Reshaping of Everyday Life, 1790–1840* (New York: Harper Perennial, 1988), xv.

4. Michael O'Malley, "Time, Work and Task Orientation: A Critique of American Historiography," *Time & Society* 1 (September 1992): 341.

5. Mark M. Smith, *Mastered by the Clock: Time, Slavery and Freedom in the American South* (Chapel Hill: University of North Carolina Press, 1997), 12–13; and Paul B. Hensley, "Time, Work, and Social Context in New England," *New England Quarterly* 65 (December 1992): 531–33, 558–59.

6. Quoted in Smith, *Mastered by the Clock,* 67–68.

7. David J. Bryden, *Sundials and Related Instruments* (Cambridge, U.K.: Whipple Museum of the History of Science, 1988), n.p.; R. Newton Mayall and Margaret Mayall, *Sundials: How to Know, Use, and Make Them* (Boston: Hale, Cushman & Flint, 1938), 26; Albert E. Waugh, *Sundials: Their Theory and Construction* (New York: Dover, 1973), 18; David Hackett Fischer, *Albion's Seed: Four British Folkways in America* (New York: Oxford University Press, 1989), 162; J. L. Heilbron, *The Sun in the Church: Cathedrals as Solar Observatories* (Cambridge, Mass.: Harvard University Press, 1999); Alice Morse Earle, *Sun Dials and Roses of Yesterday* (New York: Macmillan, 1902), 40.

8. For an overview, see Donald L. Fennimore, "The Sundial in America," *Antiques* 142 (August 1992): 196–203. For examples of public dials on a courthouse, a church, and a college campus, see *Charleston Courier,* 12 July 1806, 3, quoted in Smith, *Mastered by the Clock,* 20; Henry Spackman, *The Timepiece of Shadows: A History of the Sundial* (New York: William Comstock, 1895), 77–79; *Life of Jeremy Belknap, D.D., The Historian of New Hampshire, with Selections from His Correspondence and Other Writings Collected and Arranged by His Grand-Daughter* [Jane Belknap Marcou] (New York, 1847), 71, quoted in Allen L. King, "In Quest of a Gnomon," *Dartmouth College Library Bulletin,* November 1973, 19.

9. Advertisement from the *Boston Gazette,* 18 June 1745, quoted in Silvio Bedini, *Early American Scientific Instruments and Their Makers* (Rancho Cordova, Calif.: Landmark Enterprises, 1986), 37–38, 54.

10. W. Emerson, *Dialling,* 1770, quoted in Bryden, *Sundials,* n.p.

11. René Rohr, *Sundials: History, Theory, Practice,* trans. Gabriel Godin (Toronto: University of Toronto Press, 1970), 44; Fennimore, "Sundial in America," 198.

12. New research indicates that only in the eighteenth century did people begin to grow less fearful of the night air. See A. Roger Ekirch, "Sleep We Have Lost: Preindustrial Slumber in the British Isles," *American Historical Review* 106 (April 2001): 355. On slave life at night, see Mechal Sobel, *The World They Made Together: Black and White Values in Eighteenth-Century Virginia* (Princeton, N.J.: Princeton University Press, 1987), 33–34.

13. Jane C. Nylander, *Our Own Snug Fireside: Images of the New England Home, 1760–1860* (New York: Knopf, 1993), 238.

14. Donald Zochert, "Science and the Common Man in Ante-Bellum America," in *Science in America Since 1820,* ed. Nathan Reingold (New York: Science History Publications, 1976), 8.

15. Ralph Waldo Emerson, "Self-Reliance," in *The Complete Essays and Other Writings of Ralph Waldo Emerson,* ed. Brooks Atkinson (New York: Modern Library, 1940), 167.

16. Sarah S. Hughes, *Surveyors and Statesmen: Land Measuring in Colonial Virginia* (Richmond: Virginia Surveyors Foundation, 1979), 3; Daniel Boorstin, *The Americans: The National Experience* (New York: Random House, 1965), 241–48; Robert Multhauf, "Early Instruments in the History of Surveying," in *Plotters and Patterns of American Surveying,* ed. Roy Minnick (Rancho Cordova, Calif.: Landmark Enterprises, 1985), 59; Silvio Bedini, *Early American Men of Science* (New York: Scribner, 1975), 313–17, 328–29; Brooke Hindle, *The Pursuit of Science in Revolutionary America, 1735–1789* (Chapel Hill: University of North Carolina Press, 1956), 174.

17. J. Howard Gore, *Elements of Geodesy* (New York, 1886), 9–10; Mansfield Merriman, *The Figure of the Earth: An Introduction to Geodesy* (New York, 1881), 37–38; Josef W. Konvitz, *Cartography in France, 1660–1848: Science, Engineering and Statecraft* (Chicago: University of Chicago Press, 1987).

18. J. A. Bennett and Olivia Brown, *The Compleat Surveyor* (Cambridge: Whipple Museum of the History of Science, 1982), 14–15; A. D. Butterfield, *A History of the Determination of the Figure of the Earth from Arc Measurements* (Worcester, Mass.: David Press, 1906), 46–48; Gore, *Elements of Geodesy,* 9–10; Bedini, *Benjamin Banneker,* 108, 142.

19. J. A. Bennett, *The Divided Circle* (Oxford: Phaidon Christie's, 1987), 30–31, 179; Taylor quoted in Hensley, "Time, Work, and Social Context in New England," 540.

20. Dava Sobel and William J. H. Andrewes, *The Illustrated Longitude* (New York: Walker, 1998), and William J. H. Andrewes, ed., *The Quest for Longitude* (Cambridge, Mass.: Collection of Historical Scientific Instruments, Harvard University, 1996).

21. Alun C. Davies, "The Life and Death of a Scientific Instrument: The Marine Chronometer, 1770–1920," *Annals of Science* 35 (1978): 509–527.

22. Thornton Stratford Lecky, *"Wrinkles" in Practical Navigation,* 11th rev. ed. (London: G. Philip, 1881), 93.

23. Thomas Bond to George P. Bond, 21 February 1859, quoted in Edward S. Holden, *Memorials of William Cranch Bond and His Son George Phillips Bond* (New York, 1897), 7–8; G. P. Bond, "Memoranda relating to W. C. Bond," ibid., 11–12; *Ferdinand Berthoud, 1727–1807* (La Chaux-de-Fonds, Switzerland: Musée International d'Horlogerie, 1984), 43, 207; "La Pérouse," *Grand Larousse,* VI, 603. For background on the Bond firm, see Carlene E. Stephens, "Partners in Time: William Bond & Son of Boston and the Harvard College Observatory," *Harvard Library Bulletin* 35 (Fall 1987): 351–84.

24. Thomas B. Curtis to William C. Bond, 25 December 1818 and 21 August 1819, Bond Papers, Harvard University Collection of Historical Scientific Instruments, quoted with permission. See also Steven J. Dick, "Centralizing Navigational Technology in America: The U.S. Navy's Depot of Charts and Instruments, 1830–1842," *Technology and Culture* 33 (July 1992): 467–509.

25. Otto Mayr, "A Mechanical Symbol for an Authoritarian World," in Klaus Maurice and Otto Mayr, *The Clockwork Universe: German Clocks and Automata, 1550–1650* (Washington, D.C.: Smithsonian Institution and Neale Watson Academic Publications, 1980), 2, 8; Otto Mayr, *Authority, Liberty and Automatic Machinery in Early Modern Europe* (Baltimore: Johns Hopkins University Press, 1986), xviii.

26. John Roche, "Newton's *Principia,*" in *Let Newton Be! A New Perspective on His Life and Works,* ed. John Fauvel et al. (Oxford: Oxford University Press, 1994), 42–61; Mayr, *Authority, Liberty and Automatic Machinery,* 98.

27. Paul W. Conner, *Poor Richard's Politicks: Benjamin Franklin and His New American Order* (London: Oxford University Press, 1969), 174; I. Bernard Cohen, *Science and the Founding Fathers: Science in the Political Thought of Jefferson, Franklin, Adams and Madison* (New York: Norton, 1995), 97–108, 141–47.

28. Henry C. King, *Geared to the Stars: The Evolution of Planetariums, Orreries and Astronomical Clocks* (Toronto: Toronto University Press, 1978), 269–79. Jefferson's suggestion is in Garry Wills, *Inventing America: Jefferson's Declaration of Independence* (New York: Vintage Books, 1979), 93–110.

29. Listed in Alfred Coxe Prime, *The Arts & Crafts in Philadelphia, Maryland and South Carolina, 1786–1800.* Series Two. (Topsfield, Mass.: Walpole Society, 1932), 239, 249.

30. Mayr, *Authority, Liberty and Automatic Machinery,* 26.

31. Derek J. de S. Price, "On the Origin of Clockwork, Perpetual Motion Devices, and the Compass," *U.S. National Museum Bulletin 218: Contributions from the Museum of History and Technology, Papers 1 to 11* (Washington, D.C., Smithsonian Institution, 1959), 82–86.

32. Michael O'Malley, *Keeping Watch: A History of American Time* (New York: Viking, 1990), 11.

33. Ray A. Williamson, *Living the Sky: The Cosmos and the American Indian* (Boston: Houghton Mifflin, 1984), 59–60, 72, 81, 315; Waldo R. Wedel, "Native Astronomy and the Plains Caddoans," in *Native American Astronomy*, ed. Anthony Aveni (Austin: University of Texas Press, 1977), 131–45; Ray A. Williamson, Howard J. Fisher, and Donnel O'Flynn, "Anasazi Solar Observatories," in *Native American Astronomy*, 215.

34. Michael O'Malley, "Time, Work and Task Orientation," 347.

35. Mark M. Smith, "Culture, Commerce, and Calendar Reform in Colonial America," *William and Mary Quarterly* 55 (October 1998): 557–84.

36. Alexis McCrossen, *Holy Day, Holiday: The American Sunday* (Ithaca, N.Y.: Cornell University Press, 2000), 10–12, 16–17.

37. Eviatar Zerubavel, *Hidden Rhythms: Schedules and Calendars in Social Life* (Berkeley: University of California Press, 1985), 31–32.

38. Fray Alonso de Benavides' Revised Memorial of 1634 (1945: 101–102).

39. Alfonso Ortiz, *The Tewa World: Space, Time, Being, and Becoming in a Pueblo Society* (Chicago: University of Chicago Press, 1969).

40. Quoted in Anna B. Sands, *Time Pieces of Old and New Connecticut* ([Hartford]: Manufacturers Association of Connecticut, 1926), 7, cited in Christopher Clark, "Time-Consciousness and Social Change in Nineteenth-Century America" (copy in History of Technology Division files, National Museum of American History), 5.

41. Raoul François Camus, "The Military Band in the United States Army Prior to 1834" (Ph.D. diss., New York University, 1969), 228.

42. Hensley, "Time, Work, and Social Context in New England," 538; Peter Benes and Philip D. Zimmerman, *New England Meeting House and Church, 1630–1850* (Boston: Boston University and the Currier Gallery of Art for the Dublin Seminar for New England Folklife, 1979): 57, 58, 146.

43. For the distinction between time obedience and time discipline, see David Landes, *Revolution in Time: Clocks and the Making of the Modern World* (Cambridge, Mass.: Belknap Press, 1983), 2, 7.

44. Max Weber, *The Protestant Ethic and the Spirit of Capitalism*, trans. Talcott Parsons (New York: Charles Scribner's Sons, 1958).

45. General Court of Massachusetts, 1633, quoted in Philip Zea and Robert C. Cheney, *Clock Making in New England, 1725–1825* (Sturbridge, Mass.: Old Sturbridge Village, 1992), 11.

46. Winton Solberg, *Redeem the Time: The Puritan Sabbath in Early America* (Cambridge, Mass.: Harvard University Press, 1977); Stephen Innes, *Creating the Commonwealth: The Economic Culture of Puritan New England* (New York: Norton, 1995), 126; Hensley, "Time, Work, and Social Context in New England," 535–37.

47. Daniel T. Rodgers, *The Work Ethic in Industrial America 1850–1920* (Chicago: University of Chicago Press, 1978), 8–9, 245; Smith, *Mastered by the Clock*, 40–41; O'Malley, "Time, Work and Task Orientation," 341–58; Paul Glennie and Nigel Thrift, "Reworking E. P. Thompson's 'Time, Work-discipline and Industrial Capitalism,' " *Time & Society* 5 (3): 275–99.

48. E. R. Eschback, "The Town Steeple's Centenary Services: Historical Sermon," 27 October 1907 (copy in History of Technology Division files, National Museum of American History); Silvio Bedini, "Frederick Heisely: Clock and Compass Maker," *Rittenhouse* 3 (August 1989): 120.

49. Gerhard Dohrn-van Rossum, *History of the Hour: Clocks and Modern Temporal Orders,* trans. Thomas Dunlap (Chicago: University of Chicago Press, 1996), 146.

50. Smith, *Mastered by the Clock,* 45; O'Malley, "Time, Work and Task Orientation," 347.

51. Artisan quoted in David R. Roediger and Philip S. Foner, *Our Own Time: A History of American Labor and the Working Day* (New York: Greenwood Press, 1989), 4.

52. Patience Meannwell opinion in *Newport Mercury,* 27 July 1772, quoted in Zea and Cheney, *Clock Making in New England,* 27.

53. Robert C. Cheney, "Roxbury Eight-Day Movements and the English Connection, 1785–1825," *Antiques* (April 2000): 609, 610, 614; Anne Golovin and Rodris Roth, *New & Different: Home Interiors in Eighteenth-Century America* (an exhibition at the National Museum of American History, August 1986–September 1987), n.p.

54. Today this kind of clock is often referred to as a "grandfather" clock. Although the origin of the phrase is not entirely certain, it is likely to have originated with the publication in 1876 of the popular song "My Grandfather's Clock" by Henry C. Work.

55. The seventeenth-century improvements focused on the pendulum and the escapement, the component in the clock movement that links the wheelwork to the pendulum and brakes the clock's driving force, whether from a falling weight or unwinding spring, at regular intervals. Winthrop quoted in Hensley, "Time, Work, and Social Context in New England," 541.

56. Jefferson quoted in Sobel, *The World They Made Together*, 57; see also Silvio Bedini, "Thomas Jefferson, Clock Designer," *Proceedings of the American Philosophical Society* 108 (1964), 165–70; W. David Todd, "Thomas Jefferson's Time," paper in History of Technology Division files, National Museum of American History, 2–3; Susan Stein, *The Worlds of Thomas Jefferson at Monticello* (New York: H. N. Abrams, 1993), 276, 376–77.

57. Precisely how many clockmakers worked in America is difficult to determine. A list from Carl W. Dreppard, *American Clocks & Clockmakers* (Garden City, N.Y.: Doubleday, 1947), 197–293, analyzed in Hensley, "Time, Work, and Social Context in New England," 549, and in Smith, *Mastered by the Clock,* Table A.10, 195. For an extensive list of newspaper advertisements for clocks, watches, and horological tools and materials, see Carter Harris, "The Clock and Watch Makers American Advertiser," (copy in History of Technology Division files, National Museum of American History).

58. *Rees's Clocks, Watches, and Chronometers (1819–1820): A Selection from the Cyclopaedia, or Universal Dictionary of Arts, Sciences, and Literature* (London: David & Charles Reprints, 1970), 90–91.

59. Cheney, "Roxbury Eight-Day Movements," 613; Zea and Cheney, *Clock Making in New England,* 7, 36, 40–41.

60. Zea and Cheney, *Clock Making in New England,* 37–38; Cheney, "Roxbury Eight-Day Movements," 608, 612.

61. Zea and Cheney, *Clock Making in New England,* 41.

62. John Joseph Murphy, "Entrepreneurship in the Establishment of the American Clock Industry," *Journal of Economic History* 26 (1966), 170–71; Zea and Cheney, *Clock Making in New England,* 21–23.

63. Quoted in Barrows Mussey, ed., *Yankee Life by Those Who Lived It* (New York: Knopf, 1947), 224, quoted in Hensley, "Time, Work, and Social Context in New England," 549.

64. Zea and Cheney, *Clock Making in New England,* 24.

65. Margaret Bohn Alexander, " 'To Apprise the People of the Time': The Distribution and Uses of Clocks and Watches in Preindustrial America" (copy in History of Technology Division files, National Museum of American History), 9, 17, 38–39, analyzes data from Alice Hanson Jones, *American Colonial Wealth: Documents and Methods* (New York: Arno Press, 1977).

66. William McPherson Hornor, Jr., *Blue Book of Philadelphia Furniture* (Philadelphia: Published by the author, 1935), 129; John F. Watson, *Annals of Philadelphia* (Philadelphia, 1830), 184, cited in Sandra Narva, " 'The Hour is Often Repeated in My Ears': Women, Time, and Culture in the Early Republic," M.A. thesis, George Washington University, 1995.

67. Michael Harrold, *American Watchmaking: A Technical History of the American Watch Industry, 1850–1930* (supplement to the *Bulletin of the National Association of Watch and Clock Collectors,* No. 14, Spring 1984), 9, 12, 14–15.

68. Landes, *Revolution in Time,* 231, 287.

69. R. Campbell, *The London Tradesman* (London, 1747), quoted in *Science and Profit in 18th-Century London,* ed. Roy Porter et al. (Cambridge: Whipple Museum of the History of Science), 21.

70. Chris Bailey, *Two Hundred Years of American Clocks and Watches* (Englewood Cliffs, N.J.: Prentice-Hall, 1975), 65; Zea and Cheney, *Clock Making in New England,* 75–76.

71. Listed in Prime, *Arts & Crafts,* 238–39, 259.

72. Ibid., 264. Adam Smith identifies watch movements as those articles whose price had been most reduced (from 20 pounds to 20 shillings), despite the inflation of the previous hundred years, in *An Inquiry into the Nature and Causes of the Wealth of Nations* (Oxford: Clarendon Press, 1976; 1776) 1: 260–61.

73. Raechel Guest, "Philadelphia Watches in the Colonial Era," paper in History of Technology Division, National Museum of American History, 7; trinket ads in Prime, *Arts & Crafts,* 238, 256, 268.

74. Genevieve E. Cummins and Nerylla D. Taunton, *Chatelaines: Utility to Glorious Extravagance* (Suffolk, England: Antique Collectors' Club Ltd., 1994), 47–48. On false watches, see also Geoff Egan, "Datasheet 10: Base-metal Toys," Finds Research Group 700–1700. Thanks to Barbara Carson for this reference. Egan describes different kinds of lead-alloy "toy" watches found in archaeological digs. The surviving pieces are either cast in the form of a disc or hollow-cast. He speculates they were instructional playthings for children in the seventeenth and eighteenth centuries, but they may in fact be the false-watch fashion accessory.

75. Cummins and Taunton, *Chatelaines,* 50.

76. The Baroness D'Oberkirch reminisced in her 1785 *Memoires:* "It had been the fashion for some years to wear two watches. The watch-chains were loaded with ornaments called *breloques* – trifles which were often very expensive." Quoted in Norah Waugh, *The Cut of Women's Clothes 1600–1930* (New York: Theatre Arts Books, 1969), 122. Thanks to Claudia Kidwell for this reference. See also Cummins and Taunton, *Chatelaines,* 34, 45, 47.

77. Smith quoted in Frederick B. Tolles, *Meeting House and Counting House: The Quaker Merchants of Colonial Philadelphia, 1682–1763* (New York: Norton, 1963), 123; Narva, " 'The Hour Is Often Repeated in My Ears,' " 86–87; Sobel, *The World They Made Together,* 60.

78. Dohrn-van Rossum, *History of the Hour,* 12–14.

79. Margaret Bohn Alexander, " 'To Apprise the People of the Time,' " 2; Arthur Cole, "The Tempo of Mercantile Life in Colonial America," *Business History Review* 33 (Autumn 1959): 277–99; Melvin Maddocks, *The Seafarers: The Atlantic Crossing* (Alexandria, Va.: Time-Life Books, 1981), 83.

80. Maddocks, *The Seafarers*, 80, 86; Allan Pred, *Urban Growth and the Circulation of Information: The United States System of Cities, 1790–1840* (Cambridge, Mass.: Harvard University Press, 1973), 29.

81. Richard R. John, *Spreading the News: The American Postal System from Franklin to Morse* (Cambridge, Mass.: Harvard University Press, 1995), vii.

82. Ibid., 25–27.

83. Pred, *Urban Growth and the Circulation of Information*, 88; John, *Spreading the News*, ix, 46–47, 52.

84. Ibid., 70, 100–101.

85. Ibid., 101.

86. *Philadelphia in 1824* (Philadelphia: H. C. Carey & I. Lea, 1824), 151–52. Thanks to Barbara Carson for this reference.

87. Pred, *Urban Growth and the Circulation of Information*, 85, 92; John, *Spreading the News*, 91.

88. Quoted in John, *Spreading the News*, 17–18.

89. Ibid., 156–57, 159; Pred, *Urban Growth and the Circulation of Information*, 81.

90. John, *Spreading the News*, 37–38; Pred, *Urban Growth and the Circulation of Information*, 12–13.

91. John, *Spreading the News*, 83–89; Thomas C. Cochran, *Frontiers of Change: Early Industrialism in America* (New York: Oxford University Press, 1981), 17.

92. Robert Levine, *A Geography of Time: The Temporal Misadventures of a Social Psychologist* (New York: Basic Books, 1997), 57.

93. David Hackett Fischer, *Albion's Seed*, 158–62; Smith, *Mastered by the Clock*, 41–42; Dohrn-van Rossum, *History of the Hour*, 12–14.

94. Cochran, *Frontiers of Change*, 38–39.

Mechanizing Time 1820–1880

1. "The Great Race," *New Orleans Daily Picayune*, 3 April 1855, 2; "Nine Cheers for Lexington, *Spirit of the Times*, 7 April 1855; "The Great Match vs. Time at New Orleans," *Spirit of the Times*, 14 April 1855, 102–103; John Hervey, *Racing in America, 1665–1865* (New York: Scribner, 1944), 2: 311, 315.

2. Charles E. Trevathan, *The American Thoroughbred* (New York: Macmillan, 1905), 305.

3. John Dizikes, *Sportsmen and Gamesmen* (Boston: Houghton Mifflin, 1981), 128.

4. Roy Ehrhardt, *Waltham Pocket Watch Identification and Price Guide* (Kansas City, Mo.: Heart of America Press, 1976), 6, 21; Michael Harrold, *American Watchmaking: A Technical History of the American Watch Industry, 1850–1930* (supplement to the *Bulletin of the National Association of Watch and Clock Collectors,* No. 14, Spring 1984), 96–97; Donald Hoke, *The Time Museum Historical Catalogue of American Pocket Watches* (Rockford, Ill.: Time Museum, 1991), 111.

5. Lexington's skeleton is Smithsonian accession 121040, Record Unit 305, Smithsonian Institution Archives, Washington, D.C. Alexander's intention was reported by his agent L. Brodhead to D. D. Carter, 30 August 1875, Record Unit 52; the intention to exhibit at the Centennial Exposition in Spencer F. Baird to A. J. Alexander, 2 November 1875, Record Unit 52; and delay in the preparation of the skeleton was reported by Henry A. Ward to Baird, Record Unit 52.

6. Jack Larkin, *The Reshaping of Everyday Life, 1790–1840* (New York: Harper Perennial, 1988), xiv.

7. For an interpretation of Henry David Thoreau's *Walden* in terms of the mechanization of time and capitalism, see Leo Marx, *The Machine in the Garden: Technology and the Pastoral Ideal in America* (London: Oxford University Press, 1978), 247–48.

8. Brooke Hindle and Steven Lubar, *Engines of Change: The American Industrial Revolution* (Washington, D.C.: Smithsonian Institution Press, 1986), 205–17.

9. Quoted in Anthony Wallace, *Rockdale: The Growth of an American Village in the Early Industrial Revolution* (New York: Norton, 1980), 149.

10. Quoted in David Zonderman, *Aspirations and Anxieties: New England Workers and the Mechanized Factory System, 1815–1850* (New York: Oxford University Press, 1992), 156–57.

11. Portsmouth, New Hampshire, newspaper quoted in Hensley, "Time, Work, and Social Context in New England," 557; Gary Kulik, "Patterns of Resistance to Industrial Capitalism: Pawtucket Village and the Strike of 1824," in *American Workingclass Culture: Explorations in American Labor and Social History,* ed. Milton Cantor (Westport, Conn.: Greenwood Press, 1979), 229–30; David R. Roediger and Philip S. Foner, *Our Own Time: A History of American Labor and the Working Day* (New York: Greenwood Press, 1989), 20, 21.

40. Chauncey Jerome, *History of the American Clock Business for the Past Sixty Years and Life of Chauncey Jerome, Written by Himself* (New Haven, 1860), 62–64.

41. Chris Bailey, *Two Hundred Years of American Clocks and Watches* (Englewood Cliffs, N.J.: Prentice-Hall, 1975), 166; Douglas H. Shaffer, *A Survey History of the American Spring Driven Clock 1840–1860* (supplement to the *Bulletin of the National Association of Watch and Clock Collectors,* Winter 1973), 5.

42. Bailey, *Two Hundred Years of American Clocks and Watches,* 35–36.

43. Harrold, *American Watchmaking,* 35.

44. Joan Severa, *Dressed for the Photographer: Ordinary Americans and Fashion, 1840–1900* (Kent, Ohio: Kent State University Press, 1995), 13–14.

45. When watches were first introduced in the fifteenth century, men and women wore them on neck chains. See G. H. Baillie, *Watches: Their History, Decoration and Mechanism* (London: Methuen, 1929), 60.

46. O'Malley, *Keeping Watch,* 176.

47. Mary Booth, *New and Complete Clock and Watchmakers' Manual* (New York, 1860), 275; Harrold, *American Watchmaking,* 14.

48. David Landes, *Revolution in Time: Clocks and the Making of the Modern World* (Cambridge, Mass.: Belknap Press, 1983), 314; Harrold, *American Watchmaking,* 17.

49. Charles Moore, *Timing a Century: History of the Waltham Watch Company* (Cambridge, Mass.: Harvard University Press, 1945), 9, 17; Donald Hoke, *The Time Museum Catalogue of American Pocket Watches* (Rockford, Ill.: Time Museum, 1991), 59; Landes, *Revolution in Time,* 322.

50. Landes, *Revolution in Time,* 315; Harrold, *American Watchmaking,* 18–19; David A. Wells, ed., "The American Manufacture of Watch Movements," in *Annual of Scientific Discovery: or Year-Book of Facts in Science and Art for 1859* (Boston, 1859), 65–69, quoted in Hoke, *Time Museum Catalogue,* 83.

51. Landes, *Revolution in Time,* 317; Moore, *Timing a Century,* 50.

52. Landes, *Revolution in Time,* 319–24.

53. Hoke, *Ingenious Yankees,* 106; Landes, *Revolution in Time,* 317–18.

54. For more on this accident, see Carlene E. Stephens, "The Most Reliable Time: William Bond, the New England Railroads, and Time Awareness in 19th-Century America," *Technology and Culture* 30 (January 1989): 16–21. See also

Ian Bartky, *Selling the True Time: Nineteenth-Century Timekeeping in America* (Stanford, Calif.: Stanford University Press, 2000), 27.

55. "More Slaughter by Railroad," *New York Times*, 13 August 1853; "The Rhode Island Collision," *Illustrated News* 2 (27 August 1853), n.p.

56. Richard B. DuBoff, "Business Demand and the Development of the Telegraph in the United States, 1844–1860," *Business History Review* 54 (1980): 465. In New England, use of the telegraph for railroad dispatching met with a certain resistance until after the Civil War. See Edward C. Kirkland, *Men, Cities, and Transportation: A Study in New England History, 1820–1900* (Cambridge, Mass.: Harvard University Press, 1948), 1: 393.

57. Alexander Black, *Report, Exhibiting the Present State of the Work and Probable Progress of Operations on the Charleston and Hamburg Rail Road, Submitted to the Director, October 18, 1831* (Charleston, 1831), 13. For more on early American railroads, see Colleen Dunlavy, *Politics and Industrialization: Early Railroads in the United States and Prussia* (Princeton, N.J.: Princeton University Press, 1994).

58. Oliver W. Holmes and Peter Rohrback, *Stagecoach East* (Washington, D.C.: Smithsonian Institution Press, 1983), 23–31, 111–23, 179–81; U.S. Railway Mail Service, *History of the Railway Mail Service* (Washington, D.C., 1885), 23.

59. Act of March 3, 1845, quoted in James H. Bruns, "Star Route Service," *The United States Specialist* 56 (November 1985): 479.

60. "Report of H. Allen," in *Semi-Annual Report of the Director of the South-Carolina Canal and Rail-Road Company to the Stockholders, October 31, 1834* (Charleston, 1834), 12.

61. Alfred D. Chandler, *The Visible Hand: The Managerial Revolution in American Business* (Cambridge, Mass.: Belknap Press, 1977), 96–98.

62. The Western Railroad, "Regulations," December 4, 1843, in the Railway & Locomotive Historical Society Collection, California State Railroad Museum, Sacramento.

63. *The American Diaries of Richard Cobden*, ed. Elizabeth H. Cawley (New York: Greenwood Press, 1969), 18, 119.

64. William F. Allen, *History of the Adoption of Standard Time* (New York, 1884), 9, 14.

65. Henry David Thoreau, *Walden, or Life in the Woods* (1854; reprint, New York: New American Library, 1960), 79–80, 83. For an interpretation of Thoreau's ambivalence to the railroad, see also Marx, *The Machine in the Garden,* 248–55.

23. For a summary of arguments for and against the monastic origins of the mechanical clock, see Gerhard Dohrn-van Rossum, *The History of the Hour* (Chicago: University of Chicago Press, 1996), 10–14, 55–64.

24. See a tall case clock from 1588 by Jørgen Eckler of Copenhagen and a table clock made in Strasbourg in 1573 in *The Clockwork Universe: German Clocks and Automata 1550–1650*, eds. Klaus Maurice and Otto Mayr (Washington, D.C.: Smithsonian Institution and Neale Watson Academic Publications, 1980), 175, 178.

25. See Otto Mayr and Carlene Stephens, *American Clocks* (Washington, D.C.: National Museum of American History, 1990), 12.

26. Ward Francillon, "Some Wood Movement Alarms," *National Association of Watch and Clock Collectors* [hereafter NAWCC] *Bulletin* 14 (October 1970): 576, 578.

27. Marc Bradshaw and Howard Bradshaw, "An Alarming Time in History," *NAWCC Bulletin* 27 (August 1985): 432–33; Anthony Benis, "The Answer Box: Not All Are Typical," *NAWCC Bulletin* 12 (December 1966): 635–36; Henry Fried, "The Answer Box: 'Peep-O-Day,' " *NAWCC Bulletin* 16 (April 1974): 332; "Vox Temporis: Peep O'day," *NAWCC Bulletin* 16 (October 1974): 627–28; John R. Sangster, "Seth Thomas, a Yankee Clockmaker 1785–1859: Chapter Three, Seth Thomas Clock Company 1853–1900," *NAWCC Bulletin* 13 (October 1968): 535.

28. Bradshaw and Bradshaw, "An Alarming Time," 433; Sears, Roebuck catalog for fall–winter 1925–26, 648.

29. John M. Anderson, "Henry Warren and His Master Clocks," *NAWCC Bulletin* 33 (August 1991): 375–95.

30. Sam Bass Warner, Jr., *Streetcar Suburbs: The Process of Growth in Boston, 1870–1900* (New York: Atheneum, 1968).

31. Daniel T. Rodgers, *The Work Ethic in Industrial America 1850–1920* (Chicago: University of Chicago Press, 1978), 153–54. David Landes distinguishes between time *obedience,* when people respond to a bell rung at a particular time, and time *discipline,* when people are responsible for knowing what time it is and for appearing on time, in *Revolution in Time: Clocks and the Making of the Modern World* (Cambridge, Mass.: Belknap Press 1983), 7.

32. Helmut Kahlert, Richard Mühe, and Gisbert L. Brunner, *Wristwatches: History of a Century's Development* (West Chester, Penn.: Schiffer Publications, 1986), 10–19; Dennis Harris, "Wrist Watches 1910–1920," *Antiquarian Horology* 17 (Summer 1988): 357; Carlene Stephens, Amanda Dillon, and Margaret Dennis, "Revolution on Your Wrist," *Increase & Diffusion* (www.si.edu/i+d/time.html).

33. John H. Young, *Our Deportment or the Manners, Conduct and Dress of the Most Refined Society* (Detroit: R. B. Dickerson, 1881), 325.

34. *Horological Journal,* December 1887, 50; "Watch Fashions [from Paris]," *The Waterbury,* September 1888, n.p.; "Our Letter from Monte Carlo," *The Waterbury,* May 1889, n.p.; Nellie Bly, *Nellie Bly's Book: Around the World in Seventy-two Days* (New York: Pictorial Weeklies, 1890), Chapter 4.

Ian Bartky, *Selling the True Time: Nineteenth-Century Timekeeping in America* (Stanford, Calif.: Stanford University Press, 2000), 27.

55. "More Slaughter by Railroad," *New York Times*, 13 August 1853; "The Rhode Island Collision," *Illustrated News* 2 (27 August 1853), n.p.

56. Richard B. DuBoff, "Business Demand and the Development of the Telegraph in the United States, 1844–1860," *Business History Review* 54 (1980): 465. In New England, use of the telegraph for railroad dispatching met with a certain resistance until after the Civil War. See Edward C. Kirkland, *Men, Cities, and Transportation: A Study in New England History, 1820–1900* (Cambridge, Mass.: Harvard University Press, 1948), 1: 393.

57. Alexander Black, *Report, Exhibiting the Present State of the Work and Probable Progress of Operations on the Charleston and Hamburg Rail Road, Submitted to the Director, October 18, 1831* (Charleston, 1831), 13. For more on early American railroads, see Colleen Dunlavy, *Politics and Industrialization: Early Railroads in the United States and Prussia* (Princeton, N.J.: Princeton University Press, 1994).

58. Oliver W. Holmes and Peter Rohrback, *Stagecoach East* (Washington, D.C.: Smithsonian Institution Press, 1983), 23–31, 111–23, 179–81; U.S. Railway Mail Service, *History of the Railway Mail Service* (Washington, D.C., 1885), 23.

59. Act of March 3, 1845, quoted in James H. Bruns, "Star Route Service," *The United States Specialist* 56 (November 1985): 479.

60. "Report of H. Allen," in *Semi-Annual Report of the Director of the South-Carolina Canal and Rail-Road Company to the Stockholders, October 31, 1834* (Charleston, 1834), 12.

61. Alfred D. Chandler, *The Visible Hand: The Managerial Revolution in American Business* (Cambridge, Mass.: Belknap Press, 1977), 96–98.

62. The Western Railroad, "Regulations," December 4, 1843, in the Railway & Locomotive Historical Society Collection, California State Railroad Museum, Sacramento.

63. *The American Diaries of Richard Cobden*, ed. Elizabeth H. Cawley (New York: Greenwood Press, 1969), 18, 119.

64. William F. Allen, *History of the Adoption of Standard Time* (New York, 1884), 9, 14.

65. Henry David Thoreau, *Walden, or Life in the Woods* (1854; reprint, New York: New American Library, 1960), 79–80, 83. For an interpretation of Thoreau's ambivalence to the railroad, see also Marx, *The Machine in the Garden*, 248–55.

66. Hindle and Lubar, *Engines of Change*, 151; O'Malley, *Keeping Watch*, 67, 100; Samuel P. Langley, "The Electric Time Service," *Harper's New Monthly Magazine* 56 (April 1878): 665.

67. For more on observatory time services see Bartky, *Selling the True Time*, 59–74, 181–204; Carlene Stephens, *Inventing Standard Time* (Washington, D.C.: National Museum of American History, 1983), n.p.

Synchronizing Time 1880–1920

1. Carlton Corliss, *The Day of Two Noons* (Washington, D.C.: Association of American Railroads, 1951); William F. Allen, "Report on the Adoption of Standard Time," *Proceedings of the General Time Convention and Its Successor the American Railway Association* 1 (Appendix, 1872–1885): 703; Western Union General Superintendent Bates to William F. Allen, 17 November 1883 (William F. Allen Papers, vol. 4, 120, Manuscript Division, New York Public Library); *New York Times*, 19 November 1883, 5; *New York Herald,* November 1883, 6, all cited in Michael O'Malley, *Keeping Watch: A History of American Time* (New York: Viking, 1990), 122, 123.

2. O'Malley, *Keeping Watch,* 139–40.

3. For a brief survey of the history of standard time in the United States, see Carlene E. Stephens, *Inventing Standard Time* (Washington, D.C.: National Museum of American History, 1983). See also Ian Bartky, "The Invention of Railroad Time," *Railroad History* 148 (Spring 1983): 13–22; O'Malley, *Keeping Watch*, 99–144; Ian Bartky, *Selling the True Time: Nineteenth-Century Timekeeping in America* (Stanford, Calif.: Stanford University Press, 2000), 137–46. On the railroads, see Alfred D. Chandler, *The Visible Hand: The Managerial Revolution in American Business* (Cambridge, Mass.: Belknap Press, 1977), 81–144.

4. Charles F. Dowd, *System of National Time and Its Application by Means of Hour and Minute Indexes, to the National Railway Time-Table* (Albany, 1870); Charles F. Dowd, "Origins and Early History of the New System of National Time," *Proceedings of the American Metrological Society* 4 (1884): 90–101; Railway Association of America, Convention at New York, 14 May 1873, "Report on Adopting a Uniform System of National Time for Time Tables" (clipping from *Railroad Gazette*, 24 May 1873, in Allen Papers, box 2, folder 1).

5. *National Cyclopedia of American Biography,* s.v. "Dowd, Charles."

6. For scientists' efforts on behalf of adopting standard time, see Ian Bartky, "The Adoption of Standard Time," *Technology and Culture* 30 (January 1989): 25–56.

7. *Dictionary of American Biography,* s.v. "Allen, William Frederick"; O'Malley, *Keeping Watch,* 101–103.

8. Allen quoted in "Extract from Proceedings of General Time Convention, Held at St. Louis, Mo., April 11, 1883," William F. Allen, comp., *History of the Adoption of Standard Time* (New York, 1884), 36.

9. Carlene E. Stephens, "The Impact of the Telegraph on Public Time in the United States, 1844–1893," *IEEE Technology and Society Magazine* 8 (March 1989): 8–9. For an opposing view, see Bartky, *Selling the True Time,* 181–99.

10. Allen Papers, box 1, folder 4.

11. O'Malley, *Keeping Watch,* 130, 133.

12. Quoted in O'Malley, *Keeping Watch,* 136–37.

13. John Rogers to William F. Allen, 20 February 1882, in Allen Papers, v. 1, p. 10.

14. Quoted in O'Malley, *Keeping Watch,* 120.

15. *Clapp v. Jenkins,* No. 1171, cited in O'Malley, *Keeping Watch,* 343–44.

16. Ibid., 132–33.

17. Derek Howse, *Greenwich Time and the Longitude: Official Millennium Guide* (New York: Philip Wilson, 1997), 127–43.

18. Sandford Fleming, "Uniform Non-Local Time (Terrestrial Time)" (published by the author, 1876). The mean solar time at 0 degree longitude, formerly known as Greenwich Mean Time, is also known as UTC (Universal Coordinated Time).

19. Interstate Commerce Commission, *Standard Time* (Washington, D.C.: U.S. Government Printing Office, 1958), 2, 247; United States Department of Transportation, *Standard Time in the United States* (Washington, D.C.: U.S. Government Printing Office, 1970), 6, 7, 9; Ian Bartky and Elizabeth Harrison, "Standard Time and Daylight-saving Time," *Scientific American* 240 (May 1979): 46–53.

20. Stephen Kern, *The Culture of Time and Space 1880–1918* (Cambridge, Mass.: Harvard University Press, 1983), 11.

21. "The Waterbury Mikado Opera Rhyme," undated advertisement for Waterbury Watch Company in Collection 60, Archives Center, National Museum of American History; "Evolution," *The Waterbury* 2 (August 1888): 28.

22. George M. Beard, "Causes of American Nervousness," in *Popular Culture and Industrialism 1865–1890,* ed. H. N. Smith (New York: New York University Press, 1967), 61; "Business Habits," *The Universal Self-Instructor* (1883; reprint, New York: Winter House, 1970), 485.

23. For a summary of arguments for and against the monastic origins of the mechanical clock, see Gerhard Dohrn-van Rossum, *The History of the Hour* (Chicago: University of Chicago Press, 1996), 10–14, 55–64.

24. See a tall case clock from 1588 by Jørgen Eckler of Copenhagen and a table clock made in Strasbourg in 1573 in *The Clockwork Universe: German Clocks and Automata 1550–1650,* eds. Klaus Maurice and Otto Mayr (Washington, D.C.: Smithsonian Institution and Neale Watson Academic Publications, 1980), 175, 178.

25. See Otto Mayr and Carlene Stephens, *American Clocks* (Washington, D.C.: National Museum of American History, 1990), 12.

26. Ward Francillon, "Some Wood Movement Alarms," *National Association of Watch and Clock Collectors* [hereafter NAWCC] *Bulletin* 14 (October 1970): 576, 578.

27. Marc Bradshaw and Howard Bradshaw, "An Alarming Time in History," *NAWCC Bulletin* 27 (August 1985): 432–33; Anthony Benis, "The Answer Box: Not All Are Typical," *NAWCC Bulletin* 12 (December 1966): 635–36; Henry Fried, "The Answer Box: 'Peep-O-Day,' " *NAWCC Bulletin* 16 (April 1974): 332; "Vox Temporis: Peep O'day," *NAWCC Bulletin* 16 (October 1974): 627–28; John R. Sangster, "Seth Thomas, a Yankee Clockmaker 1785–1859: Chapter Three, Seth Thomas Clock Company 1853–1900," *NAWCC Bulletin* 13 (October 1968): 535.

28. Bradshaw and Bradshaw, "An Alarming Time," 433; Sears, Roebuck catalog for fall–winter 1925–26, 648.

29. John M. Anderson, "Henry Warren and His Master Clocks," *NAWCC Bulletin* 33 (August 1991): 375–95.

30. Sam Bass Warner, Jr., *Streetcar Suburbs: The Process of Growth in Boston, 1870–1900* (New York: Atheneum, 1968).

31. Daniel T. Rodgers, *The Work Ethic in Industrial America 1850–1920* (Chicago: University of Chicago Press, 1978), 153–54. David Landes distinguishes between time *obedience,* when people respond to a bell rung at a particular time, and time *discipline,* when people are responsible for knowing what time it is and for appearing on time, in *Revolution in Time: Clocks and the Making of the Modern World* (Cambridge, Mass.: Belknap Press 1983), 7.

32. Helmut Kahlert, Richard Mühe, and Gisbert L. Brunner, *Wristwatches: History of a Century's Development* (West Chester, Penn.: Schiffer Publications, 1986), 10–19; Dennis Harris, "Wrist Watches 1910–1920," *Antiquarian Horology* 17 (Summer 1988): 357; Carlene Stephens, Amanda Dillon, and Margaret Dennis, "Revolution on Your Wrist," *Increase & Diffusion* (www.si.edu/i+d/time.html).

33. John H. Young, *Our Deportment or the Manners, Conduct and Dress of the Most Refined Society* (Detroit: R. B. Dickerson, 1881), 325.

34. *Horological Journal,* December 1887, 50; "Watch Fashions [from Paris]," *The Waterbury,* September 1888, n.p.; "Our Letter from Monte Carlo," *The Waterbury,* May 1889, n.p.; Nellie Bly, *Nellie Bly's Book: Around the World in Seventy-two Days* (New York: Pictorial Weeklies, 1890), Chapter 4.

35. David Landes, "Watch and Clock Trade," in *Encyclopedia of Time*, ed. Samuel L. Macey (New York: Garland, 1994), 660–61.

36. Harris, "Wrist Watches 1910–1920," 357–58, 360–64.

37. Marvin Whitney, *Military Timepieces* (Cincinnati: AWI Press, 1992), 533; Marco Richon, *Omega: The History of a Great Brand* (Bienne, Switzerland: Omega SA, 1994), 7; NMAH Cat. No. 1997.0144.05, wristwatch made in Switzerland marked: "Cyma/Signal Corps/U.S.A."

38. Whitney, *Military Timepieces*, 533; Edward Blunden, *Undertones of War* (1928; reprint, New York, 1965), 171, and John Keegan, *The Face of Battle: A Study of Agincourt, Waterloo and the Somme* (New York, 1976), 241, cited in Kern, *Culture of Time and Space*, 288.

39. "Wrist Watches," *Horological Journal*, October 1916, 18–19.

40. Ibid.

41. Benrus advertisement in *Liberty* magazine (Warshaw Collection, box 1, AC, NMAH); "Watches and Their Wearers in War Time," *American Horologist*, February 1943, 23.

42. Michael Harrold, *American Watchmaking: A Technical History of the American Watch Industry, 1850–1930* (supplement to the *Bulletin of the National Association of Watch and Clock Collectors*, No. 14, Spring 1984), 3, 4, 49–51, 59; Donald Hoke, *The Time Museum Catalogue of American Pocket Watches* (Rockford, Ill.: The Time Museum, 1991), 27.

43. Hoke, *American Pocket Watches*, 24; O'Malley, *Keeping Watch*, 174.

44. This chapter defines a presentation watch as any watch given by one person to another. In the early twentieth century, watch companies called their most expensive models presentation watches. See Willis I. Milham, *Time and Timekeepers* (New York: Macmillan, 1929), 120; for a history of gold and silver objects given on special occasions, see David B. Warren et. al, *Marks of Achievement: Four Centuries of American Presentation Silver* (New York: Abrams, in association with Museum of Fine Arts, Houston, 1987).

45. NMAH Cat. No. 335,239; Silvio A. Bedini, "The Touch of Time: Helen Keller's Pocket Watch," typescript in files of History of Technology Division, NMAH.

46. *Ladies' Home Journal* 28 (December 1911): 76, pictured in William B. Waits, *The Modern Christmas in America: A Cultural History of Gift Giving* (New York: New York University Press, 1992), 114; *Saturday Evening Post* 186 (December 1913): 34, pictured in Waits, *Modern Christmas*, 136; *Saturday Evening Post*, 23 May 1925, 67.

47. Kern, *Culture of Time and Space*, 6, 18–19, 33, 81; Linda Dalrymple Henderson, *The Fourth Dimension and Non-Euclidean Geometry in Modern Art* (Princeton, N.J.: Princeton University Press, 1983).

48. For the history of the automobile before 1920, see James J. Flink, *America Adopts the Automobile, 1895–1910* (Cambridge, Mass.: MIT Press, 1970); Michael L. Berger, *The Devil Wagon in God's Country: The Automobile and Social Change in Rural America, 1893–1929* (Hamden, Conn.: Archon Books, 1979); Clay McShane, *Down the Asphalt Path: The Automobile and the American City* (New York: Columbia University Press, 1994); Stephens W. Sears, *The American Heritage History of the Automobile in America* (New York: American Heritage, 1977); and Reynold M. Wik, *Henry Ford and Grass-Roots America* (Ann Arbor: University of Michigan Press, 1972).

49. Larry McKilwin, "Keeping the Land Yacht Shipshape," *Harper's Weekly* 53 (2 January 1909): 10, quoted in Flink, *America Adopts the Automobile*, 101–102; "Where the Charm Is," *Motor World* 2 (16 May 1901): 127, quoted in Flink, 102.

50. Edison interview in *New York World*, 1895, quoted in Sears, *History of the Automobile*, 52.

51. Ibid., 61, 62, 64.

52. Quoted in Claude S. Fischer, *America Calling: A Social History of the Telephone to 1940* (Berkeley: University of California Press, 1992), 138.

53. Berger, *Devil Wagon*, 16–17.

54. McShane, *Down the Asphalt Path*, 200–201; James Michael Brodie, *Created Equal: The Lives and Ideas of Black American Innovators* (New York: Morrow, 1993), 94–95, 99, 113–14.

55. Norman T. Moline, *Mobility and the Small Town, 1900–1930: Transportation Change in Oregon, Illinois* (Chicago: University of Chicago Department of Geography, 1971), 59–60; McShane, *Down the Asphalt Path*, 127.

56. Moline, *Mobility and the Small Town*, 5–6; Berger, *Devil Wagon*, 125–26; Kern, *Culture of Time and Space*, 217; Fischer, *America Calling*, 10–11.

57. Berger, *Devil Wagon*, 133–37, 144; Alexis McCrossen, *Holy Day, Holiday: The American Sunday* (Ithaca, N.Y.: Cornell University Press, 2000), 79–92.

58. Kern, *Culture of Time and Space*, 69.

59. Steven Lubar, *InfoCulture: The Smithsonian Book of Information Age Inventions* (Boston: Houghton Mifflin, 1993), 120.

60. Fischer, *America Calling*, 41, 42, 81; Kern, *Culture of Time and Space*, 214.

61. Lubar, *InfoCulture*, 124; Fischer, *America Calling*, 42.

62. Kern, *Culture of Time and Space*, 66, 67.

63. Ibid., 68, 112.

64. Ibid., 68–70.

65. Ibid., 38–39; Marvin, *When Old Technologies Were New*, 203–205.

66. Paul Israel, *Edison: A Life of Invention* (New York: John Wiley & Sons, 1998), 142–47; David Morton, *Off the Record: The Technology and Culture of Sound Recording in America* (New Brunswick, N.J.: Rutgers University Press, 2000), 3. For efforts to develop a talking clock from Edison's phonograph, see René Rondeau, *Tinfoil Phonographs* (Corte Madera, Calif.: published by the author, 2001), 71.

67. Morton, *Off the Record*, 78.

68. Marvin, *When Old Technologies Were New*, 79–80.

69. Kern, *Culture of Time and Space*, 29; Murray Melbin, *Night as Frontier: Colonizing the World After Dark* (New York: Free Press, 1987), 3.

70. Melbin, *Night as Frontier*, 13–14.

71. David Nye, *Electrifying America: Social Meanings of a New Technology, 1880–1940* (Cambridge, Mass.: MIT Press, 1995), 2, 29, 382.

72. Ibid., 382.

73. Melbin, *Night as Frontier*, 29–52.

74. Kern, *Culture of Time and Space*, 21, 29–30; Lubar, *InfoCulture*, 198.

75. Marta Braun, *Picturing Time: The Work of Etienne-Jules Marey (1830–1904)* (Chicago: University of Chicago Press, 1992), 187–91, has analyzed the relationship of Edison to the cinema work of Eadweard Muybridge and Etienne-Jules Marey. See also Charles Musser, *Before the Nickelodeon: Edwin S. Porter and the Edison Manufacturing Company* (Berkeley: University of California Press, 1991).

76. Tom Gunning, *D. W. Griffith and the Origins of American Film Narrative: The Early Years at Biograph* (Urbana: University of Illinois Press, 1991), 85; O'Malley, *Keeping Watch,* 204–205.

77. O'Malley, *Keeping Watch,* 206–209.

78. Gunning, *D. W. Griffith,* 88–90.

79. Ibid., 95–96, 195–204, 206.

80. O'Malley, *Keeping Watch,* 218–19.

Saving Time 1920–1960

1. *Transferring Eggs* (Storrs, Conn.: Motion and Time Study Laboratory, University of Connecticut, 1953), in Frank and Lillian Gilbreth Collection, Purdue University Libraries, Special Collections and Archives.

2. For an introduction, see Thomas P. Hughes, *American Genesis: A Century of Invention and Technological Enthusiasm 1870–1970* (New York: Viking, 1989); David F. Noble, *America by Design: Science, Technology, and the Rise of Corporate Capitalism* (Oxford: Oxford University Press, 1977), 261, 264.

3. Lindy Biggs, "The Engineered Factory," *Technology and Culture* supplement to 36 (April 1995): S175; idem, *The Rational Factory: Architecture, Technology, and Work in America's Age of Mass Production* (Baltimore: Johns Hopkins University Press, 1996), 3–7; Daniel T. Rodgers, The Work Ethic in Industrial America 1850–1920 (Chicago: University of Chicago Press, 1978), 24.

4. Herbert Applebaum, *The American Work Ethic and the Changing Work Force: An Historical Perspective* (Westport, Conn.: Greenwood Press, 1998), 68, 154.

5. Richard Whipp, " 'A Time to Every Purpose': An Essay on Time and Work," in *The Historical Meanings of Work,* ed. Patrick Joyce (Cambridge: Cambridge University Press, 1987), 211.

6. Benjamin Kline Hunnicutt, *Work Without End: Abandoning Shorter Hours for the Right to Work* (Philadelphia: Temple University Press, 1988), 1–3, 9–16.

7. International Time Recording Co., "Minutes Turned to Gold," quoted in Joseph M. Gensheimer, "The International Time Recording Company: The First Ten Years," *Bulletin of the National Association of Watch and Clock Collectors* 37 (June 1995): 293.

8. For an example, see David A. Zonderman, *Aspirations and Anxieties: New England Workers and the Mechanized Factory System, 1815–1850* (New York: Oxford University Press, 1992), 158.

9. Saul Engelbourg, *International Business Machines: A Business History* (Arno Press, 1976; 1954), 27, 32–33; "The Bundy Time Recorder," *Engineer* 85 (11 March 1898): 239; "An Accurate Automatic Time Recorder," *Scientific American* 66 (18 June 1892): 386; "The Bundy Automatic Time Recorder at the Exposition," *Scientific American* 69 (16 December 1893): 389.

10. Engelbourg, *International Business Machines,* 28; "The 'Rochester' System of Time-Recording," *Scientific American* 89 (24 December 1897): 404; Gensheimer, "International Time Recording Company," 292.

11. For examples of cards printed with time stamps and their uses, see Hugo Diemer, *Factory Organization and Administration* (New York: McGraw-Hill, 1910), 185–97; Engelbourg, *International Business Machines,* 35.

12. International Time Recording Co., "The Connecting Link between Employer and Employee," 1918; idem, "Electric Time Recorders," 1920, both in History of Technology Division file, National Museum of American History; Engelbourg, *International Business Machines,* 251–52.

13. IBM sold its time equipment division to Simplex, another time system manufacturer, in 1958. Gensheimer, "International Time Recording Company," 301.

14. David Landes, *Revolution in Time: Clocks and the Making of the Modern World* (Cambridge, Mass.: Belknap Press, 1983), 4.

15. Howard P. Emerson and Douglas C. E. Naehring, *Origins of Industrial Engineering* (Atlanta: Institute of Industrial Engineers, 1988), 36.

16. Noble, *America by Design,* 274; Hughes, *American Genesis,* 188; Frederick W. Taylor, *The Principles of Scientific Management* (New York: Harper, 1919), 7.

17. See Hugh G. J. Aitken, *Scientific Management in Action: Taylorism at Watertown Arsenal,* 1908–1915 (Princeton, N. J.: Princeton University Press, 1985) and Daniel Nelson, *Frederick Taylor and the Rise of Scientific Management* (Madison: University of Wisconsin Press, 1980).

18. Harry Braverman, *Labor and Monopoly Capital: The Degradation of Work in the Twentieth Century* (New York and London: Monthly Review Press, 1974), 67–68.

19. Lillian Gilbreth, *The Home-Maker and Her Job* (New York: Appleton, 1927), 78–79.

20. Peter Liebhold, "Seeking 'The One Best Way': Frank and Lillian Gilbreth's Time-Motion Photographs 1910–1924," *Labor's Heritage* 7 (Fall 1995): 19–33, 56–59.

21. For biographical material, see Lillian Gilbreth, *As I Remember* (Norcross, Ga.: Engineering and Management Press, 1998); Laurel Graham, *Managing on Her Own: Dr. Lillian Gilbreth and Women's Work in the Interwar Era* (Norcross, Ga.: Engineering and Management Press, 1998); Jane Lancaster, " 'Wasn't She the Mother in *Cheaper by the Dozen?*': A Life of Lillian Moller Gilbreth, 1878–1972" (Ph.D. diss., Brown University, 1998).

22. Susan Strasser, *Never Done: A History of American Housework* (New York: Pantheon, 1982), 214–19; Frederick quote, 218.

23. Ibid., 203.

24. Graham, *Managing on Her Own,* 179–80.

25. *The New York Herald-Tribune Institute Presents Four Model Kitchens* (New York: New York Herald-Tribune Institute, 1931); *The Model Kitchen Is Remodeled* (New York: New York Herald-Tribune Institute, 1935), both in Frank and Lillian Gilbreth Collection, Purdue University Libraries; Lancaster, " 'Wasn't She the Mother,' " 399.

26. *Planned Motion in the Home Saves: Time–Energy–Money* (Frank and Lillian Gilbreth Collection, Purdue University Libraries, Special Collections and Archives); Lancaster, " 'Wasn't She the Mother,' " 400.

27. Graham, *Managing on Her Own,* 238–39.

28. "Easier Housekeeping," *Life,* 9 September 1946, 97, 105.

29. See Ruth Schwartz Cowan, *More Work for Mother: The Ironies of Household Technology from the Open Hearth to the Microwave* (New York: Basic Books, 1983).

30. See John C. Burnham, *Bad Habits* (New York: New York University Press, 1993); Joseph R. Gusfield, "Passage to Play: Rituals of Drinking Time in American Society," in ed. Mary Douglas, *Constructive Drinking: Perspectives on Drink from Anthropology* (Cambridge: Cambridge University Press, 1988; and Patricia Tice, *Altered States: Alcohol and Other Drugs in America* (Rochester, N. Y.: The Strong Museum, 1992).

Expanding Time 1960 to the Present

1. Murray Melbin, *Night as Frontier: Colonizing the World After Dark* (New York: Free Press, 1987), 3, 7.

2. Ibid., 51, 29–52.

3. Kevin Coyne, *A Day in the Night of America* (New York: Random House, 1992), xv.

4. Harriet Presser, "Job, Family, and Gender: Determinants of Nonstandard Work Schedules Among Employed Americans in 1991," *Demography,* November 1995, 577–78.

5. For the compelling story of the discovery and exploration of time genes, see Jonathan Weiner, *Time, Love, Memory: A Great Biologist and His Quest for the Origins of Behavior* (New York: Knopf, 1999). See also "How Biological Clocks Work," NIH Publication No. 01-4604 (www.nimh.nih.gov/pulicat/bioclock.chm); and Franz Halberg interview in Jeremy Campbell, *Winston Churchill's Afternoon Nap: A Wide-Awake Inquiry into the Human Nature of Time* (New York: Simon & Schuster, 1986), 122.

6. See Otto Mayr, *Authority, Liberty and Automatic Machinery in Early Modern Europe* (Baltimore: Johns Hopkins University Press, 1986), 7, 21–26.

7. Christine Kleinegger, " 'You Snooze, You Lose': Sleep and Time in Modern Life" (paper presented at the On Time Conference, Liverpool, England, September 1999); Carol M. Worthman and Melissa K. Melby, "Toward a Comparative Developmental Ecology of Human Sleep," in *Adolescent Sleep Patterns: Biological, Social, and Psychological Influences,* ed. Mary Carskadon (New York: Cambridge University Press, forthcoming).

8. Harriet B. Presser, "Nonstandard Work Schedules and Marital Instability," *Journal of Marriage and the Family* 62 (February 2000): 93–110.

9. Martin Moore-Ede, *The Twenty-Four-Hour Society: Understanding Human Limits in a World That Never Stops* (Reading, Mass.: Addison-Wesley, 1993); U.S. Congress Office of Technology Assessment, *Biological Rhythms: Implications for the Worker* (Washington, D.C.: U.S. Government Printing Office, 1991); Melbin, *Night as Frontier,* 134.

10. Melbin, *Night as Frontier,* 10–14; Wolfgang Schivelbusch, *Disenchanted Night: The Industrialization of Light in the Nineteenth Century,* trans. Angela Davies (Berkeley: University of California Press, 1988; 1995); David E. Nye, *Electrifying America: Social Meanings of a New Technology, 1880–1940* (Cambridge, Mass.: MIT Press, 1992), x.

11. Nye, *Electrifying America,* 193.

12. Michael Lamm, "Dollars Ex Machina," *Invention & Technology* 16 (Summer 2000): 48–49.

13. For an original interpretation relating the American Sunday to changing notions about work, rest, and leisure, see Alexis McCrossen, *Holy Day, Holiday: The American Sunday* (Ithaca, N.Y.: Cornell University Press, 2000).

14. "On the Seventh Day?," *Newsweek* 51 (21 April 1958): 72, quoted in Alan Raucher, "Sunday Business and the Decline of Sunday Closing Laws: A Historical Overview," *Journal of Church and State* 36 (Winter 1994): 24.

15. McCrossan, *Holy Day, Holiday*, p. 107; *McGowan v. Maryland*, 366 U.S. 420 (1961): 495, 551, cited in Jerome A. Barron, "Sunday in North America," *Harvard Law Review* 79 (1965–66): 42; Candida Lund, "The Sunday Closing Laws and the Law" (Ph.D. diss., University of Chicago, 1963), 2–3.

16. Raucher, "Sunday Business," 25–26.

17. For detailed background on *Two Guys v. McGinley*, a case originating in Allentown, Pennsylvania, and *Gallagher v. Crown Kosher Super Market*, from Worcester, Massachusetts, see Lund, "Sunday Closing Laws and the Law," 32–86.

18. McCrossen, *Holy Day, Holiday*, 105–10; Raucher, "Sunday Business," 31–32.

19. An alternative to the almanac, widely used in Great Britain from the mid-eighteenth century, was Robert Dodsley's *Memorandum-Book*. See Stuart Sherman, *Telling Time: Clocks, Diaries, and English Diurnal Form, 1660–1785* (Chicago: University of Chicago Press, 1996), 171–72.

20. *Lefax*, July 1916, 2, 55–58; Lillian M. Gilbreth, *As I Remember* (Norcross, Ga.: Engineering and Management Press, 1998), 132.

21. William G. Ross, *The Honest Hour: The Ethics of Time-Based Billing by Attorneys* (Durham, N.C.: Carolina Academic Press, 1996), 14–22; Robert Dorney, interview by author, Allentown, Pennsylvania, 23 August 1999.

22. Ibid.

23. Steven R. Covey, A. Roger Merrill, and Rebecca R. Merrill, *First Things First* (New York: Simon & Schuster, 1994), 326–27.

24. Ida Sabelis, "Time Management: Paradoxes and Patterns," *Time & Society* 10 (September 2001): 389–90.

25. Ibid.

26. In 1956 by international agreement, the second was defined as the fraction 1/31, 556, 925.9747 of the tropical year for 0 January 1900, at midnight Ephemeris Time. Tony Jones, *Splitting the Second: The Story of Atomic Time* (Bristol, UK: Institute of Physics Publishing, 2000), 17–24.

27. Warren A. Marrison, "The Crystal Clock," *National Academy of Sciences Proceedings* 16 (July 1930): 504. See also W. R. Topham, "Warren A. Marrison – Pioneer of the Quartz Revolution," *National Association of Watch and Clock Collectors Bulletin* 31 (April 1989): 126.

28. Patrick R. J. Brown, "The Influence of Amateur Radio on the Development of the Commercial Market for Quartz Piezoelectric Resonators in the United States," *Proceedings of the 1996 IEEE International Frequency Control Symposium,* 58–60.

29. Virgil Bottom, "A History of the Quartz Crystal Industry in the USA," *Proceedings of the 35th Annual Frequency Control Symposium,* 1981, 10–11.

30. For historical studies of atomic clocks, see Paul Forman, "The First Atomic Clock Program: NBS, 1947–1954," *Proceedings of the Seventeenth Annual Precise Time and Time Interval (PTTI) Applications and Planning Meeting, Washington, D.C., December 3–5, 1985* (Washington, D.C.: U.S. Naval Observatory, 1986), 1–17; idem, "Atomichron®: The Atomic Clock from Concept to Commercial Product," *Proceedings of the Institute of Electrical and Electronic Engineers,* 73 (1985): 1181–1204; and idem, "Inventing the Maser in Postwar America," *Osiris,* 2nd series, 7 (1992): 105–34.

31. Don Sullivan quoted in Verlyn Klinkenborg, "The Best Clock in the World," *Discover,* June 2000, 57. Thanks to him for references to the new clock: S. A. Diddams, Th. Udem, J. C. Bergquist, E. A. Curtis, R. E. Drullinger, L. Hollberg, W. M. Itano, W. D. Lee, C. W. Oates, K. R. Vogel, and D. J. Wineland, "An Optical Clock Based on a Single Trapped 199 Hg+ Ion," *Science* 293 (2001): 825–28; and J. C. Bergquist, S. R. Jefferts, and D. J. Wineland, "Time Measurement at the Millenium," *Physics Today* 54 (2001): 37–42.

32. Robert Drullinger cited in Gary Taubes, "A Clock More Perfect Than Time," *Discover,* December 1996, 70.

33. L. Alberto Cangahuala, "Interplanetary Navigation Overview," *Proceedings of the 2000 IEEE/EIA International Frequency Control Symposium and Exhibition,* 618–21; William G. Melbourne, "Navigation Between the Planets," *Scientific American* 234 (June 1976): 59, 61. Thanks to John D. Prestage for these references.

34. Jones, *Splitting the Second,* 155; see also L. Casey Larijani, *GPS for Everyone: How the Global Positioning System Can Work for You* (New York: American Interface Corporation, 1998).

35. Geoff Chester, U.S. Naval Observatory, telephone conversation with the author, 19 July 2001.

36. Jones, *Splitting the Second,* 82.

37. This section derives from Carlene Stephens and Maggie Dennis, "Engineering Time: Inventing the Electronic Wristwatch," *British Journal for the History of Science* 33 (2000): 477–97; Maggie Dennis and Carlene Stephens, "Giving Time a New Face: Digital Watch Displays and Changing Perceptions of Time" (paper presented at the annual meeting of the American Historical Association, Boston, January 2001); and Maggie Dennis, "Wrist Computer and Babe Magnet: Masculinity and the Origins of the Digital Watch" (paper presented at the annual meeting of the Society for the History of Technology, Munich, August 2000).

38. David Landes, *Revolution in Time: Clocks and the Making of the Modern World* (Cambridge, Mass.: Harvard University Press, 1983), 338–60.

39. *New York Times,* 21 July 1973.

40. Milton C. Stevens, "The Watchmakers' Position in the World of Quartz/Electronic Watches," *American Horologist and Jeweler* 42 (December 1975): 56.

41. "GH Institute's Complete Guide to Digital Watches," *Good Housekeeping,* May 1976, 192.

42. Georgia Dullea, "Digital Watches: The Technologically Chic Way to Tell Time," *New York Times,* 31 December 1975, 26.

43. Quoted in Michael Stroh, "Keeping Time to the Same 'Beat,' " *Baltimore Sun,* 8 April 1999.

illustration credits

Illustrations are listed by page number and location on the page. All photographs are courtesy of the Smithsonian Institution unless noted otherwise. Smithsonian Institution photo numbers for objects and graphics in Smithsonian collections are in parentheses, as are the names of Smithsonian photographers, when attributed. Smithsonian photo numbers for loan objects are also provided.

Telling Time

20	Maryland Historical Society, Baltimore, Maryland
22	Abby Aldrich Rockefeller Folk Art Museum, Williamsburg, Virginia
25 top	(74-222)
25 bottom	Library of Congress
26 left	(74-7088)
26 bottom right	Watson, Little Ltd.
26 top right	All rights reserved, The Rhode Island Historical Society, Rhi(x3)2633.
27 top	(Richard Strauss, 99-36455)
27 bottom	(Richard Strauss, 2001-13213-09)
28 left	(98-4653) Smithsonian Institution Libraries
28 right	(Lynette Chewning and Bill Kendrick, 91-10383)
30	(99-36578)
31	By permission of The British Library, ships glasses by Blanckley's *A Naval Expositor*, 1651/806
33 left	National Maritime Museum, London
33 right	(Richard Strauss, 99-36532)
34	(Dane Penland, 83-9987)
35	The Library Company of Philadelphia
36 left	(Richard Strauss, 99-36700)
36 right	(Richard Strauss, 99-36701)
37 left	(Richard Strauss, 99-36702.1)
37 center	(Richard Strauss, 99-36702.6)
37 right	(Richard Strauss, 99-36702.5)
38	National Park Service, Chaco Culture NHP Museum Collection & Archive, photographer Dabney Ford
40	(Richard Strauss, 96-2519)
41 top	Library of Congress
41 bottom	U.S. Military Academy Library
42 top	(99-36555) Collection of First Congregational Church of Whately, Massachusetts
42 bottom	The Connecticut Historical Society, Hartford, Connecticut
43 top	Copyright © The British Museum
43 bottom	(Terry McCrea, 99-36562)
45	(Rick Vargas, 96-2222-3)
46	(Richard Strauss, 97-1652)
47 top	(Richard Strauss, 97-1678)
47 bottom	(Richard Strauss, 97-1676)
49	(Richard Strauss, 99-339)
50	(Dane Penland, 83-9981)
51	(Dane Penland, 83-9971)
53	(Richard Strauss, 2001-13211-1)
54	*Daniel Boardman*, by Ralph Earl, Gift of Mrs. W. Murray Crane, photograph © 2002 Board of Trustees, National Gallery of Art, Washington, D.C., 1789
55	Albany Institute of History and Art
56	(98-3024)
57	Collection of The New-York Historical Society, acc.1907.32
58	(98-3065)
59	Old Sturbridge Village photograph by Henry E. Peach
61	(95-465) Collection of the National Postal Museum, Smithsonian Institution

Mechanizing Time

68	(98-151)
69	(Dane Penland, 90-14476)
70	(98-2420) Collection of National Museum of Natural History, Smithsonian Institution
71 right	George Eastman House
71 left	Smithsonian Institution Libraries
72	Hagley Museum and Library
73 top	(Harold Dorwin, 2001-9119)
73 bottom	(Harold Dorwin, 2001-9120)
76 left	Library of Congress, Historic American Buildings Survey, photograph by Alex Bush, 1934
76 right	The Museum of the Confederacy
77	Abby Aldrich Rockefeller Folk Art Museum, Williamsburg, Virginia

78	Schlesinger Library, Radcliffe College, photograph by W. F. Lengenheim
79	(97-4634) Smithsonian Institution Libraries
80 left	(Hugh Talman, 99-36617)
80 right	(99-36605)
81 left	(99-36594)
81 top right	Hampton University Archives
81 bottom right	National Anthropological Archives, Smithsonian Institution, photograph by Allen & Rowell (54544-B)
83	(99-36723) Collection of Kristina Johnson
84	Collection of the Mattatuck Museum, Waterbury, Connecticut
85	American Clock & Watch Museum
86	(Dane Penland, 83-9972)
87 bottom	(Dane Penland, 83-9979)
87 top	Enoch Pratt Free Library
88 top	(Dane Penland, 83-9982)
88 bottom	(Dane Penland, 83-9973)
89 left	(98-4718)
89 right	The Valentine Museum/Richmond History Center
90	Deborah F. Cooney
92 left	Deborah F. Cooney
92 right	National Archives and Records Administration
93 left	The American Museum in Britain
93 center	(Hugh Talman, 99-36504)
93 top right	(Richard Strauss, 99-36453)
93 bottom right	(Richard Strauss, 99-36459)
94 top	(Dane Penland, 82-3763)
94 bottom	(74-4796) Collection of Massachusetts Charitable Mechanic Association
95 top left	(Richard Strauss, 94-5318)
95 bottom left	(Richard Strauss, 96-2466)
95 right	(98-4787)
96	(98-41007) Warshaw Collection, Archives Center, National Museum of American History
97	(93-2780) Smithsonian Institution Libraries
98	George Eastman House
99	(Richard Strauss, 99-36662)
101	Collection of Historical Scientific Instruments, Harvard University
104 left	(10611)
104 center	Smithsonian Institution Libraries
104 right	Smithsonian Institution Libraries

Synchronizing Time

110	Library of Congress
111 left	(Dane Penland, 83-9986)
111 right	(99-36570)
112	Smithsonian Institution Libraries
113	Association of American Railroads
114 and 115 right	William Frederick Allen Papers, Rare Books and Manuscripts Division, The New York Public Library, Astor, Lenox and Tilden Foundations
117 top left	Smithsonian Institution Libraries
117 bottom left	National Maritime Museum
120	National Archives and Records Administration
121 top left	Canadian Pacific Railway Archives, image NS5573
121 bottom left	(Rick Vargas, 91-2029)
121 right	Division of Rare and Manuscript Collections, Cornell University Library, from *Uniform Non-Local Time (Terrestrial Time); a memoir by Sir Sandford Fleming*, History of Science QB43.A16 no. 18
123	(2001-4268) Princeton Poster Collection, Archives Center, National Museum of American History
124	(98-41031)
125	Library of Congress
126 left	(99-2346) DeVincent Collection, Archives Center, National Museum of American History
126 right	(Hugh Talman, 97-9009)
127	(98-4132) Warshaw Collection, Archives Center, National Museum of American History
128 left	(Hugh Talman, 97-9011)
128 right	(Hugh Talman, 97-9021)
130	(Hugh Talman, 99-36512)
131 left	(Richard Strauss, 99-36653)
131 right	(Richard Strauss, 99-36654)
132	Shelly Foote
133	(Richard Strauss, 99-36713)
134	National Archives and Records Administration
135 top left	National Archives and Records Administration
135 bottom left	(Richard Strauss, 99-36670)
135 right	(Hugh Talman, 99-36465)
136 top	(Hugh Talman, 99-36467)
136 bottom	(Hugh Talman, 99-36475)
137 left	(Terry McCrea, 99-36680)
137 right	(Richard Strauss, 96-2458)
138 left	(Richard Strauss, 99-36645)
138 right	(Richard Strauss, 99-36646)
139	Library of Congress
140	*Rush Hour, New York*, by Max Weber, Gift of the Avalon Foundation, photograph © 2002 Board of Trustees, National Gallery of Art, Washington, D.C., 1915
141	AIP Emilio Segrè Visual Archives
147	State Historical Society of Wisconsin, Neg. No. WHi(K91)356

148	Schenectady Museum Archives
152	Quigley Photographic Archives, Special Collections Division, Georgetown University

Saving Time

158	Purdue University Libraries Special Collections and Archives: Frank and Lillian Gilbreth Collection
160	Library of Congress
161 top	(Richard Strauss, 99-36541)
161 bottom	(Richard Strauss, 99-36542)
162 left	(98-2481) Smithsonian Institution Libraries
162 right	(98-2480) Smithsonian Institution Libraries
163 top	Maryland Historical Society, Baltimore, Maryland
163 bottom	(Hugh Talman, 99-36544) Collection of National Clock & Watch Museum
164 left	(99-36573)
164 right	(98-4135)
165 left	(Richard Strauss, 99-36710)
165 center	(Dane Penland, 83-9977)
165 right	(Richard Strauss, 99-36709)
168 left	Western Reserve Historical Society
168 right	(98-2418) Smithsonian Institution Libraries
169 left	(Richard Strauss, 98-5238)
169 right	(98-3828) from Ralph Barnes, *Motion and Time Study: Design and Measurement of Work,* 4th ed. (New York: John Wiley and Sons, Inc., 1961).
170	(99-36598)
171	(99-36580) Princeton Poster Collection, Archives Center, National Museum of American History
172	Library of Congress
173	SuperStock, Inc.
174 left	Purdue University Libraries Special Collections and Archives: Frank and Lillian Gilbreth Collection
176	(89-1270)
177 left	(97-3500)
177 right	(97-3541)
178 left	Purdue University Libraries Special Collections and Archives: Frank and Lillian Gilbreth Collection
178 right	(85-133)
179, 181 top and bottom	Purdue University Libraries Special Collections and Archives: Frank and Lillian Gilbreth Collection
182 left and right	Archives and Special Collections, University of Connecticut, Storrs

183	Gjon Mili/ Life Magazine © Time Inc.
184 left	(Richard Strauss, 99-36621)
184 right	Culver Pictures, Inc.

Expanding Time

189 top	(2001-10162) Illustration © Ernie Hergenroeder
190	NASA
191	(Rick Vargas, 96-2501-4)
192 left	(owl, 99-36585; rooster 99-36586) Courtesy of 7-Eleven®, Inc.
192 right	Mark Peterson/Saba
193	(John Wooten, 77-14756)
195 top	Peter Arnett
195 bottom	Bancroft Library, University of California, Berkeley
197	Library of Congress, Prints and Photographs Division, Look Magazine Collection, LC-L9-66-2990-V, frame 31
198	(99-1591) Smithsonian Institution Libraries
200	(99-36657) Smithsonian Institution Libraries
201 top left	(Hugh Talman, 99-36690)
201 bottom left	(99-36724)
201 right	(99-36725)
203	By permission of Dave Coverly and Creators Syndicate, Inc.
204	(99-501) Smithsonian Institution Libraries
207	Property of AT&T Archives. Reprinted with permission.
208	National Institute of Standards and Technology
210	Department of Defense, Defense Visual Information Center; photograph by SPC Gerald James, 55th Signal Company
211 left	(Harold Dorwin)
211 right	U.S. Naval Historical Center
212	*Popular Mechanics,* December 1968
213	Illustrations by Ray Pioch
214 left	(Eric Long, 96-1972-6)
214 right	(Eric Long, 96-1977)
215 top	(98-4540)
215 bottom	Centre Suisse d'Electronique et de Microtechnique
216 left	(Eric Long, 96-1971-6)
216 right	(Eric Long)
217	"Curv Your Dog by Scott Bookner"
219 left	The Swatch Group, Ltd.
219 right	(73-7565)

index

Numbers in *italics* refer to pages on which illustrations appear.

Abbe, Cleveland, 113
Abell, Mrs. L. G., 79
Académie Royale des Sciences, 30
acorn shelf clock, *88*
aerial photographer wearing wristwatch (c. 1918), *134*
African-Americans
    clockmakers, 19-20, 28
    and drums, 42, *43*
    enslaved, 12, 28, 41, 43, 53, 76-77
    photograph of couple, *90*
    slave drivers, *76*
    timetable of school for, *81*
agricultural society. *See* preindustrial society
"Alarm Clock Blues," 126
    sheet music, *126*
alarm clocks, 125, 126-128, *126, 127, 128*
    electric, *128,* 128
Alexander, A. J., 68
Alger, Horatio, 135
Allan, James, and Company, 111
Allegheny Observatory, *104,* 104
Allen, Frederick Lewis, 142
Allen, William Frederick, 109, *113,* 113-114
almanac, 18, 19-21, *27, 28,* 28, 29, 199, 209
    Banneker's, 19-21, *20*
    British *Nautical,* 120
    and Christian calendar, 40
    Elgin, *97*
    German-language, *25*
    Poor Richard's, 35, *41*
    Poor Robin's, 23
American Association for the Advancement of
    Science, 112
American Federation of Labor, 161
American Frugal Housewife, The (Childs), 77
American Heart Association, 182
American Metrological Society, 112
American Revolution. *See* War of Independence
American Society of Civil Engineers, 112
American Stage Coach (Storer painting), *59*
American Watch Company (Waltham,
    Massachusetts), 52, 94-96, 135, 136
    chronodrometer (horse-timing watch) made by,
        68, *69,* 166
    presentation watches made by, *95, 137*
    See also Waltham watches
Anasazi Indians, 38
Andrews, Rev. Lorrin, 83
Anheuser-Busch brewery time clock, *165*
Annual of Scientific Discovery, 91
Ansonia Clock Company, 89, 127
Appleton's Railway and Steam Navigation Guide, 111

"Arbitration is the True Balance of Power" (*Puck*
    cartoon), *160*
Armitage, F. S., 151
Arnett, Peter, *195*
Around the World in Eighty Days (Verne), 120
Arthur, Chester A., 113
artificial light, 28, 74-75, 141, 148-149, 191, 194.
    See also nighttime
Arnold, John, 32
Arnold & Dent (London), 33
astrology, 20, 23
astronomy, 19, 20
    astronomical clocks, 36, *111*
    astronomical observatories, *104,* 104, 206; private,
        decline of, 116
    and "clock stars," 29
    and longitude, 32
    physics takes over from, 206
asylums, 82
ATM machines, 194-195
atomic clocks, 207-210, *208*
Aurora Watch Company, 135
automatons, clockwork, *37, 193,* 193
automobile, the, 141-144
Ayres, Waldemar, 181

Baker City Tavern (New York City), 57
balance-wheel escapement, 127
Baltimore & Ohio (B&O) Railroad, 10-11
Baltimore Gas & Electric, workers at, *161*
banjo clocks, 49, *50,* 77, 127
Banneker, Benjamin, 19-20, 21, 30
Barnes, Ralph, 169
Barraud & Lund (London), 99
Barth, Carl, 168
Beard, Dr. George M., 125
Beecher, Catharine, *78,* 78
Beecher, Lyman, 78
Bell, Alexander Graham, 96, 139, 146
    and Bell Telephone Company, 144
Bell, Chichester, 146
Bell Telephone Laboratories, 206-207
bells
    church and mission, *41,* 41-42
    community, 44-45
    factory, 72, 73-74, 162
    prison and asylum, 82
    plantation, 76, *76*
    school, 80
Benedictine Order, 41
Benrus watches, 135
Bergey, John, 215
Berliner, Emile, 146
Bernard Rice's Sons, 184
Berthoud, Ferdinand, 32, 34
Berthoud Frères, 219
Bhopal disaster, 194

Bigger, Gilbert, 52
Black Ball Company (packet line), 58
Blanckley, Thomas Riley, 31
Bleyer, Dr. J. Mount, 146
blue laws, 40-41, 43, 195, 196-197
Bly, Nellie, 133
Boardman, Daniel, portrait of, *54*
Boer War, 134
Bond, William Cranch, 34, 52
Bond, William & Sons, 99
Bono, Sonny, 216
Boston & Providence Railroad, time rules, *101*
Boston City Council, 119
Bourke, John Gregory, 41
Boyle, Charles, earl of Orrery, 35
"Boy with watch" (Shute painting), *93*
Bradley, Abraham, 59-60
Brady, Matthew, 92
Brasier, A., 52
brass-movement clocks, 47, 49-50, 88-89, 127
Braunfeld v. Braun, 197
"Breakfast time," *124*
Britain
    adopts Gregorian calendar, 40, 41
    clock- and watchmaking in, 28, 32, 34, 35, 133;
        British soldier's watch, *53;* exports, 46, 47, 51-
        52, 92; lantern clock, *46;*
    geodetic surveys by, 30
    Nautical Almanac, 120
    packet service to U.S., 58
    post coach service in, 60
    warships run aground (1707), 32
brooch watches, 91, *93,* 133
Brooklyn Borough Gas Company, 180
Brown University, 175
Bryan, C. W., 198
Bundy, Willard, and Bundy time clocks, 162-163
Bureau International des Poids et
    Mesures (BIPM), 210
Bureau of Labor Statistics, U.S., 192
Bush Terminal (New York City), *162*
button promoting eight-hour day, *161*

Cadmus, Philip, 137
calendar, 20, 21
    calendar-based rituals, 39-41
    day planners, 199-200, *201, 202*
    desk, advertisement for, *200*
    French revolutionary, 219
    hand-drawn, 200, *201*
    Gregorian replaces Julian, 40, *41*
    patent specification for, *198*
    See also almanac
Callaghan, Jane, 157, 158
Calvinism, 44, 62
Camden & Amboy Railroad, 113
    train wreck, 99

Campbell, Charles, 36
Canadian Institute time zone committee, 112
Canadian Pacific Railway, 121
Catholic Church, 41, 43, 83
Centennial Exposition (1876, Philadelphia), 68, 96
Chan, Shee Wong and grandchildren reading
    Sunday funnies, *195*
Chandlee, Goldsmith, 25
Chandler, Alfred, 102
Charleston & Hamburg Rail Road, 100, 102
Chase, Amanda Matthews, 125
chatelaine watch set, *130*
Cheaper by the Dozen (Gilbreth), 178
Cheney, Benjamin and Timothy, 49-50
Cheney, Orin, 168
Chernobyl meltdown, 194
Cheshire & Monadnock Railroad broadside, *115*
Cheshire Watch Company, 135
Chicago world's fairs (1893-94, 1933), 149, 181
child care center (Toyota factory), *192*
children
    time discipline taught to, 80
    time management for, 189; book cover
        illustration, *189*
    watches for, 52, 53, 135, 139
    painting of "boy with watch," *93*
Childs, Lydia Maria, 77
Christianity, 39-41, 43-44
chronodrometer (horse-timing watch), 68, *69,* 166
chronograph, *104,* 166
chronometers, 32, *33,* 34
    rated, 117
church and mission bells, *41,* 41-42
Cincinnati *Commercial Gazette,* 119
circadian rhythms, 192-193
Civil War, U.S., 95, 96
Clapp, Horace, 119
Claudy, C. H., 149
clock
    in American culture, 11-14, 25, 44, 47-51, 73
    atomic, 207-210, *208*
    brass-movement, 47, 49-50, 88-89, 127
    and clockwork as metaphor, 34-36, 41, 103
    cost of, 44, 47, 49-50, 86, 87, 88-89, 127-128
    as domestic furnishing, 14, 47, 48, 85, *89,* 89
        (*see also* shelf [or half] clock)
    in European Scientific Revolution, 13
    factory, *see* factories
    free-pendulum, 205-206
    imported, *46,* 47, 49, 51
    lantern, *46,* 47
    mantel, *89*
    mechanical, invention of, 13, 20, 36, 122, 126
    musical, *37*

one-handed, *46, 47,* 47
origin of word, 44
pillar-and-scroll, 86, *87*
quartz, 206-207, *207,* 212
railroad, 99-100, 102, 103
shelf, *see* shelf (or half) clock
with springs, *88,* 89
as status symbol, 44, 47-51
striking, 86, 127
as symbol of time control, 14
tall case, *see* tall case clock
wooden, 47, 49-50, *85,* 85-87, 88, 127
See also Connecticut clocks and clockmakers;
    Pennsylvania clocks
clock dials, 11, *37*
digital v. analog, 216-218
factory clock, *73*
learning to read, 80; lesson card for, *80*
with moon phases, *28, 28, 36*
tower clock, *10*
white-painted, 28
*Clockmaker, The: or the Sayings and Doings of Samuel
    Slick, of Slicksville* (Haliburton), illustration
    from, *87*
clockmaking in America, 27, 48-51
by African-Americans, 19-20, 28
factory workers, *84*
geographical distribution of, 48
innovations in, 89 (*see also* interchangeable parts;
    mass production)
clock sales
by peddlers, 87-88, 95
showroom (1840 advertisement), *89*
"clock stars," 29
clock towers. *See* towers and tower clocks and bells
clockwork as metaphor, 34-36, 41, 103, 193
clockwork automatons, *37, 193,* 193
CNN (Cable News Network), 195
Cobden, Richard, 102
cocktail hour, the, *184,* 184
cocktail set, *184*
Colles, Christopher, 26
Columbian Exposition (1893-94), 149
Columbus Watch Company, 135
Comet Theater (New York), *152*
community life, 42, 44-45
Computing Scale Company, 164
conch shell, *42,* 76
Congress, U.S., 29, 122, 161
Connecticut clocks and clockmakers, *27,* 48, 50, *51,*
    85-89, 127
and watchmaking, 52
workers at clock factory, *84*
Continental Congress, 56
Cooper, D. M., 163
Corliss, George, 96
Covey, Steven, 202
Coyne, Kevin, 192
Crabtree, Willy, 215
Cummings, Frederick A., 119-120
curfew, 73
Curtis, Samuel, 94
Curtis, Capt. Thomas B., 34
Cuyler, Hannah Maley, portrait of, *55*
Cyrus, USS (1818), 34

Dana, Richard Henry, 83
Davidson, Elizabeth Grant, 81
Davis, Joseph H., drawing by, *77*
Davis, Sammy Jr., 216
day, length of, 27, 206
daylight saving time, 122
poster promoting, *123*
Day-Timer planner, 202
prototype for, *201*
decimal watch (early French), *219*
Defense Meteorological Satellite
    Program, 190
Democracy in America (Tocqueville), 83
Dennison, Aaron, 94
Depression
    1837, 88
    1857, Panic of, 95
    1930s, 161, 181
desk, Gilbreth Management, *178, 181,* 181
digital watches, *213, 214,* 214-219, *216, 217*
v. analog, 216-218
District of Columbia surveyed, 30
Dixon, Jeremiah, and Mason-Dixon line, 30
"dollar" watch, *135,* 135
Dorney Printing Company, 202
Dow, Jesse, 60
Dow Chemical Company, 170
Dowd, Charles F., *112*
Drinker family (Philadelphia), 53
drums as time signals, *42, 42,* 43
Duryea brothers, 142
Dwight, Timothy, 50

Earl, Ralph, 54
Earnshaw, Thomas, 32
Easter in church calendar, 40
Edison, Thomas, 142, 146, 148, 150
Edison phonograph, *147*
Edwards, Jonathan, 50
efficient use of time. *See* time control
    ("scientific management")
E. Howard and Company. *See* Howard, Edward
eight-hour day, watch fob and button promoting,
    161. See also work hours
E. Ingraham and Company, 89, 135
Einstein, Albert, 109, *141,* 141
electricity, 141, 148-149, 191, 194-195
electric alarm clock, *128,* 128
Franklin's experiments, 35
Electro-Data company, 215
Elgin National Watch Company, 96, 133, 135, 139
advertisement by, *139*
Almanac published by (1871), *97*
Elizabeth I, queen of England, 129
Ellery, William, 95
Elliott, Major Andrew, 30
Ellicott, George, 19
Ellicott, Joseph, 35, 36, *37*
Emerson, Ralph Waldo, 29, 91
English, L. I., 81
Enlightenment, the, 35, 36, 73
E. N. Welch Manufacturing Company, 89
Equation of Time, The, *26, 27,* 27
"Everybody Hustle" (office sign), *172*

factories, *71*
bells of, 72, 73-74, 162
clockmaking, 85-86
clockmaking, workers at, *84*
clocks in, *73,* 73-74 (*see also* time clocks, factory)
mill timetable, 72
as symbol of new industrial order, 159
watchmaking, 94-96, *95*
Farmer's Almanac, 66
Farmers' Monthly Visitor (periodical), 61
fashion items. *See* watch; wristwatch
"Father Time," 66, 96
Featherstonhaugh, George, 85
Feiss Company, Joseph, time study, *168*
Female Seminary (D.C.), 81
Fier, Neuman, 126
Filofax, 200
F. Kroeber Clock Company, 127
Fleming, Sir Sandford, *121,* 121
"Foolish Carriage" (Gilbreth family automobile),
    178
Ford, Gerald and Betty, 216
Ford, Henry, 142
Ford Motor Company, 159
Forestville Manufacturing Company, 88
Fort Bell (New York City, 1733), 45
France
    decimal watch from, *219*
    geodetic surveys by, 30
    marine timekeepers of, 32, 34
    wristwatches as fashion in, 133
Franciscan Order, 41
Frankfurter, Felix, 197
Franklin, Benjamin, 35, 41, 56, 62
Frederick, Christine, 180
Frederick, Maryland, tower clock of, 44, *45*
free-pendulum clocks, 205-206
French Revolution, 219
Frisius, Gemma, 32

Galaup, Jean-François de, 34
Gallagher v. Crown Kosher Super Market, 197
General Electric Company, 128, 207
General Time Convention (St. Louis, 1883),
    113-114
geodetic surveys, 30
Geography (Morse), 60
Georgia Institute of Technology, 169
German Admiralty (1880s), 134
German Reform Church (Frederick, Maryland),
    clock movement, 44
Gilbert, William L., Clock Company, 89, 128
Gilbreth, Frank, 175-178, 179, 200
Gilbreth, Lilian, 157, 175-178, 179-183
Gilbreth Management Desk, *178, 181,* 181
"Global City Lights," *190*
gnomon, 27
Goddard, Luther, Daniel, and Parley, 27, 52
Gold and Stock Telegraph Company, 111
Good Housekeeping magazine, 217
GPS satellites, 209
    GPS receivers, *210,* 218
graphophone and gramophone, 146
Greenleaf, Stephen, 25
Greenwich (England) as prime meridian, 114,

120-121
Gregory XIII (pope), and Gregorian calendar, 40
Griffith, D. W., 151
Guest, Edgar, 129
Guy, Francis, 57

Halberg, Franz, 193
half-dollar bill, Franklin's design for, *56*
Haliburton, Thomas, 87
Hall, Basil, 76
Hall, J. G., 92
Hall, Joseph, 46
Hamilton Watch Company, 96, 135, 136, 214-216
    Pulsar wristwatch, *214,* 214-216, *216*
Hampden Watch Company, 96, 135
Hampton Normal and Agricultural Institute
    (Virginia), 81
Hanks, Benjamin and Truman, 73
"happiness minutes." *See* home management
"happy hour," 184
Harland, Thomas, 52
Harper's New Monthly Magazine, illustrations from,
    71, 104
Harper's Weekly, 141
Harrison, John, 32, 34
Harvard University, 35
Hawaiian Tract Society, 83
Hawthorne, Nathaniel, 66
Haymarket Riot (Chicago, 1886), 160
Healey Picture Completion Test, *124*
Hicks, Edward, 22
Hill, Peter, 28
Hine, Lewis, 135
Hitz, John, 139
Hoadley, Silas, 84, 85
Hodgson, Adam, 24
holidays, 83. *See also* leisure time; Sabbath
    observance
Hollerith punch card machines, 164
Holmes, Judge Oliver Wendell, 119
Holy Name parish (Washington, D.C.), office of, *172*
Holyoke Mills, timetable of, *72*
Home-Maker and Her Job, The (Gilbreth), 177
home management, 77-78, 79, 175-184
    for the disabled, *182,* 182
    "happiness minutes," *174,* 175, 183
    "how to make a bed," *183*
    kitchen floor plans, *179, 181*
    management desk, *178, 181,* 181
    and "therbligs," *177*
Hope-Jones, F., 205
Hopper, Admiral Grace, *211*
Horatio Allen's Novelty Works (New York), work
    schedule of, 73
horns as time signals, 42, 76-77
Horological Journal, 134, 204
horse-training watch
    (chronodrometer), 68, *69,* 166
hourglass. *See* sandglass
Household Engineering (Frederick), 180
housework. *See* home management
Howard, Edward, 94, 96
    E. Howard and Company, 10, 93, 111, 135,
    136, 139
    Howard & Davis, 94

Howard, Davis & Dennison, 94
"How to make a bed," *183*
Hughes, Thomas, 167
Hussein I, king of Jordan, 216

IBM (International Business Machines), 159, 164,
        165, 178, 181
idleness as disgrace. *See* work ethic
Illinois Watch Company, 96, 135
Industrial Revolution, American, 13, 51, 70, 73,
        77, 85
Ingersoll Watch Company, 133, 135
Ingraham, E., and Company, 89, 135
intelligence test, *124*
interchangeable parts, 85-86, 88, 94, 133, 135
International Association of Machinists, 161
International Geographical Congress (1871), 120
International Meridian Conference (1884), *120*, 121
International Time Recording
        Company (ITRC), 159, 164, 165. *See also*
        IBM (International Business Machines)
Internet, the, 195, 210, 219, 220
        "Internet time," *219*, 219, 220
Interstate Commerce Commission, 167
Iran, Shah of, 216
Ives, Joseph, 89

James Allan and Company, 111
James Bond film, 216
James Monroe (merchantman), 58
Japanese quartz watches, 214, *215*
Jefferson, Thomas, 11, 35, 47-48, 53
Jefferson Junior High School
        (Washington, D.C.), wall clock from, *80*
Jefferts, Steve, *208*
Jerome Brothers (Chauncey and Noble), 88-89
jeweled watches, 96, 135, *135*
Jewish calendar, 40, 41
Jews and the Sabbath, 196, 197
Johnson, Betty Jane, 157, 158
Johnson, Prince (former slave), 76
Joseph Feiss Company time study, *168*

Keith, William, 52
Keller, Helen, pocket watch presented to, *138,* 139
Kendal, Thomas, 43
Kendall, Larcum, 32
Kid's Guide to Managing Time, A (Wilt), 189
        cover illustration, *189*
Kinetoscope, 150
Kissinger, Henry, 199
kitchen design, *178, 179,* 180-182, *181, 182*
        "the Kitchen Practical," *174, 180,* 180-181
Knickerbocker Watch Company, 135
Kreuger, Edgar and Jennie, 1905 photograph of, *147*
Kroeber, F., Clock Company, 127

labor. *See* factories; plantation
        life; strikes; work ethic; work hours
Ladies' Home Journal, 139, 180
Lancaster Watch Company, 135
Landes, David, 214
Langley, Samuel P., 103, *104,* 104
lantern clock, *46,* 47
Larcom, Lucy, 80

latitude and longitude, 32-34
Lawyer's Day calendar, *201,* 202
Lazar, W. H., 76
LCD (liquid crystal display) watches, 216, 217
Leavit, Jacob, 25
Lecomte (racehorse), 67
LED (light-emitting diode) watches, 214, 215, 216,
        217
Lefax, Inc., 200
leisure time, 41, 75, 157
        the automobile and, 143-144
        the cocktail hour, *184,* 184
        time management and, 183
LeRoy, Pierre, 32
Leslie, Robert, 48
letter and envelope (1797), *61*
Lexington (racehorse), 67-68, *68, 70*
Liebenroth, Von Auw & Company, 200
Life magazine, 183
Life of an American Fireman (film), 151
Lindsay family calendar, *201*
Live and Let Die (film), 216
Logan, James, 35
Lonely Villa, The (film), 151
longitude, determination of, 32, 34
Los Angeles Coliseum, night rodeo at (1927), *148*
Low, Nathanael, 18
Lynd, Robert and Helen, 143, 144

Macaroni, the (London dandies), 53
McCay, James T., 203
McCormick Harvesting Machine Company, 159,
        160
McGowan v. Maryland, 196
Mackay, C., 52
Mackenzie, Alec, 203
McLean, John, 61
Maine, State of, and standard time, 119-120
Management of Time, The (McCay), 203
Manhattan Watch Company, 135
mantel clock. *See* shelf (or half) clock
Marrison, Warren, 206-207, 212
Marsh, Oliver B. and David, 94
Mason, Charles, and Mason-Dixon line, 30
Massachusetts clocks, 48, 49. *See also* Waltham
        watches
Massachusetts Superior Court, 119
mass production
        of clocks, 49, 70, 85-89, 127, 128
        of watches, 68, 70, 91, 94-96, 133, 135
mean time, 27, 120
Mechanics Bell (New York City), 74
Meekhof, Dawn, *208*
Melbin, Murray, 191
meridians, 29, 30, 32
        Greenwich as prime meridian, 120-121
        meridian markers, 25
*Middletown: A Study in Contemporary
        American Culture* (Lynd and Lynd), 143
Midvale Steel Company, 167
minute, concept of, 47
MIT (Massachusetts Institute of Technology)
        Media Lab, 220
Model Kitchen is Remodeled, The (New York Herald-
        Tribune Institute), 178

plans from, *179*
Monroe, Marilyn, 188
moon, phases of. *See* clock dials
Moore, Roger, 216
Morgan, Garrett, 143
Morse, Jedediah, 60
Moss, Brittney, *192*
motion and time studies. *See* time control
        ("scientific management")
Motion and Time Study (Barnes), 169
Motion and Time Study Laboratory
        (University of Connecticut), 157, 158
Motor World magazine, 142
Mount Royal station, Baltimore, *10,* 11
movies, the, 149-152
        of time and motion studies, 176
Mudge, Thomas, 32
Mumford, Lewis, 13, 108
Mundel, Marvin, 183
musical clocks, *37*

nanosecond, representation of, *211*
NASA (National Aeronautics and Space
        Administration), 209, 215
National Institute for Standards and Technology,
        208, 210
National Museum of American History
        (Smithsonian Institution), 11, 13, 70
Native Americans, 38, 39
        students at Hampton Institute, *81*
Naval Expositor, A (Blanckley), 31
Naval Observatory, U.S., 116, 119, 209, 210
        time-signal room in (late 1800s), *117*
Navy, U.S., 34
Negroponte, Nicholas, 220
neon sign, *191*
New England Butt, 177
New Haven Clock Company, 89, 128
New Haven Watch Company, 135
New Housekeeping, The (Frederick), 180
Newport, Rhode Island, public bells, 45
Newsweek magazine, 196
Newton, Sir Isaac, *35*
        and Newtonian philosophy, 35, 36, 73, 109, 141,
        148
New York and New Jersey Telephone Company,
        144-145
New York Herald-Tribune Institute, 178, 179, 181
New York Standard Watch Company, 135
New York Times, 99, 199, 217
New York Tribune, 109
Night as Frontier (Melbin), 191
nighttime, 28, 29
        and artificial light, 74-75, 148-149, 191, 194
        "Global City Lights," *190*
        night rodeo (1927), *148*
        night workers, 191-194
        "24/7" mentality, 12, 41, 191-197
Nixon, Richard, 216
Nye, David, 194

octant, use of, *33*
O'Farrell, Dr. G. D., 95
"Ogee" clock case, *88,* 88
Omega watches, 133, 134

omer, *40*
On Time (Smithsonian exhibition), 11, 13
Opticks (Newton), 35
Oriani, Thomas, 137
orrery, 35-36, *37*
Osgood, Samuel, 59

packets (ships), 58
        notice of arrival, *58*
Panic of 1857, 95
Parker, John Clinton, 200
Parker Clock Company, 127
Parry, John J., 52
Passover, 40
Past and Present (historical journal), 13
Pathfinder ("dollar" watch), *135*
Patrick, Gil, 67
peddlers, 87-88, 95
Peep O'Day alarm clock, 127
        advertising card for, *127*
Pennsylvania clocks, 35-36, *36, 47,* 48
Pennsylvania Railroad, 103, 104, 136
Peoria Watch Company, 135, 136
"Perfect Clock, The," advertisement for, *204*
Perkin, Morris, 200, 202
        hand-drawn calendar made by, *201*
Persian Gulf War, 195
Peyton, General and Mrs., 89
Philadelphia Centennial Exposition
        (1876), 68, 96
"Philadelphia Standard Time," 111
Philosophiae Naturalis Principia Mathematica
        (Newton), 35
Phonogram, The (periodical), 146
phonograph, the, 146
        Edison's (1905 photograph), *147*
photography in motion and time studies, 176, *177.*
        See also movies
pillar-and-scroll clock, 86, *87*
Plains Indians, 39
plantation life, *76,* 76-77. *See also*
        African-Americans
pocket watch, 129-130, 134-139, *135, 136, 137*
        advertisements for, *125,* 125
        Helen Keller's, *138*
        railroad, *136,* 136
        and watch pocket, 52, 53, 91, 130
        See also watch chains and fobs
Polaris (star), 32, 33
Poor Richard's Almanac, 35, *41*
Poor Robin's Almanac, 23
Pope, Joseph, 35
Porter, Edward and Levi, 85-86
Porter, Edwin S., 151
Post Office, U.S., and postal service, 57, 59-61, 83,
        100
        letter and envelope (1797), *61*
Post Office Act (1792), 59
post roads, 59, 60
Potts, William, 143
Pratt, Daniel Jr., 89
preindustrial society, 13, 14, 19-21, 23-36
        agricultural, 23-24, 48, 70, 76, 78, 118, 122;
        depicted, *22*
        See also plantation life

presidential election returns, 145
Primer for Foreign Speaking Women (Chase), 125
Princeton University, 35
prison life, 82
productivity. *See* work ethic
Prohibition and repeal, 184
Protestant Ethic and the Spirit of Capitalism, The (Weber), 43
Protestantism, 39, 43-44, 78, 83
Providence & Worcester Railroad train wreck, *98, 99, 101*
Puck cartoon (1886), *160*
Pueblo people, 39, 42
Pulsar watch, *214,* 214-216, *216*
punctuality
  of early U.S. postal service, 59-61; railroads and, 100
  emphasis on, 14, 80, 104, 125-126, 128, 152, 161-162
  school certificate of (1844), *81*
  as term, 61-62
Purdue University, 178, 183
Puritans, the, 40-41, 43-44, 50, 62, 80, 195

quartz clocks, 206-207, *207,* 212
quartz wristwatches, 212-217, *213, 214, 215, 216*

racehorse (Lexington), 67-68, *68, 70*
railroads, U.S., *70,* 167
  clocks and watches of, *10,* 10, 98, *99,* 99-102, 103, 111, *136;* pocket watches and standards for, 136
  first interregional, 102
  Standard Railway Time, 109, 114, 115, 116, 119; Allen's plan for, *114*
  time service used by, 104
  timetables of, 99-100, *101,* 102, 109, 113, 218
  and time zones, 12, 102-103, 104, 109, 111, 112-114, 116, 118-119, 141; announcements of, *115*
  train wrecks, *98, 99,* 101, 102
Railway Age magazine, 112
Railway Association of America, 112
Ramsey, Mrs., wearing watch (Brady photograph, c. 1865), *92*
RCA (Radio Corporation of America), 215
Reader, Mr. and Mrs. Foster M., 184
religious rituals, 38, 39-42
Remington Typewriter Company, 176
  slogan, 156
Residence of David Twining, 1787, The (Hicks painting), *22*
Rittenhouse, David, 35
Robbins, Royal, 95
Robinson, Harriet Hanson, 74
Rockford (Illinois) Watch Company, 93, 135
Rogers, Admiral John, 119
Rogers, John (machinist), 73
Roosevelt, Franklin D., 122, 161
Royal Society (Britain), 30
Rush Hour, New York (Weber painting), *140*

Sabbath observance, 40-41, 43, 83, 144, 160
  Sunday shopping, 195-197, *197*
Sabbath Whaling: or Is It Right to Take Whales on the

Sabbath? (Andrews), *83*
sandglass, *30,* 30, *31,* 32
  as gravestone motif, *43*
  watch supplanting, 66
school clocks and schedules, *80,* 80, *81*
Scientific American magazine, 149
"scientific management." *See* time control
Scientific Revolution (Europe), 13
Sears, Roebuck and Company, 128
seasonal time, 23-24, 42
second, definition of length of, 208
Seiko (Japan), 215
Self-Winding Clock Company (Brooklyn, New York), 116
Seth Thomas Clock Company, 89, 127, 135
7-Eleven signs, *192*
Seventh-Day Adventists, 196
shelf (or half) clock, 49, *71, 88, 89,* 127
  by Eli Terry, *27,* 86, *86, 87*
Shippen, Nancy, 53
ships' arrivals, notice of, *58*
Sholes and Glidden typewriter, 96
Shop Management (Taylor), 167, 168
Shortt, William, 205
Shute, Ruth Whittier and Samuel Addison, 93
Signal Corps, U.S., 134
Simultaneous Motion Chart (simochart), 176
Skillful Housewife's Complete Guide to Domestic Cookery, Taste, and Economy, A (Abell), frontispiece, *79*
slavery. *See* African-Americans
sleep and sleep deprivation, 192-194. *See also* nighttime
"Slick, Samuel" (fictional clock peddler), *87,* 88
Smith, John, 53
Smithsonian Institution, 104
  National Museum of American History, 11, 13, 70
Society of Friends, 53
Southern Railway Time Convention, 113, 114
space age. *See* technology
speed limits, 142-143
Springfield (Massachusetts) Armory, 94
springs, clocks with, *88,* 89
Spruck, Peter, 48
Standard Railway Time, 109, 114, 115, 116, 119
  Allen's plan for, *114*
standard time. *See* time, standardization of
Standard Time Stamp Company, 163
Star Theater (film), 151
steam whistle, *164*
Steiger, Jimmy, 126
stem-winder watch, 92, *93*
Stipp, Augusta Frances, 137
stopwatch, 12, 68, *69*
  use of, in time control, 166-169, *168, 169;* pamphlet defending, *170*
Storer, T., 59
Stowe, Harriet Beecher, 78
Stretch, Peter, 47
strikes, 74, 160, 168, 169
striking clocks, 86, 127
Struggling Upward (Alger), 135
Suffolk Watch Company, 135
Sullivan, Don, 208

Sunday shopping. *See* Sabbath observance
sundials, *25, 26, 27, 56,* 122, 218
sun time, 24-27
  and rituals, *38*
  vs. standard and daylight saving time, 118, 119, 122
Supreme Court, U.S., 196-197
surveying, 29-30
Swatch (Swiss firm), 219-220
Swiss watches, 92, 96, *131,* 133, 134, *138,* 166, 219-220
  quartz, 214, *215*
  showing "Internet time," *219*
Synchronome Company, advertisement for, *204*

Tabulating Machine Company, 164
Tainter, Charles Sumner, 146
tall case clocks, *28,* 28, 35, *36, 47, 49, 51,* 51
  with wooden movements, 50, *85,* 85
Taylor, Rev. Edward, 32
Taylor, Frederick Winslow, and Taylorism, 157, 167-169, 175
Technics and Civilization (Mumford), 13, 108
technology, 10-11, 13
  Centennial display of, 96
  medieval, 44
  space-age, 209-210, *211,* 215, 216, 220
  and time consciousness, 109, 141-152
  and twenty-four-hour needs, 194-195
  watch, 51
  See also interchangeable parts; mass production
Telechron electric alarm clock, *128,* 128
telegraph, the
  invention of, 61
  railroads and, 100, 102
  time relayed by, 25, 104, 109, 110, 116; time ball in New York City, *117*
telephone, the, 96, 139, 144-145, 146
Temple Grove Ladies Seminary, 112
Ten Broeck, Richard, 67
"Ten-Hour Bell," 74
Terry, Eli, 27, 51, 85-86, 87, 88
Terry, Eli Jr. and Henry, 86
Terry, Samuel, 86, 87
Texas Instruments, 215, 216
textile workers, *71,* 74
"therbligs," 176, *177*
Thiess, George, 215
Thomas, Seth, 85, 86, 89, 135
Thompson, E. P., 13-14, 43-44
Thompson, Sanford, 169
Thoreau, Henry David, 103
Thornhill plantation bell, *76*
Three-Mile Island, 194
Tiananmen Square, 195
Tiffany & Company, 215
time
  colonizing, 191
  "Cosmic," watch dial showing, *121*
  daylight saving, 122; poster promoting, *123*
  deviation in length of day, 206
  efficient use of, *see* time control ("scientific management")
  as "fourth dimension," 109, 141
  "Internet," *219,* 219, 220
  learning to tell, 80

mariner's, 30-34
  as money, 57-62, 73, 77, 161
  North American regional, 12, 101, 102-103, *110,* 111, 112-114, 118-120
  seasonal, 23-24, 42
  standard, *see* time, standardization of
  star, 29-30, 104
  sun, 24-27; v. standard and daylight saving, 118, 119, 122
  world, standardized, 120-121, *121*
time, standardization of
  importance of, 122
  North American: Gregorian calendar, 40, *41;* opposition to, 118-120; railroad bulletin, *101;* time zones established, *see* time zones
  "Philadelphia Standard Time," 111
  Standard Railway Time, 109, 114, 115, 116, 119; Allen's plan for, *114*
  world, 120-121, *121*
time clocks, factory, 12, *159,* 161-164, *162, 163, 164, 165,* 199
time consciousness
  artificial lighting and, 148
  and digital v. analog dials, 217-218
  emergence of modern, 11-14, 24, 42, 85; railroad and telegraph and, 104
  the movies and, 149-150, 151
  standardization of time and, 122
  technology and, 109, 141, 152
  under slavery, 77
  watches as symbol of, 126
time control ("scientific management"), *159,* 161
  clock as symbol of, 14
  in home management, 175-184
  and leisure time, 183
  motion and time studies, *158, 168, 176, 177, 179;* by Gilbreths, 175-183; Taylor's system, 157, 167-169
  pamphlet illustrating workplace system of, *164*
  productivity urged, 12, 161, *171, 172, 173*
  and self-management: advice on, 203; day planners, 199-200, *201,* 202
  students learning, 169
  time management cartoon, *203*
  "24/7" mentality, 12, 41, 191-197
  use of stopwatch in, 166-169, *168, 169;* pamphlet defending, *170*
Time Machine, The (Wells), 141
Timers for Ordnance Symposium, 215
time service, 104, 116. *See also* telegraph, the
timetables
  mill, *72*
  railroad, 99-100, *101,* 102, 109, 218; monthly catalog, 113
  school, *81*
Time Trap, The (Mackenzie), 203
time zones,
  American, regional, 24, 102-103, *110,* 111
  American, standardized, 12, *101,* 103, 104, 109, 112-114, 116, 118-120, 152; Allen's plan, *114;* announcement of, *115*
  world, standardized, 120-121; Fleming's scheme for, *121*
Tocqueville, Alexis de, 83
Todd, Lt. James, 53
Tontine Coffee House, New York City, *57,* 57

Tornado alarm clock, *128,* 128
towers and tower clocks and bells, 10-11, 44-45
    Frederick, Maryland, 44, *45*
    Mount Royal station (Baltimore), *10,* 11
town clock, 11, 74
town criers, 42
Townsend, Christopher Jr., 26
Toyota child care center, *192*
traffic lights, 143
Transferring Eggs (time and motion study film), *158*
Travelers' Official Guide of the Railway and Steam
    Navigation Lines in the United States and
    Canada, The, 113, *115*
Travels Through the States of North America, and the
    Provinces of Upper and Lower Canada, 59
Treatise on Domestic Economy, A (Beecher), 78
Trenton Watch Company, 135
"24/7" mentality, 12, 41, 191-197
Two Guys v. McGinley, 196
Two Slave Drivers and a Backwoodsman with His
    Rifle (detail from etching), *76*
2001: A Space Odyssey (film), 215
Two Years Before the Mast (Dana), 83

Uncle Tom's Cabin (Stowe), 78
Uniform Time Act (1966), 122
United States
    -Britain packet service, 58
    clocks and watches in culture of, *see* clock; watch
    industrialization in, 75 (*see also* factories;
        Industrial Revolution, American)
    postal system, 57, 59-61
U.S. Watch Company, 135
Universal Self-Instructor, The (1883), 125
University of Connecticut School of Home
    Economics, 157, 158, 182
University of Pennsylvania, 35
Upson, Rensselaer, 87
UTC (Coordinated Universal Time), 210

Van Horne, Emma, *132*
Vermont Central Railroad, 99
Verne, Jules, 120, 133
Virginia Gazette, ship arrival notice in, *58*
Volta Bureau, 139

Wabash (Indiana) *Plain Dealer,* 148
wages, 73, 74
Wagnitz, Don, 170
Waldo, Leonard, 113
wall clocks, *79, 80*

Waltham watches, 68, 91, 92, *94,* 96, 133,
    135, 135, *137. See also* American Watch
    Company (Waltham, Massachusetts)
Walton, Richard, 215
War of 1812, 34, 52, 61
War of Independence, 52, 60-61, 87
    British watch taken in, *53*
Warren, Chief Justice Earl, 197
Warren, Henry E., and Warren Clock Company,
    128
Washington, George, 23, 61
Washington Post, 216
watch

in American culture, 11-14, 25, 47, 50, 51-53,
    66, 91; as essential tool, 11, 126
child's, 52, 53, 135, 139; painting of "boy with
    watch," *93*
cost of, 47, 52, 94-95, 135, 139, 215-216
dial showing "Cosmic Time," *121*
digital, *213, 214,* 214-219, *216, 217*
"dollar," *135,* 135
in European Scientific Revolution, 13
as fashion item, 14, 52-53, *53, 54, 55,* 90, 91-92,
    92, 93, 129-133, 215-216
French decimal, *219*
imported, 47, 92, 94 (*see also* Swiss watches)
jeweled, 96, 135, *135*
ladies', 11, 52, 53, *55,* 91-92; chatelaine set *130*;
    Helen Keller's, *138,* 139; lapel, 130, *131, 132*;
    pendant or brooch, 91, *92, 93,* 130, 133
mass-produced, 68, 70, 91, 94-96, 133, 135
mechanical, drawing of parts of, *212*
open-face (v. "hunting"), 92, *93*
presentation, 11, 53, *95,* 136, *137, 138,* 139
railroad, 98, *99,* 99-100, 111, 136, *136*
stem-winder, 92, *93*
See also pocket watch; stopwatch; wristwatch
watch chains and fobs, 52-53, *53, 54,* 90, 91, *93,*
    129, 130, *161. See also* pocket watch
watch glass. *See* sandglass
watchmaking, 51-52, 91
    factories, 94-96, *95*
watch papers, *26, 27,* 27
watch pockets. *See* pocket watch
Waterbury Clock Company, 89, 126
Waterbury Supplement (watch advertisement in), *96*
Waterbury Watch Company, 135
    advertisements for, *96, 125*
water-powered machinery, 85, 86
Watertown (Massachusetts) Arsenal, 168, 169
Weather Bureau, U.S., 113
Weber, Max (painter), 140
Weber, Max (sociologist), 43-44
Welch, E. N., Manufacturing Company, 89
Weld, Isaac Jr., 59
Wells, H. G., 141
Westclox, 128
Western Railroad (New England), 102
Western Union Telegraph Company, *117*
    time ball, 109, 114, 116, *117*
whaling and the Sabbath, 83
whistle, steam, *164*
White, Rev. William B., 119
Willard & Frick, 163
Willard brothers (Simon, Aaron, Benjamin) 49-50,
    52, 86, 94, 127
William L. Gilbert Clock Company, 89, 128
Wilson, Woodrow, 122
Wilson Clock Dial Manufactory (England), 28
Wilt, Joy, 189
Winthrop, John, 47
women
    economic role of, 77-78
    factory workers, *71,* 80, 86, 94, *135, 168*
    and home management, 175-184
    time and motion studies of, *168, 176*
    watches for, *see* watch (ladies'); wristwatch
    (ladies')

wooden clock movements and clocks,
    47, 49-50, 85, 85-87, 88, 127
Woodman, L. H., 170
work ethic, 43-44, 62, 78
    idleness as disgrace, 43, 80
    productivity urged, *171, 172, 173*
    "24/7" mentality, 12, 41, 191-197
    See also punctuality
work hours, 13, 73-75, 160-161
    fixed, 184
    night workers, 191-194
    "nontraditional," 192
world's fair, 194
    Chicago (1893-94), 149
    Chicago (1933), 181
    Philadelphia (1876), 68, 96
world time standardized, 120-121, *121*
World War I, 122, 134, 145
    poster for war work, *171*
World War II, 89, 122, 206
    office workers, *173*
    postwar concerns for disabled, 182
Wright, Isaac and William, 58
Wright, L., 98
wristwatch, *133, 134,* 135
    for children, 139
    as fashion item, 129, 133, 134-135, 139
    ladies', 129-135, *135,* 139
    LED and LCD, 214-217
    for men, 129, *134,* 134-135, 215-216
    quartz, 212-217, *213, 214, 215, 216*
    "wrist radio" (fictional), 218
    and "wristwear," 219

"Yankee Doodle" (song), 75